Ma'at Magic: Renewal Unveiled

Nadim Nahas

ABSTRACT

In searching for restorative stories that elevate understanding and engender the capacity for seeing through the cultural chaos and confusion of modern times, this dissertation turns to Egypt at the beginning of its recorded history, approximately 3100 BCE. The ancient Egyptians faced many of the same challenges facing the world today, and they learned to weather them by creating a resilient cultural model that endured cycles of growth and decline. Their culture perpetuated while adapting and transforming. In their surviving records are some of their rituals, practices, and beliefs that provide much-needed perspectives, observations, and stories that contributed to their own renewal and capacity to regenerate their culture.

The mythological roots of renewal in ancient Egypt reveals one deity in particular who embodies the capacity to harmonize and balance the opposites—Ma'at. She is central to the act of fostering daily reciprocal relationship and maintaining the flow of energy between the divine and the human realms. She is both the daughter of the solar god Re and his source of life. She is the embodiment of the cosmic patterns and natural laws. She is the incarnation of the offerings to the gods and their reciprocal response flowing back to the human realm. She governs the tides of justice, truth, balance, and harmony.

The collective psyche's inherent capacity for renewal and resilience is revealed through Ma'at's story and prominence in Egyptian history. Their images and literature reveal that in the presence of Ma'at, it is possible for human consciousness to discover

the transcendent space where opposites reconcile to initiate new harmony, create unity,

and guide all things to their rightful place. Balancing and harmonizing any duality creates

a continuous circulation of energy in the psyche. This circulation has the potential to birth

a conscious, ethical heart, an awakened heart which—as these ancient people would

say—directs our saying and our doing. By recognizing Ma'at's essential characteristics,

understanding her relationship with her fellow deities, and identifying her foundational

role within the ancient Egyptian civilization it is possible to participate in the awakening

of Ma'at's roots of renewal in our own times.

Table of Contents

Chapter 1. Seeking Stories of Harmony and Renewal

If we can recover the values intrinsic to the ancient participatory

way of knowing without losing the priceless evolutionary

attainment of a strong and focused ego, together with all the

discoveries we have made and the skills we have developed, we

could heal both the fissure in our soul and our raped and

vandalized planet. (Baring 131)

In *The Dream of the Cosmos*, depth psychologist and scholar of mythology Anne
Baring explores the evolution of human consciousness. In her poignant observations she
chooses strong words, stating that our planet is "raped and vandalized." These words
identify major challenges facing our society. Baring points to the numerous ways that the
grave split between intuition and intellect, psyche and matter, religion and science, nature
and human impacts our lives. Others[1] have noted the intersection between our
predominant style of consciousness that views nature and other peoples as resources or
commodities to be used and consumed, and the alarming degradation of our biosphere.
This conditioned belief is a contributing factor in numerous out-of-balance concerns.

Introduction: Healing the "Fissure in Our Soul"

Baring names this split, this rupture in the collective consciousness, a "fissure in
our soul," which squarely indicates the first steps toward healing, for the soul, the psyche,
is within each individual's purview. She directs our attention to the starting point in our
individual quest, to heal the fissure in our own psyche and, in so doing, tend to the soul of
the world. This "fissure in our soul" is related to a separation and denigration of one half

---

[1] Carolyn Merchant, Jeffery Kiehl, and Jimmy Carter are authors who note the connection between how
women and girls are treated in their culture and how nature is viewed.

of the duality that is a fundamental, constitutive part of the phenomenal world. This results in a blindness to other perspectives, and a failure of imagination that arises from it. Our lack of emotional connection to instinctual knowing and our failure to see how our actions impact the quality of life for all are symptoms of this malady.

Medicinal Myths[2]

> In recent times, the term "myth" has come to signify falsehood, but when we examine myths we find that they are a high form of truth. They are the deepest, innermost cultural stories of our human journeys toward spiritual and psychological growth. An essential part of myth is that it allows for our return to the creation, to a mythic time. It allows us to hear the world new again. (Hogan 51)

Myths emerge from the archetypal layers of the collective psyche, "from the mystical region of essential experience" (Campbell and Kudler xix). Both oral and written stories can carry medicinal properties, as certain stories have the capacity to strike a chord within, awakening feelings and stimulating reflection. Wounds of the deepest grief, outrage, joy, delight, hardship, and insights are just a few examples of the range of experiences and emotions personified in mythologems.[3]

In his book *Ego and Archetype,* depth psychologist Edward Edinger explores the nature of what Campbell calls the "mystical region of essential experience," identifying it with the "archetypal psyche" (3). Edinger describes the archetypal psyche as originating

---

[2] Modern thinkers who explore the healing potential of myths and dreams, and who have influenced my own understanding of this rich realm, include C. G. Jung, Marie-Louise von Franz, Marion Woodman, Michael Meade, and Joseph Campbell.

[3] Basic mythological themes that appear in the stories of cultures from around the world, such as death, self-sacrifice, betrayal, birth of the divine child, descent into the underworld, love, and magical aide from animals and nature.

in the "pre-personal or transpersonal dimension which is manifested in universal patterns and images such as are found in all the world's religions and mythologies" (3). The archetypal psyche "has a structuring or ordering principle which unifies" its contents (3). He describes these archetypal patterns as arising from a source that is beyond human consciousness, from "the realm of eternal forms" (*Anatomy of the Psyche* 98).

Mythologist Sean Kane points out that the "proper subject of myth is the ideas and emotions of the Earth" (34). Kane's word-image suggests that Earth itself is a source of myths, of the eternal forms. This echoes Linda Hogan's recognition that myths "allows us to hear the world new again" (51). It is returning to this imaginal wellspring that propels us on "our human journeys toward spiritual and psychological growth" (51). Like Baring, Hogan also points out that we live in a time of broken connections, "not only in language and myth but [also] in our philosophies of life. There is a separation that has taken place between us and nature. Something has broken deep in the core of ourselves" (52). This broken connection has resulted in a fragmentation that is experienced in both the inner and the outer realms.

The recovery of the natural instinctive psyche[4] has a long history with many branches. Depth psychologist Monika Wikman identifies the "schism" at the heart of our times (xix). In her book *Pregnant Darkness: Alchemy and the Rebirth of Consciousness*, she traces the loss of "connection with the spirit in the core of all beings" and identifies the consequence—namely, "our consciousness becomes one-sided, dry, and cut off from the natural sources of renewal in the psyche" (xviii). To respond to what is needed to heal this rent in the fabric of the individual and collective psyche, each of us must become an

---

[4] See the work of C. G. Jung and Marie-Louise von Franz, who developed psychological distinctions and methodologies for recovery of the natural instinctive psyche.

astute observer and a deep listener. Inner guidance is accessible, and its source is not just the human intellect; all nature, the ancient ancestors, and our own hearts hold often-ignored wisdom. Instinctual archetypal energies are available to aid us—when we are open to their communications.

The old stories and myths carry the wisdom of the deepest patterns, arising from the collective archetypal layer of our psyche with symbolism that spans multiple cultures and time periods. Depth psychologist Clarissa Pinkola Estés defines her book *Women Who Run with the Wolves* as a "psychic-archeological" dig into the underworld to recover the feminine psyche's gold (3). Pinkola Estés believes the depth psychological methods she employs enable the recovery of the "natural instinctive psyche" (4). Her work has inspired my own for years. Her rich selection, retelling, and amplification of old folk and fairy tales reveals archetypal patterns within this often-undervalued genre of literature.

Recovering the ancient participatory way of knowing, bridging the schism, and recovering the natural instinctive psyche are intimately related, and these processes begin with the act of recovery. Reclamation of the ancient healing myths and stories reveals the outlines of the archetypal patterns. These patterns hold evidence of the rituals and practices that reflect the ancient participatory way of knowing. The old stories hold the wisdom and the models so needed to make meaning of life's challenges. Because medicinal stories activate the archetypal patterns, they have the potential to activate the multiple levels of the psyche, both collectively and individually, awakening our deepest knowing, our heart's wisdom.

Turning to the book *Magical Child Matures* provides a developmental perspective on human consciousness. Its author, Joseph Chilton Pearce, states that the human's psyche is encoded with a storytelling capacity, a creative process or "blueprint," which is "ready for activation by the appropriate models . . . Speak the Word, and the inner reality forms" (58). Chilton Pearce details the process, explaining that initially language shapes our experience of the sensory world, and then at around age two the language of storytelling begins to shape our internal world; at this point, our imagination births the next rung of our development with the combination of metaphor and image (58).

The ancient stories are also enacted in rituals and sacred practices as well as images and metaphors. Rituals have the potential to promote and ensure a healthy society and bestow life-giving energy and vitality. Rituals can foster an ever-evolving balance between the opposites of creation and destruction, light and dark, life and death, compassion and greed. Rituals and myths enliven and renew community, family, and the individual, for they mark our most sacred occasions as well as the worldly ones.

But myths eventually lose their elasticity, and the life-giving rituals diminish in vitality and become rote. When we fail to honor our inherent interdependency and connections with the natural world, life on earth fails to thrive. What we resist, persists. What we reject, activates. What we deny, demands. What we suppress, rages.

Focus on Ancient Egyptian Mythology

In searching for restorative stories that elevate understanding and engender the capacity for seeing through the cultural chaos and confusion of modern times, I turn to Egypt at the beginning of its recorded history, approximately 3100 BCE. Over five thousand years ago these ancient people began writing down their cosmologies, observations, ideas, insights, histories, and stories, providing us with a rich perspective on the human condition. Their surviving records expose some of their rituals, practices, and beliefs that may provide much-needed perspectives, observations, and stories that contributed to their own renewal and capacity to regenerate their culture when the systems failed and the political and societal structure broke down. They have much to teach us, if we are willing to listen with our hearts (as they did) as well as our intellect.

The ancient Egyptians' archetypal patterns are still alive, and they speak to us—for when we uncover their relics, learn to read their image-rich language, understand their social structure, trace their history, and grasp their speculations about sacred science, philosophy, and religion, insights spontaneously arise and our own consciousness expands. These long-ago people tantalize us with their images and culture, grab us with their unfamiliar ways and customs, and stretch our capacity to think outside our own conditioning as we try to see through the evidence and reconstruct their fertile culture.

As I dove into their rich and varied history, culture, and mythology, all my previous assumptions about ancient Egypt were challenged. I discovered that their history was not static and unchanging, though it is often portrayed as such in present-day representations of their culture. Like the much shorter-lived cultures of the contemporary world, it was a rich civilization that experienced many upheavals, traumas, and setbacks. Over ancient Egypt's more than thirty-five hundred years of recorded history, despite incompetent leaders, political upheaval, environmental crises, plagues, famine, and hostile takeovers, the people renewed their culture so that it maintained a recognizable coherency. This realization stimulated a question that began to shape my research: What unifying elements gave the ancient Egyptian civilization its vibrant, creative resilience and its capacity for renewal?

The ancient Egyptians were the most thorough of all the early peoples in recording and preserving their thoughts on everything from the mundane to the sublime. They inscribed their writing on bone, wood, stone, metal, linen, and papyrus scrolls. They also developed a number of literary genres that came to a glorious pinnacle in the Middle Kingdom (*c.* 2055–1650 BCE) and that continued evolving until the end of their civilization in approximately 395 CE. Their sacred science, philosophy, religious speculations, and material developments influenced many of the later civilizations and religions of the Mediterranean basin, in particular the Greek and Judeo-Christian traditions.[5]

At times this study may seem to idealize the ancient Egyptian culture despite facts that reveal "ample evidence of dysfunctional, destructive, and unenlightened behaviour among the [ancient] Egyptians" (Hayen 3). One goal of this study is to uncover a "model of excellence" for their times and our own. Therefore, the focus is on articulating the qualities of ancient Egyptian thought and culture that supported renewal and regeneration.

The movement of renewal we so urgently need now must be imagined and held in our hearts before it will become a reality. By necessity this imagined model of excellence must be articulated as an ideal, with its highest values and goals explicated. Contemporary culture is experiencing perilous times that call forth the very opposite of these, as the depth psychologist C. G. Jung noted in his copious writings during the previous century. If we have no imagining of those archetypal energies, the ensuing

---

[5] Several scholars—Walter Burkert, Henri Frankfort, Martin Bernal, and R. A. Schwaller de Lubicz—challenge the notion of the so-called Greek miracle and recognize the influences and achievements that originated in ancient Egypt. Ancient Greek sources also cite numerous ancient Egyptian contributions and accomplishments.

chaos as they attempt to differentiate their attributes could be deeply disruptive and violent.

The ancient Egyptians faced many of the same challenges we are facing today, and they learned to weather them by creating a resilient cultural model that endured cycles of growth and decline, including the invasion of foreign powers, incompetent leadership, corruption and political infighting, and natural disasters. Their culture perpetuated while adapting and transforming. Significant periods of decline, identified by modern Egyptologists as the First, Second, and Third Intermediate Periods, "saw the continuation of Egyptian civilization, often with the introduction of new ideas and concepts" (Wilkinson, *Reading Egyptian Art* 12). This is one of the main reasons I selected ancient Egypt as the focus of this study. Furthermore, the ancient and widespread fascination with all things Egyptian is a testament to the collective psyche's longing for and interest in the ingredients contained within its cultural remnants.

Of particular interest to this study are the main components that contributed to ancient Egypt's resilience, flexibility, and renewal. As a mythographer, I focus my interest on their texts, inscriptions, papyri, images, and symbols, with an eye to uncovering the archetypal energies at the heart of their culture. These sources reveal the prominence the ancient Egyptians placed on the concept of renewal. The focus on death, regeneration, and rebirth, so evident in the culture at large, are all aspects of renewal and can be traced in the symbolism represented in their mythology and art. One way they expressed renewal was through daily practices that fostered a reciprocal relationship with the divine and ancestral realms. It is clear from the evidence that these rituals cultivated the sense of renewal they valued so highly.

Roots of Renewal in Ancient Egypt

Recognition of their relational stance to nature and the divine, and the practices and rituals the ancient Egyptians created to embody this reciprocity, recollects Baring's call for attention and differentiation. As I was researching the mythological roots of renewal, one deity in particular emerged from the array of Egyptian divinities. She is central to the act of fostering daily reciprocal relationship and maintaining the flow of energy between the divine and the human realms. She is both the daughter of the solar god Re and his source of life. She is the embodiment of the cosmic patterns and natural laws. She is the incarnation of the offerings to the gods and ancestors and their reciprocal response flowing back to the human realm. She governs the tides of justice, truth, balance, and harmony. Her name is Ma'at.[6]

The ancient Egyptians personified the archetypal forces, differentiating their characteristics and bringing them into the light, where the people consciously built reciprocal relationships with these energies, honoring their numinous power. These people also recognized that the psyche is a source of overpowering, destructive energies; this darker aspect, too, was personified and made conscious. They incorporated it into their mythology and practices, recognizing the jackal-headed god Seth, driven by the raw strength of unrestrained appetites, creating chaos; the rampant, lioness-headed goddess Sekhmet, consumed by battle rage, wantonly devouring humanity; the gigantic serpent Apophis emerging from the undifferentiated depths, capturing all life in its dark coils.

---

[6] Ma'at is often referenced as an abstract concept or principle in modern scholarship, but it seems doubtful that the ancient Egyptians experienced their gods and goddesses as abstract concepts. Because the intention of this study is not to iterate and reinforce our own conventions, but to uncover the ancient Egyptian perspective as much as possible, this study refers to Ma'at by her name or with a gendered pronoun.

Far more than most modern cultures do, the ancient Egyptians personified the restoration of balance, order, and renewal through the harmonizing of opposites. Consider the word *harmony*, which comes from the Greek *harmonía*, meaning "joint, framework, agreement," and from the verb *harmozō*, meaning "fit together, join" ("Harmony," Dictionary.com). This capability—the fitting and joining of opposites in agreement—is centrally personified in the goddess Ma'at. Thus this study unearths the roots of renewal in ancient Egyptian culture through their portrayal of the goddess Ma'at and her companions as a *remedy* for challenging and potentially catastrophic times.

Thesis Statement and Research Questions

This study explores the ancient Egyptian cultural emphasis on awakening wisdom from the energy that flows among polarities, to bring forth a flourishing individual life and dynamic transformative traditions. The collective psyche's inherent capacity for renewal and resilience is revealed through Ma'at's story and prominence in Egyptian history. By recognizing her essential characteristics, understanding her relationship with her fellow deities, and identifying her foundational role within their civilization, we can trace an expansion of consciousness over the long history of the ancient Egyptians.

In ancient Egyptian mythologems, we discover dimensions of the psyche that honor the relational unity among complementary opposites. Critical to their beliefs is the insight that when united and harmonized among complementary pairs, the exchange of energy between the two poles reestablishes and rebuilds what is critical for transformation and renewal to occur. They envisioned this transformative action as the purview of the goddess Ma'at.

One outcome of balancing and harmonizing any duality is the continuous circulation of energy in the psyche. This circulation can give birth to a conscious, ethical heart, an awakened heart—then and now—which, as the ancient Egyptians would say, directs our saying and our doing. Their practices promoted this renewal that kept alive their connection to their spiritual wellspring despite the challenges and setbacks that they experienced as individuals and as a culture. Their images and literature reveal that in the presence of Ma'at, it is possible for human consciousness to discover the transcendent space where opposites join to initiate new harmony, create unity, and guide all things to their rightful place within the laws of nature.

The following questions—which mark a journey from the ancient to the contemporary, from the personal to the societal, and from the philosophical to the practical—shape this inquiry:

1. What unifying elements give the ancient Egyptian civilization its vibrant, creative resilience and its capacity for renewal?

2. How do the ancient Egyptians depict their experience of the archetypal energies of Ma'at and the renewal that she represents?

3. What do the myths, rituals, and prescriptions surrounding Ma'at reveal about the participatory way of knowing and the power of renewal derived from seeking harmony with Ma'at?

Exploring this culture-wide devotion to fostering reciprocal relationships with the divine provokes comparison with the profane and materialistic style of consciousness prevalent in our culture today. For students of depth psychology, a pivotal question naturally follows: What guidance does this ongoing relationship with Ma'at offer our society today, as we struggle to evolve, regenerate, and live in harmony? By exploring Ma'at's interwoven relationships within the divine and the human realms, we may find it possible to participate in the shift of consciousness that is currently under way in our own times and to encourage the awakening of the heart's wisdom.

Review of the Literature

> The protean mythologem and the shimmering symbol express the processes of the psyche far more trenchantly and, in the end, far more clearly than the clearest concept; for the symbol not only conveys a visualization of the process but—and this is perhaps just as important—it also brings a re-experiencing of it. (Jung, *CW* 13 para. 199)

As Jung points out, the psyche's multiple perspectives revealed in mythologems and symbols evoke the essence of culture in a way that is superior to rational concepts or logical conclusions. Symbols and myths have the capacity to touch an experiential chord within, awakening feelings and resonating with intuitive knowing. The artifacts, images, and literature of ancient Egypt provide ample examples of this resonance within the psyche through contact with the primordial archetypes, once one learns to understand and read their symbolic images.

The symbolism imparted through myths and rituals contributes to the revitalization of the individual and the collective culture. This study weaves together ancient cultural influences to provide a contrast and point of reflection on modern practices and beliefs. In working with images, myths, and other sacred texts, and in employing the depth psychology method of amplification, it endeavors to bring the archetypal images alive. In addition, circumambulating the images repeatedly invites deeper layers of rich symbolism to reveal themselves, and in the process our own consciousness is expanded and enriched.

The following review is a brief introduction to the literature consulted throughout my research process, starting with the translators of the primary sources of ancient Egyptian literature that are utilized in the study. In employing a multidisciplinary approach, I rely on renowned authors who are well-recognized in the fields of Egyptology (which includes Egyptian history and archaeology), mythology, and depth and archetypal psychology. These contemporary scholars provide the necessary grounding for analysis and amplification of the primary source material. Their contributions and insights will be noted in the citations and footnotes.

Translators of Primary Sources

Translating hieroglyphic writing is an art form based on scientifically gathered evidence, but nevertheless it comes down to interpretation. The written language of the Egyptians is complex, multifaceted, and filled with subtle puns and innuendos that are often lost on contemporary scholars. In addition, the hieroglyphic symbols are a combination of ideographs and phonograms that can function as both sounds and symbolic images. Therefore, it is difficult to walk the line between unearthing the best literal translation and honoring the music of the language. The latter approach is arguably the most valuable, as it brings us closer to the feeling of this ancient and poetic, metaphor-rich language. The translators listed in this section subscribe to both methods.

The translations of the ancient Egyptian texts used throughout this study are the work of the following Egyptologists: Miriam Lichtheim (*Ancient Egyptian Literature*

Vols. 1–3; *Ma'at in Egyptian Autobiographies and Related Studies*), R. O. Faulkner (*The Ancient Egyptian Coffin Texts*), Ogden Goelet, Jr. (*The Egyptian Book of the Dead: The Book of Going Forth By Day, being the papyrus of Ani*, coauthored with Faulkner), James P. Allen (*Middle Egyptian: An Introduction to the Language and Culture of Hieroglyphs*), R. T. Rundle Clark (*Myth and Symbol in Ancient Egypt*), and John L. Foster (*Hymns, Prayers, and Songs: An Anthology of Ancient Egyptian Lyric Poetry*). Many of these authors make use of the prescribed scientific methods of Egyptology, working directly with copies or photographs of the hieroglyphic inscriptions and cross-referencing their translation with other translations, noting any inconsistencies in their footnotes.

Egyptology

There is ample historical evidence that other cultures in the Mediterranean basin, in particular ancient Greece, were of the opinion that the Egyptian civilization was far older and more advanced and had much to teach them. Garth Fowden, the author of *The Egyptian Hermes: A Historical Approach to the Late Pagan Mind*, grounds this opinion with the following: "Even the wisest representations of other traditions—Moses among the Jews, Solon, Pythagoras and Plato of the Greeks—were acknowledged to have sat at the feet of Egyptian priests" (15).

Egyptologist Henri Frankfort (1897–1954) published seminal books on Egyptology in the first half of the twentieth century, including *Kingship and the Gods: A Study of Ancient Near Eastern Religion as the Integration of Society and Nature* and *Ancient Egyptian Religion: An Interpretation*. Frankfort's work begins from the premise that the ancient Egyptian style of consciousness "can be comprehended once its own peculiar coherence is discovered" (*Ancient Egyptian Religion* xi). One of his major books focuses on kingship in ancient Egypt, which is pertinent for a study of Ma'at's influence, for she is a Daughter of Re and a constant companion of his, traveling in the Solar Barque both day and night, providing Re the protection and companionship necessary for his successful renewal and thus the renewal of all life.

R. T. Rundle Clark (1909–1970), in *Myth and Symbol in Ancient Egypt*, focuses on the mythology and symbolism of ancient Egypt, in particular the Osiris mythologem with its theme of regeneration and renewal. In Clark's opinion, the aim of Egyptian mythology was to "provide a series of symbols to describe the origin and development of consciousness" (33). He captures the essence of ancient Egypt's interwoven view of creation, stating, "Gods, men, animals, plants and physical phenomena all belonged to the same great order. . . . Conception, germination, sickness or chemical change were just as much god-directed as the motions of the stars or the beginnings of the world" (26).

Erik Hornung (b. 1933), is an eminent contemporary Egyptologist and author of (among other fine works) *Conceptions of God in Ancient Egypt*, *Idea Into Image*, and *Akhenaten and the Religion of Light*. He also coauthored the seminal *Knowledge for the Afterlife*, which details the symbolism of the journey leading to daily renewal, with the Egyptologist and depth psychologist Theodore Abt (b. 1947). Their book serves as a model for this study's approach to amplifying mythological themes in the ancient texts.

Jan Assmann (b. 1938), who explores the themes of death and renewal in such works as *Death and Salvation in Ancient Egypt*; *The Mind of Egypt: History and Meaning in the Time of the Pharaohs*; *The Search for God in Ancient Egypt*; and *Egyptian Solar Religion in the New Kingdom*, concludes, "Living with the dead and with death is one of the most normal manifestations of human culture, and it presumably lies at the heart of the stuff of human existence" (*Death and Salvation* 1). His work is most useful for examining the disconnect between the reality of death and contemporary culture's denial of death.

Alison Roberts—author of *Hathor Rising: The Power of the Goddess in Ancient Egypt* and *My Heart My Mother: Death and Rebirth in Ancient Egypt*—has contributed to Egyptology through her focus on the divine Feminine and on Hathor in particular. Her presentation of the moderating and influential relationship between Hathor and Ma'at is a refreshing look into the interwoven relationships of the ancient Egyptian deities and serves as a model for this study's examination of the wreath of archetypal patterns that surround Ma'at.

Mythology

Anne Baring (b. 1931) and Jules Cashford's *The Myth of the Goddess: Evolution of an Image* adds immensely to current scholarship on the evolution of the divine Feminine in Western and Near Eastern cultures. They begin with the Paleolithic Period and trace her shapeshifting forms to present times. They conclude their examination of ancient cultures by applying their findings to contemporary concerns, weaving together the archaic and present-day mythological landscapes to illuminate our collective condition. Their example has inspired my own approach to this challenge of weaving and contrasting the ancient and the contemporary.

Jane Ellen Harrison (1850–1928), author of *Themis: The Study of the Social Origins of Greek Religion*, was a founding member of the Cambridge Myth and Ritual school of thought, along with Sir James Frazer and Gilbert Murray. She contributed greatly to the development of archaeology when she recognized that ancient Greek ceramics were decorated with images of rituals, as well as gods and goddesses, and could be "read" like a written text. Her method of reading the images on ancient artifacts is especially useful for working with ancient Egyptian artifacts, for the images are truly multilayered texts.

Mythologist Joseph Campbell (1904–1987), author of the ground-breaking work *The Hero with a Thousand Faces* and also of *Myths of Light: Eastern Metaphors of the Eternal* (with David Kudler), introduced the mythologem of the Hero's Journey in terms of phases of actions and revealed how this myth is cross-cultural. The Hero's Journey can be traced in the solar god's daily journey of renewal, with a significant difference: the solar god/hero is never a solo voyager. This is an important distinction for this study.

The work of mythologist Michael Meade (b. 1944), including *Why the World Doesn't End: Tales of Renewal in Times of Loss*, focuses on the healing capacity of myths and storytelling. His tales of renewal and his lively, experiential way of working with myth and the psyche are an art form. His enthusiasm for mythology resonates with my own. His example of weaving together the threads of mythology and storytelling with promoting healing through sparking consciousness aligns with my intent for this study. Chapter 2 employs this method to enliven the ancient Egyptian physical and mythological worlds, as an offering to the *spirit of the depths*.[7]

Depth and Archetypal Psychology

Four depth psychologists who have employed the fertile Egyptian symbolism in their quest to map the psyche are Marie-Louise von Franz (1915–1998), author of *Aurora Consurgens: A Document Attributed to Thomas Aquinas on the Problem of Opposites in*

---

[7] Jung's term for the unconscious, from the *Red Book*.

Alchemy, Alchemy: An Introduction to the Symbolism and the Psychology, and *On Dreams and Death*; Erich Neumann (1905–1960), author of *The Origins and History of Consciousness* and *The Great Mother: An Analysis of the Archetype*; Theodor Abt (whose work with Hornung is mentioned above) and *Tutankhamun—Reviving Egypt's Past for the Future: The Story of the Facsimile of the Tomb of Tutankhamun and the Meaning of the Pictures in its Burial Chamber*; and Andreas Schweizer, author of *The Sungod's Journey Through the Netherworld: Reading the Ancient Amduat*. Abt and Schweizer are eminent scholars of Egyptology as well. Their books are an invaluable resource in working with the complex and multilayered symbolism that richly illustrates ancient Egyptian images and texts. The psychic processes that Jung spent his lifetime exploring have a particularly potent expression in ancient Egypt, where they began from the premise of respecting and valuing the psyche's many perspectives.

I am using depth psychology as the bridge between the traditional, scientific Egyptological interpretation and the amplification of the mythological material of the psyche's many voices. With its rich tradition of cross-cultural studies for mapping the processes of the psyche, this method of working with archetypal images enlivens the sometimes obscure symbolism, because its metaphors and imaginal depths are so foreign to contemporary thought. Depth psychology recognizes that within the psyche there exist numinous archetypal patterns that speak to us in a metaphoric, image-laden language.

Organization of the Study

Chapter 2. Ancient Egyptian Wisdom: A Holoscopic Perspective

This chapter introduces the unique landscape of ancient Egypt and imagines how it influenced and shaped the cosmologies and consciousness of its people—in particular how they embraced a flexible viewpoint that incorporated multiple perspectives under the umbrella of a unified metaphorical and material outlook. It also explores the nature of hieroglyphic writing in ancient Egypt, focusing on the treatment of symbols, words, and images as sacred, living texts, in dramatic contrast to our own alphabetic writing system and our perspective on it.[8] Specific terminology surrounding the concepts of *renewal, rebirth, harmony,* and *balance*—all of which are sorely missing in today's world—was ever-present in ancient Egyptian society and culture, and warrants reevaluation with an eye to revival.

This chapter also puts into context key elements of ancient Egyptian mythology, including participation in the rhythms and cycles of nature (particularly from life/creation to death/rebirth); an interpretation of their pantheon of gods and goddesses (*neters*) as active rather than static beings; the consequences of their surprising spatial and temporal orientation; and the pragmatic and philosophical aspects of the culture. It concludes with a reverie on renewal and rebirth, life and death, past and present, which serves to expand the boundaries of these concepts before realigning them with the goals and nature of this study.

Chapter 3. Who Is This Ma'at?

This chapter introduces the goddess Ma'at and articulates the ancient participatory way of knowing, including the wreath of archetypal energies, symbols, and unified opposites that exemplify Ma'at's powerful essence and her role as the root of renewal for this ancient culture. Although underrepresented in modern study, Ma'at was in fact foundational for ancient Egypt—not only as an integral part of the cherished land, the

---

[8] The material history of Egypt is a vast subject with numerous facets. It is outside the scope of this study to provide an in-depth review on the many avenues of ancient Egyptian history. Footnotes, quotes, and citations will provide pertinent sources.

heavens, and underworld, but also as the focus of daily rituals performed by the king and his high priests to maintain order, unity, harmony, and balance, and thus to uphold natural laws and cosmic patterns. Ma'at symbolized what was essential in order to perpetuate the paradigm of renewal—the keystone for the building blocks on which this ancient culture was built. Indeed, Ma'at was the heart's blood of ancient Egyptian beliefs.

Chapter 4. Order and Reciprocity: Ma'at's Mighty Influence

Using the depth psychological technique of letting the texts speak for themselves, this chapter analyzes several significant genres of ancient Egyptian works from the Old, Middle, and New Kingdoms—from the *Autobiography* in tombs and on stelae to *Wisdom Literature* to texts dealing exclusively with the afterlife. The sacred *Pyramid Texts, Coffin Texts,* and *Book of Going Forth Into Day*[9] celebrate the harmony of nature with the divine, while *The Complaints of Khakheperre-Son*; the *Coffin Texts*, Spell 330; and *The Eloquent Peasant* paint a picture of both turmoil and opportunity. The popular and instructive *The Contendings of Horus and Seth* explores the potential for opposites to bring renewal and regeneration to all life. This chapter introduces dynamics of social breakdown and political upheaval in ancient Egypt and traces the practice of "saying" and "doing" Ma'at as it expanded from royalty alone during the Old Kingdom to become the responsibility of the entire New Kingdom population.

Chapter 5. Ma'at: The Framework for Stability and Renewal

This chapter investigates the universe of knowledge about the multifaceted Ma'at and her role in ancient Egypt, speculates on Ma'at's relationship to the principles associated with her, and establishes her position as a foundational, coherent pattern that

---

[9] *Book of the Dead* is the misleading name assigned to this genre of sacred texts by an early Egyptologist. It is a misnomer. Therefore, this study prefers the literal translation of the ancient Egyptian name—*Book of Going Forth Into Day*. Readers will occasionally be reminded of this throughout the dissertation.

organizes all life. The ancient Egyptians believed that the rigor with which they attended to Ma'at determined whether or not their civilization flourished. Maintaining a reciprocal relationship with the divine, therefore, was a top priority and responsibility of the king and, in later periods, of society as a whole in order to ensure stability if possible—and resilience when necessary. The chapter highlights Ma'at's place in the Heliopolitan cosmology and the understanding that alignment with her natural order and principles—and paying the proper attention to this flow of reciprocity between the human and divine realms—would support harmony, balance, and renewal in the world.

Ma'at's structural importance for this culture can be understood as inhabiting spheres of influence in three broad areas—creation, kingship, and the afterlife—presented here through the lens of several literary and artistic works. Ma'at's place in creation myth is explored in several genres and texts, including Spell 80 of the *Coffin Texts*, which reveals that Ma'at's breath is the essence of life, the source of awakening and rejuvenation. The Presentation of Ma'at, from reliefs inscribed on temple walls by kings over the long history of Egypt, portrays a daily ritual that validated the king's right to rule by acknowledging Ma'at's authority and thus renewing the reciprocal relationship between the human and divine realms. Her dominion in the underworld is revealed in the Weighing of the Heart scene, from a papyrus that is central to the *Book of the Dead*. And the Twelfth Gate, a hieroglyphic image from the *Book of Gates*, depicts the final passage of the solar god and his accompanying deities from the underworld, illuminating a critical aspect of the nightly renewal process, underscoring that it takes a community effort—and the presence of Ma'at—to ensure the renewal of life.

Chapter 6. Restoring Balance: Seti I's Temple at Abydos

This chapter focuses on the pivotal New Kingdom and a series of transformations by a succession of rulers who differed in their approach to Ma'at and the cosmic order. The destruction and rebuilding of religious temples coincided with the growing movement toward an ever-greater sense of personal piety—and a return to a deeper intimacy with and devotion to deities and recognition of their underlying oneness. The result was a wider commitment to Ma'at and, more specifically, to *doing* Ma'at, or pledging oneself to the service of justice and unity. The chapter carefully forms an intimate view of the impressive Temple of Seti I at Abydos and deconstructs exciting images found there, offering a new take on the symbols and the story that speak volumes about Ma'at's mythemes of unification, stability, and eternal renewal.

Chapter 7. Navigating Transformation: The *Hymn to Ma'at*

This chapter analyzes a critical work in the comprehension of Ma'at and exposes the truth about her role in the renewal of society. The *Hymn to Ma'at*, inscribed late in Egypt's history on a wall of the Temple of Amun at el-Hibis, gives voice to the ancient Egyptians' profound and lasting dedication to Ma'at as the foundation of their society, even in times of turmoil. This chapter identifies the central role of this feminine co-creator in the main cosmologies of Egyptian mythology and illustrates her enduring, multifaceted influence as the goddess who brought balance to the sacred order. The hymn focuses on upholding Ma'at through the actions of *speaking* and *doing*—a result of listening to the wisdom of the heart and aligning one's thought, words, and deeds with her natural laws. Further analysis of the hymn reveals Ma'at as the source of the wisdom and the power behind the ebb and flow of life, and underscores how Ma'at and her counterparts symbolize *sema*, or "union"—the ordering and harmonizing of all things, that her people hoped would continue long into the future.

Chapter 8. Conclusion: Finding Renewal in Ma'at

This chapter begins by summarizing the study and the conclusions drawn, returning to the thesis and research questions as it synthesizes our understanding of Ma'at and renewal in an interwoven cosmos. After reviewing the principle themes and cultural mysteries at the foundation of the study, this chapter consider how alignment with Ma'at-like principles can allow human consciousness to transcend opposites, achieve order and balance, and awaken the collective psyche's inherent capacity for resilience.

The chapter then turns to suggestions for future lines of inquiry revealed by the work, questioning the potential to open pathways to new insights and a much-needed transformation of consciousness. In these Sethian[10] times, can we modern humans translate the guidance of the ancient Egyptians into our struggling society and implement this heart's awakening in our own civilization? Can weaving new energy patterns and following Ma'at's ethical model help us replenish the living imagination, remedy polarization, rediscover unity, and resolve widespread conflict? Will we awaken to the dire consequences of our actions on humanity and the earth itself? How might we recreate our culture with the people of Ma'at as our template for renewal and harmony? Can Ma'at and her people show us the way?

Methodology: Multiple Channels of Perception

This study delves into ancient Egyptian mythological offerings and amplifies their abundant symbolism using the methodology of intuitive inquiry. It is not the intention of

---

[10] Seth is the god in ancient Egypt most often associated with chaos and discord, though, like all archetypal energies, he embodies both creative and destructive dynamisms.

this study to generate a historical Egyptological analysis; these are readily available from

eminent Egyptologists, many of whom are cited in this study. Instead the ancient

Egyptian mythology and images that are attested to in the earliest evidence and

maintained throughout their history are the focus of my exploration.

In ancient Egyptian writing, images hold the same value as the hieroglyphic

symbols that were used to express sounds and concepts, and in much of the evidence

presented in this study the images are the main carriers of meaning. Images hold a

treasure trove of complex information which can be read from multiple perspectives. As a

visual and intuitive thinker, this style of consciousness resonates with my own psyche in

particular. I will use the depth psychology method of amplification of the archetypal

images and texts to explore the symbolic images and mythological themes. Occasionally

mythological material from other cultures will be brought into this study to amplify

Egyptian examples.

Ma'at: Abstract Concept and Goddess

Egyptologists focus on the grammatical structure of ancient Egyptian writings in

order to decipher the complex web of meaning conveyed by hieroglyphic symbols and

images. They use grammatical analysis to interpret their meaning. The grammatical rules

tell us that the word *Ma'at* is both a goddess and "an abstract noun derived from the verb

maa, meaning 'direct' or 'guide'" (Allen 147). Ma'at refers to the natural order of the

cosmos and essentially means "the way things ought to be" (Allen 147). Ma'at is also

related to the concept of time that is eternal, fixed, perfected, which the Egyptians called

djet. The idea that Ma'at is both a goddess and an "abstract concept" is related to these

grammatical facts. To distinguish between the goddess and the abstract concept, some

Egyptologists employ the device of capitalizing the proper noun "Maat" when they describe her as a goddess and italicizing the abstract noun "*maat*" for all her other functions. When they are referring to *maat* as an abstract concept, they also use the genderless pronoun *it*.

An explanation is necessary, for this study does not follow these conventions. In maintaining Ma'at as an "abstract concept" it is too easy to lose sight of the fact that the ancient Egyptians lived in an interdependent and participatory cosmos. They did not see through the materialistic viewpoint which has conditioned the contemporary style of consciousness and greatly influences the modern interpretation of mythological and cosmogonical metaphors.

This study maintains that the tendency to split apart Ma'at and her many attributes into two categories—one of which is identified as an abstract concept—acts to depersonalized her and makes it difficult to bring her alive. Without the web of relationship, the divine energies never activate and all the psychic energy they hold stays disembodied, as a mere collection of thoughts, facts, and ideas. Referring to Ma'at as an abstract concept makes it very difficult to activate a spark of connection.

Since one goal of this study is to bring Ma'at alive, I have found it necessary to put aside the grammatical distinction. Creating a personal connection with Ma'at awakens the heart and engages the commitment to understanding her, to creating relationship with her, and through her, the Egyptian people and their unique consciousness that still feels very active. This is also the essential core of the intuitive inquiry methodology.

In addition to developing relationship with the gods and goddesses of ancient Egypt, the deities themselves are portrayed in relationship with one another, as is true in all mythologies. This understanding is the basis of the psychological method of amplifying imagery—in teasing apart the relationship threads we enter into the dance of relationship with the archetypal reality of the gods and goddesses and this activates our own emotional centers. This activation allows deeper regions of the psyche to open up and revel their mysteries. This is the heart of the participatory way of knowing. Relationship is the key to creating this deeper understanding. A respect for the many constituents of the mystery of life arises from relationship with the divine.

This study does acknowledge that Ma'at's name cannot be interpreted with just one word. She is a complex archetypal energy and the ancient Egyptians were masters of fine distinctions and differentiation. Therefore, each time Ma'at's name is used, it calls forth her many characteristics, such as order, balance, harmony, truth, justice, rightness, straightness, joy. She embodies cosmic patterns as well as the natural order. Like you or I, to understand and relate to Ma'at, it is essential to acknowledge all her traits and essences. Her many characteristics combine to make her who she is—Ma'at.

As a goddess, Ma'at retained her importance throughout the history of ancient Egypt. The renowned philologist Miriam Lichtheim attests to this in her observation that in the late New Kingdom, "[l]ife is still governed by Maat, the divine order; and as ever success depends on living in accord with Maat"[11] (*Ancient Egyptian Literature* 2: 7). In addition, it is widely recognized in the scholarship that Ma'at was experienced as every

---

[11] Like Hebrew, the ancient Egyptian written language did not include vowels; thus Egyptian hieroglyphic symbols are transcribed using only consonants. To create letter signs that are more familiar to our notions of written language Egyptologists insert vowels—commonly *e*, though this is not strictly standard. This results in a variety of spellings for Ma'at's name (and other words), depending on the modern translator's preference.

ritual offering placed upon the altars throughout Egypt: "It was said that the gods 'lived on' Maat, as if partaking of her as their food. In that way they could maintain the cosmic order she represented" (Lesko 268–69).

Further evidence for this is the common ancient Egyptian phrase "Do Maat, say Maat, for Maat is your bread and beer," which can be interpreted as stating that the goddess Ma'at is the staff of life. This metaphor resonates with similar metaphors used in the worship of Osiris (Egyptian), Dionysos (Greek), and Christ (Christian). When the fact that Ma'at was seen as all of the offerings placed upon the altars throughout Egypt daily is taken into account, the evidence suggests that Ma'at held a similar archetypal energy for the ancient Egyptians. But this interpretation is never ventured, and I suspect this is due to the fact that Ma'at has been split in two—and thus divided and depotentiated.

A didactic text from the Middle Kingdom, *The Eloquent Peasant,* will be explored in chapter 4 and it offers ample examples of Ma'at's significance to the ancient Egyptians. Numerous examples of Ma'at's prominence are explored in each of the following chapters, and with each Ma'at's standing within the ancient Egyptian culture becomes more evident. Each new piece of evidence reveals yet another layer her essence.

Intuition Points the Way

Employing intuition heightens awareness of synchronicities through attuning to what has resonance. Resonance has both emotional and physical characteristics. It is like a pull or magnetic attraction that creates a spark of interest, discharging energy—it can feel like waking up more fully, a shift in consciousness, recognition, an "Aha!" Tuning in to this energy during research is much like engaging in any intuitive process or working with dream imagery, the resonance calls attention to correlations and connections, and points to the next right step.

Myth literally takes on a life and energizes itself as it activates the psyche. It draws consciousness into the alive presence and structure of the story and returns consciousness to daily life, renewed and transformed. Handling the myths of Ma'at from various texts and time periods in Egyptian history, enable Ma'at's mysteries to activate in our current times. The ancient Egyptians' archetypal patterns are still alive, for when we uncover their relics, learn to read their image-rich language, understand their social structure, and trace their history, philosophy, and religion, insights spontaneously arise and our own consciousness expands.

Four innovative educators—Michele Cassou, Robert Romanyshyn, William Braud, and Rosemarie Anderson—have informed my understanding of intuitive inquiry as a research methodology. Each of these authors directly experienced a unique approach to intuitive inquiry in their personal journeys that they outline in their books. Those experiences led them to formalize their methodology and teach it to others. Intuitive inquiry is a hermeneutical research method that joins intuition to intellectual investigation. As a method, intuitive inquiry seeks to describe what is and to envision new possibilities for the future through an in-depth process of interpretation and reflection.

Cassou is the creator of a method of self-inquiry that (in her 2001 book *Point Zero Painting: Creativity without Limits*) she calls "point zero painting," or "the painting experience." The method encourages development of one's capacity to attune to intuition, or inner knowing, for guidance while simply painting spontaneously. Accessing the intuition involves learning to hear and trust its guidance. One does this by paying attention to the flow, or lack of flow, of energy in the body as this is an innate guide that informs the process. Insights occur naturally, as does healing, generating a sense of aliveness. In her own painting practice, Cassou discovered that opening herself to the deepest levels of the psyche through creative expression and self-inquiry carried a healing energy. When she began teaching this to others she observed that this energy was uniquely tailored for each person. She articulates her process and discoveries she gleaned from working with thousands of students for more than forty years in her books: *Point Zero: Creativity Without Limits* and *Life, Paint and Passion: Reclaiming the Magic of Spontaneous Expression* offer succinct overviews of the fundamentals of a process-painting practice.

Romanyshyn is a depth psychologist whose book *The Wounded Researcher: Research with Soul in Mind* offers a depth psychological and archetypal approach to researching and writing a dissertation from an embodied, soulful position. He encourages research that ensouls scholarly research, refocusing the direction of research questions themselves and what this calls forth from the researcher. It is an embodied methodology based in phenomenological hermeneutics. Depth psychology recognizes that an archetype never exists alone and always includes both positive and negative attributes, and Romanyshyn's lens opens the door to a deeper understanding of this study's central questions and how they are indeed interconnected at the most fundamental levels.

Braud and Anderson are the coauthors of *Transpersonal Research Methods for the Social Sciences: Honoring Human Experience.* Anderson states that intuitive inquiry is a transpersonal approach that brings together a heuristic and phenomenological focus using intuition as a focus (30). Braud and Anderson also encourage access to the transpersonal and alternative states of consciousness through the use of intuition, creative expression, compassion for self and others, discernment, and imaginal techniques such as gathering and amplifying dreams and active imagination. These are characteristics of the methodology that informs this study. Intuitive inquiry endeavors to intimately connect the researcher with the subject of their research, to enliven both. This point of connection creates a heart-connection that awakens transformational energies on the mental, emotional, spiritual, and physical levels of being and works to expand consciousness.

The ancient Egyptians acknowledged the heart as the seat of intelligence, emotion, and self-reflection that leads to wisdom. I like this definition because it infers that the heart makes it possible to expand one's consciousness through learning and enacting ethical practices and mindfulness. In this study, the phrase "heart's wisdom" will be used to express this.

Intuitive process painting, journaling, and tending to my dreams are the center of my personal practice of renewal and self-discovery and have been for many years. Through these avenues into the depths of my psyche self-reflection has generated the recognition of a host of perspectives. In rich, multi-layered images these seemingly paradoxical viewpoints communicate, interact, and inspire new insights. A sense of renewal and release comes from giving these contradictory flows of energy a path of expression. Insights come too, but that process usually take time to percolate and emerge.

It is my willingness to be with the spontaneous images coming through my intuition and onto the paper that a host of responses surface. My practice is to witness my emotions, memories, thoughts with a compassionate awareness, but not to collapse into them or attach heightened meaning to them, which only serves to add to the 'story' I

already know. There is a deep wisdom in the psyche that creativity flows from,

communicating with consciousness.

Intuition Sparks the Inspiration

Illustrating this methodology of intuitive inquiry is the synchronicity that led me

to Ma'at. While researching ancient images of masculine and feminine archetypes—in

particular Thoth as a representative of *eros*—I came upon an ancient *Book of the Dead*

papyrus whose Weighing of the Heart scene arrested my attention utterly (fig. 1). In this

papyrus, the priestess Nisti-ta-Nebet-Taui, who commissioned the work, has just been

"justified," or found "true of voice," for the scale is in perfect balance.

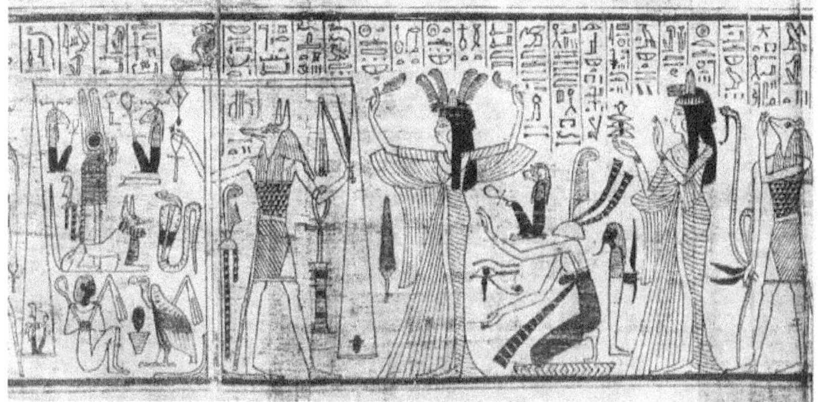

Figure 1. Papyrus of Nisti-ta-Nebet-Taui: Weighing of the Heart scene in Papyrus #8
(Piankoff and Rambova, *Mythological Papyri*). The papyrus is in the collection of the
Cairo Egyptian Museum. Public domain.

Nisti-ta-Nebet-Taui's jubilation and confidence in the afterlife offer a compelling

resonance over the ages. What gave her the assurance that she would be welcomed as a

denizen of the afterlife, to live forever with the gods and goddesses and the other Blessed

Dead who preceded her? What was the meaning behind the esoteric images and symbols on her treasured scroll, her *Book of Going Forth Into Day*?

How did the ancient Egyptians depict their experience of the archetypal energies of renewal? What might individuals past and present, struggling to survive and evolve, learn from this ancient and venerable nation? These questions pointed my exploration toward the mysteries of renewal central to the ancient Egyptian culture. Here I would uncover new perspectives—both personal and cultural—on the flourishing of life through learning how to honor the processes of regeneration, renewal, and rebirth.

Personal Call to Action

It's August 2005, and I am standing on the Continental Divide with my teenage son, daughter, and niece. We are looking out over the western slope of the Rocky Mountains, where millions upon millions of rust-colored pines stretch out as far as the eye can see. The pine beetles are killing them, thanks to an infestation spurred on by warmer winters and less precipitation. In this moment, climate change becomes much more than a theory or a collection of statistics. The beauty I've always known—the mountain landscape I've counted on sharing with my children and grandchildren, just as my parents and grandparents shared it with me—is forever altered and diminished. A harsh realization settles in: human actions that contribute to global warming are destroying the world I love.

In the years following this heartbreaking moment, guilt, hopelessness, and ultimately resignation take hold. Then, on Labor Day 2010, an explosive forest fire begins just one mile from my home. In over twenty years of living in the foothills west of Boulder, Colorado, I had yet to experience the numbing fear that settles heavily over one's consciousness when the call to evacuate comes. Driven by high winds, this hungry, erratic wildfire consumes thousands of acres of forest and 168 of my neighbors' homes before the firefighters contain it at last, five days after our evacuation. Our home is miraculously spared from the blaze, yet my sense of helplessness deepens.

Two weeks later, I begin a doctoral program in mythological studies. I spend the next four years concentrating not on environmental disaster and heartbreak, but on various cultures and their spiritual traditions. After completing my coursework and gaining approval for my dissertation concept, *Eros and the Fierce Feminine,* I dive into my research on emerging archetypal energies—until a poem comes to my attention that hits a nerve with unusual force, nudging me in a new direction.

hieroglyphic staircase

It's 3:23 in the morning

and I'm awake

because my great grandchildren

won't let me sleep

my great grandchildren

ask me in dreams

what did you do while the planet was plundered?

what did you do when the earth was unraveling?

surely you did something

when the seasons started failing?

as the mammals, reptiles, birds were all dying?

did you fill the streets with protest

when democracy was stolen?

what did you do

once

you

knew?

(Dellinger *love letter* 1–3)

Dellinger imagines the future generations as his relatives, his great-great-grandchildren, and he hears them demanding an accounting of our individual parts in stemming the multipronged catastrophes that are unfolding. This poem resonates deeply within me, requiring a descent into the very darkness I had pulled back from in recent years. I am soul-struck[12] by the poem's haunting images and questions, its insistence that the many crises plaguing our world can no longer be ignored. *The Earth is unraveling,* it cries to me. *What are you doing about it?*

An inner knowing demands that I find a way to deepen my understanding of these very concerns. I resist, doubting that I can face these issues without succumbing to despair. I question my credibility, my right to speak to these matters. I reason with myself. After all, what can I offer to the conversation? I am neither a climate scientist nor an expert. I am an artist . . . a scholar of world cultures . . . a mother. Yet I am in the grip of this *need* to address the unrest within me, which by now has transformed from

---

[12] *Soul-struck* is a feeling akin to a sudden, penetrating recognition, like an arrow. It is a hallmark of eros and an awakened heart. Repression of its call to attention, or action, results in the loss of connection to what has the most meaning and passion in life, leading to restriction of life's sustaining flow of energy. It is the Call to Action Campbell outlined as part of the Hero's Journey, and rejection of the Call has dire consequences.

uneasiness into pure outrage: *This is not the world I want to be handing over to my children and their children!*

Still I resist, and my research process becomes ever more complex, abstract, and disembodied. At last, I hit an immovable wall. Confusion and desolation envelop me. At the eleventh hour, with my dissertation committee challenging me to speak with an authentic voice, a *woman's* voice, I struggle to understand what my work is missing.

In the midst of my soul-searching, many memories surface, both fear-filled and love-filled. In one, I am a wee child, snuggled against my grandmother Larsen. She reads me a story from a precious twelve-volume set of world mythologies, the same treasured books she read to my father when he was a boy. As wonder-filled images of ancient gods and goddesses flow through my imagination, her warm voice washes over me and a visceral feeling of security wraps around me, fostering a sense that *all is well.*

I have always loved storytelling, whether making up stories with my children or reading books aloud for hours. And this, I suddenly realize, is the missing link: my willingness to witness, my need to speak out. My memories are pointing to a path forward, inescapable and implacable. My dissertation must be an offering to the flow of stories pressing on humanity, those stories that need to be told. It must speak to those hearts longing to awaken to their own wisdom and stories in the hearing.

In accepting this task, my work shifts. The underlying framework—and the pattern for weaving together all the facets—presents itself, and this dissertation begins to emerge from the swirling maelstrom of fear and loss. My great-great-grandchildren—like Dellinger's—deserve an accounting. This accounting must begin in an attempt to differentiate the psychological and archetypal forces that inhibit our actions, our willingness to address the crises of our contemporary world. *What can I do,* I ask, *as the world unravels, as the seasons fail, as the many beings die?* I am determined to discover the answers to these questions by seeking the wisdom embedded in the stories and cosmic worldview of the ancients.

Recognition of the consequences of our nation's inaction and my own complacency is my personal call to action. I feel I must not be resigned to handing on these pressing, multipronged issues to my beloved children and their children. It is past the time to begin differentiating the pernicious roots feeding the multitude of crises in our world while simultaneously taking action to stem the rising destruction, no matter how modest the contribution. *The movement of renewal we so urgently need must be imagined and held in our hearts before it will become a reality—and each of us is capable of that!*

Chapter 2. Ancient Egyptian Wisdom: A Holoscopic Perspective

For [the ancient Egyptian], heaven and earth, beings and things,

gods and their creations were all parts of an animated universe

permeated with manifestations of divine power. (Žabkar 15)

As one delves into Egyptian mythology, it quickly becomes apparent that specific

characteristics and spheres of influence are not assigned to just one particular goddess or

god. Our contemporary style of consciousness prioritizes scientific evidence, well-

delineated categories, and linear timelines that include a beginning, a middle, and an end.

This is true for literature as well as the sciences. But the ancient Egyptian perspective was

not based on this style of consciousness, and *not* because they were less evolved,

primitive, or illogical, as a number of historians have assessed. To move beyond the

categories and the quest for cold, hard facts that modern scientific methodologies depend

on requires a transformation in our relationship with the ancient Egyptians and their

symbolic images and texts.

Differentiation and Pragmatism: The Ancient Egyptian Style of Consciousness

The Egyptians were not drawn to a concept of "one truth," nor did they create a

single codified text containing an apportioned, delineated pantheon. Their gods and

goddesses were not represented in only one particular form or even one species, nor did

they assume a consistent, predictable place in neatly arranged groupings. The people who

belonged to this culture seem to have understood that the creative imagination opens up

"a space, a cosmos, in which all these styles [of consciousness] coexist" (Cheetham 111).

The ancient Egyptians were also profoundly pragmatic. Indeed, this culture is an

early example of interest in making and recording scientific explorations in such areas as astronomy and human anatomy. They were well aware of the subtle body energies, and like many ancient cultures, they relied on this knowledge in both medicinal and religious practices. The authors of *The Medicine of the Ancient Egyptians* offer an in-depth analysis of the extant medical papyri that attest to sophisticated medical knowledge "unparalleled in other cultures" (Strouhal, Vachala, and Vymazalová 3).[13]

Furthermore, they were unparalleled observers of nature, noting the finest details of all the life that surrounded them. The artistic renderings of the myriad life forms living in and along the Nile that I saw inscribed on the walls of a tomb in Egypt forty years ago left a profound impression on me. The lovingly rendered fish, birds, papyrus bushes—the Nile teeming with life—conveyed a love of living and a reverent appreciation for every creature.

Differentiation is foundational to the ancient Egyptian style of consciousness. It can be discerned in the development of their sacred sciences, from astronomy, mathematics, architecture, medicine, and a sophisticated calendar based on 365 days to metallurgy, stone working, hydraulic irrigation systems, and so on (Thompson 17). The ancient Egyptians also developed the first nation-state and the accompanying administrative layers required to maintain this form of government. For the ancient Egyptians there was no division between church and state; instead "all acts were played out against a background of divine patterns" (Clark 26).

Their religious and philosophical speculations were original and complex, evolved over the millennia, and "penetrated and informed every aspect of life" (Clark 26). Pivotal to their spiritual beliefs was the potent insight that the One becomes the

---

[13] The authors are archaeologists and Egyptologists, and Eugen Strouhal is one of the founders of the field of paleopathology.

Many without losing its inherent oneness. Differentiation does not annul the primordial unity, which continues to underlie all that appears separate, including many aspects of the divine.

Embodying this idea are a dream message and image that came to me as I was exploring the goddess Ma'at's symbolism: Ma'at, appearing as the Wild Cow, emerged from a cave to greet the dead. She was wearing her crown, a vermillion sun disc, between her long, gracefully curved horns, with two huge ostrich feathers, back-to-back, rising up from the central solar disc. The message that accompanied her appearance was: *Until we realize that the gods and goddesses are multiple perspectives—holoscopic—they don't come alive. They are like a kaleidoscope: composed of all the same elements, but with changing patterns that express the differences endlessly.*

This revelation has informed my approach to the exploration of Ma'at and her compatriots. The original term *holoscopic* is a perfect way to describe this perception. It comprises a combination of actual Greek words that work together seamlessly to describe the style of consciousness prevalent in ancient Egypt. *Holo-* comes from the Greek word *holos*, meaning "whole, entire, complete," and *-scopic* comes from *scope,* which is related to the Latin word scopo "aim, purpose, object, thing aimed at, mark, target," and the Greek word *skopos*, meaning "aim, target, object of attention" and "watcher, one who watches" ("Holos"; "Scope" Etymonline.com). Therefore, a holoscopic viewpoint recognizes that life comprises innumerable interwoven facets, patterns that together create and participate in a whole system that is observable.

Examples of the holoscopic perspective in renewal symbolism abound in ancient Egyptian iconography. This study focuses on the symbols of the divine Feminine, specifically those that relate to Ma'at: the raising of the primordial mound; the active Eye, the cobra, and the *uraeus*; the Two Ladies who embody the Crowns of Upper and Lower Egypt; the Throne and Sacred Enclosure as the Lap, Womb, and Tomb of the divine Feminine; the Day and Night Barques as the means for renewal and rebirth; the double lion as the liminal gates of the east and the west, of sunrise and sunset; and complementary duality as it gives shape to time. These images (which are further articulated in chapter 3) point to the core concept of renewal, and yet each grouping also emphasizes particular characteristics of renewal, circulation, and regeneration.

A Unique Landscape: Egypt as a "Gift of the River"

> In ancient times, people had the feeling that in the part of the world
> they inhabited, the whole was experienced as present. . . . In this
> macrocosmic experience of landscape people saw universal,
> spiritual forces active and immanent in the desert and flood, the
> course of the sun, the dome of the sky, and throughout the
> phenomenal world. (Naydler, *Temple of the Cosmos* 11)

A mighty river created the fertile river valley that stretches the length of Egypt's lands, flowing from south to north. To these ancient people, it was unique and holy. With little to no annual rainfall in Egypt, all water came from the Nile. The Nile literally and figuratively shaped not only the landscape and the lives of all those who dwelled near its banks, but also ancient Egyptian consciousness.

The Nile river valley itself is an essential example of renewal. Its fertility was a result of the river's annual cycle of inundation and was the source of all life in ancient Egypt. The substantial base of alluvial soil, which had built up over the millennia, provided a deep layer of rich humus in an otherwise arid, barren desert. The ancients named their fertile land *Kemet*, "Black Lands," due to the rich black silt deposited each year during the floods. The surrounding desert was known as the "Red Lands." The ancient Egyptians called their river simply "River" or "Great River."

In his reflections on ancient Egypt, the Greek historian Herodotus (*c.* 484–425 BCE) astutely observed that "the Egypt to which the Hellenes sail is land that was deposited by the river—it is the gift of the river to the Egyptians" (Strassler 118). The portion of the river known as the White Nile begins its 4,180-mile journey from Lake Victoria, in central Africa, and flows toward the north. The portion known as the Blue Nile—source of the precious silt that ensured the valley's lands were arable for thousands of years, until the Aswan Dam[14] curtailed the annual cycle—originates in the Ethiopian highlands. Where these two mighty tributaries join, it becomes the river we know today as the Nile.

Arriving in midsummer, the Nile's annual inundation literally meant life or death. If the water levels were too low to fertilize sufficient farmland, low crop yields resulted in hunger and drought was a distinct possibility. If the inundation was too abundant, entire villages were swept away, causing significant loss of life and damage to essential infrastructure such as dikes and irrigation canals. Recordings of water levels using a device historians call a "Nile-o-meter" attest to the importance the ancient Egyptians placed on closely observing nature. Judging from early evidence, historians speculate that the need to record the annual inundation spurred the development of writing.

---

[14] Built in the 1960s, the Aswan Dam was envisioned as the answer to Egypt's growing energy needs and its desire to manage the annual inundation. In reality, the dam interrupted a cycle of renewal that was critical to the land's fertility and the delta watershed. Nature had evolved the perfect method for washing away naturally occurring salts while depositing fertile silt and plant matter each year.

The prevailing winds blow across this land from north to south. The north wind was equated with the breath of life, symbolized by the *ankh*. This breeze was envisioned as restorative, bringing life to the land and to the deceased as they entered the afterlife. This relatively steady breeze also made transportation on the Nile by boat possible. Boats traveled with the south–north current of the Nile or used sails, oars, and tow ropes to move against the current going from north to south.

Despite the challenges and dangers the river presented—from the annual inundation to the daily threats of crocodiles and hippopotami—humans living along the Nile were inextricably intertwined with its cycles, with the numerous ecosystems along its banks, and with the animals, birds, and reptiles that shared these habitats. Reverence for and connection to the land and its life forms were deeply entrenched in the ancient Egyptian psyche. The people loved their lands along the Nile, considering them holy and imbued with divine presence. Their intricate observations of the land, the animals, the river, the stars, and the moon and sun gave rise to their mythological and cosmological imagery.

From what can be discerned in their writings and from their lifestyle (as is revealed in later chapters), the ancient Egyptians' pragmatic mind-set focused on harmonizing opposites and accepting the paradoxical foundation of life. This is especially evident in their view that "it was always possible to bring a negative or imperfect condition back […] to its perfect state at the time of creation" (Hornung, *Idea Into Image* 91). It stands to reason that the river's cyclic dual nature—creation and destruction—had a hand in shaping this unique consciousness of the people, encouraging them to harmonize with its paradoxical nature.

Into the Landscape: An Imaginal Journey

Imagine living enveloped in the natural rhythms of the earth, with its multitude of facets sparked with consciousness and creativity. Overhead, a vast sky stretches from horizon to horizon in all directions, where the orderly procession of celestial bodies marks the twelve hours of the day and the twelve hours of the night. The stars blazing in their ordered configurations, wheeling night after night in the velvet blackness with rhythmic precision, set the mind to observation, measurement, and proportion.

Imagine the silvery moon above, a luminous orb that increases and decreases with rhythmic precision, influencing the tidal pull of fluids and emotions within the human body. The brilliant blue of the daytime sky begins and ends with the golden sun emerging from and disappearing behind shining mountains. The sun's passage orchestrates life's movements and commerce, encouraging verdant fertility with its warmth or wilting all life with its intense hot eye. In this astronomical landscape, arising and dying are ever-present events—a natural part of the eternal return, the circle of repetition.

There is nothing to compare to the beauty of a sunset in the desert. The setting sun's mellow light illuminates the sky, transforming it from below the horizon with a palette of red, orange, pink, and purple. As the air cools, the earth radiates its solar warmth and proceeds toward night. The stars begin to pop into view until at last the black sky is ablaze with their fiery light. Night after night, the moon moves through its phases in this skyscape, with its predictable, measured waxing and waning light.

Imagine a narrow, fecund river valley burgeoning with life, surrounded by arid desert and forbidding mountains. Here, with one foot placed upon fertile black alluvium of the river valley and the other planted on the barren red soil of the desert, a person can literally straddle the divide between life and death. Ma'at's cosmic patterns of renewal and regeneration shape the landscape and fill the sky with celestial beings that can be relied upon, provided the reciprocal relationships are maintained and honored with the fitting devotion.

The signs of life and cyclic rounds of nature fired the hearts and imaginations of these ancient desert dwellers, just as nature inspires artists and poets today. Nature in all its glory gave the ancient Egyptians an imaginal series of images for interpreting the processes of life and death. The sun's disappearance behind the western mountains symbolized the solar god's death and entrance into the netherworld, referred to as the "beautiful West" (Faulkner 50). The dawn's light was envisioned as the renewed sun, rebirthed after having regained its youthful vigor and strength during its underworld journey.

These insights into aging and dying are especially useful for our own modern times, because we have purged our imaginal cache of complementary images related to (on the one hand) old age and death and (on the other) the renewal promised with the coming of dawn.

Ma'at, Who Links Above and Below

Human consciousness is structured by the psyche's image-rich, metaphorical communication style, with its inherent storytelling power that is employed by the meaning-seeking mind. This system uses creative means to express the mysteries of life and death and to imbue our collective and individual journeys with meaning. The psyche also connects to a dimension that is beyond or below individual consciousness, and for the ancient Egyptians this dimension permeated all life.

As described above, these people were keen observers of nature, enlivened by a deeply rooted sense of pragmatism. The celestial bodies they scrutinized, as well as the terrestrial and metaphysical forms of energy they discerned, are expressions of archetypal patterns that inspired the felt sense of a cosmic presence. In ancient Egypt it was the goddess Ma'at who personified this presence—who "establishe[d] the link between above and below" (Uždavinys, *Philosophy and Theurgy* 295).

Over the centuries, the people increasingly recognized that living within the natural boundaries of the cosmic patterns and being directed by Ma'at's natural laws reaped the best rewards for their personal lives and their society. Therefore, they focused on harmonizing their actions with the world order that, according to their system of beliefs, was established by Ma'at at the time of creation. Living enfolded within nature, and working to balance and order their lives to Ma'at's sacred harmony, awakened their hearts and ignited an evolution of consciousness, birthing self-reflection and a sense of right proportion for more and more of the population as time marched on.

Cosmic Order: A Living, Breathing Tapestry

Holoscopic wisdom lent flexibility to the ancient Egyptians' explorations of metaphysical questions and fostered depth and breadth of consciousness. Although it embraced multiple perspectives, the culture shared a vision of unification and order that could be expressed both materially and metaphorically. The archetypal pattern of unity sustained their civilization over the millennia and, in times of discord and political unrest, was available as a model for reweaving harmony and balance. As chapter 4 explores, to be in balance meant to be in harmony with Ma'at's cosmic order.

Neters: The Gods and Goddesses

> The gods were still present in the land of Egypt, for nature was still
> transparent, not yet solid and opaque. Nature mediated divine
> energies that people became aware of by "seeing through" the
> phenomenal world to the numinous presences beyond. (Naydler,
> *Future of the Ancient World* 90)

For the people of ancient Egypt, spiritual energies—including the features of the landscape, the natural elements, all creatures, even time and space—were alive and permeated every aspect of life. Theirs was a living tapestry of vibrant interwoven threads of life and death, light and dark. All life was rooted in the imaginal and arose organically from the fertile soil of the Nile valley through awareness of and connection to the spiritual energies recognized and related to over the eons.

"For them, these invisible beings [deities] were imaginal in precisely the sense that they were objectively real" (Naydler, *Future of the Ancient World* 138). Opposites existed not as a question of either/or, but as a continuum, with the two poles actively exchanging energy—either harmonized and working together to amplify one another's energy, or disharmonious and disruptive to one another. Just as their great river flowed and inundated the land each year since time-out-of-mind, their myths represented living, breathing, interactive presences that required constant attention to foster the reciprocal relationship that ensured the flourishing of life. If we discount this way of seeing as "primitive" or dismiss it as "unreal," we miss the opportunity of seeing the world as the ancient Egyptians did, of learning from them and expanding our own consciousness.

"Archetypes are really verbs" (Howell 164) as opposed to nouns. The ancient

Egyptian deities, or *neters*, express archetypal patterns and primordial principles; they are

envisioned as actions, not as static beings. They are intertwined in all phenomena, and

they exist in a divine realm that exists alongside our worldly realm. These principles

inspired a sense of cosmic presence and holiness in all life, including the mountains and

stones, the river, the wind, the sun and stars, the seeds and fertile soil.

Though modern science describes much of the natural world as "dead matter"—

and many humans no longer believe in gods and goddesses per se—experiences in nature

still conjure a sense of restoration and reverence. Given nature's inherent capacity to

encourage renewal and emotional healing, it behooves us to become astutely aware of

this connection and to ask how we can promote a more conscious relationship with this

energy of renewal.

Creation: From Chaos to Order

> Myths of creation have a fundamental, exemplary importance in
>
> every culture: only the recollection of an ideal, perfect beginning
>
> of the world and of human existence enables us to overcome crises
>
> and begin anew . . . [T]he world could become repeatedly as new
>
> and perfect as at the time of its origin. From this conviction they
>
> drew much of the creative power that continues to impress us
>
> today. (Hornung, *Idea Into Image* 40)

In ancient Egyptian cosmology, there are at least six variations of creation—

additional proof of the holoscopic perspective that seeks to explore the mysterious,

complex idea of creation from multiple vantage points. Continuous creation is not a onetime event but reoccurs in many ways. Every dawn is a return to First Time. Each year the cosmic patterns renew, announced by the heliacal rising[15] of the star Sirius, heralding the return of the inundation. The death of the king, and the coronation of the new king, resets historical time while maintaining the connections with the past. Each of these events is experienced as a return to the beginning, to the creation of all things.

Creation is known as *tep zepy*, literally meaning "First Occasion"—first breath, first light, first sound. All cosmologies in ancient Egypt begin in the Nun, a watery realm where *tep zepy* initiates and all life forms emerge. The Nun is both the source of creation and inertia. Ma'at's order comes forth from the inert stillness of Nun along with the breath of life; the creator exhales, or releases the spoken word (which is simply another way to envision the breath, in resonant chant or sung prayer), and the primordial mound rises or the eternal lotus blooms. Ma'at's cosmic order and patterns of nature begin to give shape to all creation. Perfection of her natural laws and cosmic patterns provides the potential for both society and individual to reset whenever balance is disrupted and chaos reigns.

When I think of the word *chaos,* I see a swirling confusion of discordant energies, but the ancient Egyptians knew another way to see chaos as undifferentiated inertia. For them, standstill and inertia were abhorrent. To be alive was to be in motion, to have the ability to use one's limbs, to work, to enjoy life's offerings. Their response to the image of Nun's inertia was akin to the fear of becoming a rotting corpse. And yet from the homogenous abyss of Nun's still and watery realm, myriad life forms were born. This is

---

[15] "Heliacal rising" refers to a group of stars that disappear below the horizon for a period of time before reappearing in the night sky. Sirius is the brightest star in the night sky by a magnitude of -1.46, and its ancient Greek name means "glowing." The ancient Egyptians named this star Sopdet and (in later times) related her to Isis, just as Osiris became equated with Orion. Her rising, after seventy days' absence when she was thought to be in the underworld with Osiris, coincided with the arrival of the inundation.

yet another example of the holoscopic viewpoint that weds the paradoxical opposites into a relationship of both/and.

Renewal Through Death and Resurrection

For the ancient Egyptian, death was not the end but, like birth, simply a passage or an initiation (Kristensen 56). Death was a threshold that gave way to afterlife. Like creation, death was envisioned in multiple ways, not as one codified story. Egyptologists have charted the evolution of the beliefs surrounding death, through discoveries in tombs and grave goods as well as in the contemporary literature. The main thesis of Jan Assmann's book *Death and Salvation in Ancient Egypt* is that "death is the origin and center of culture" (1)—not just in Egypt but in all cultures:

> Living with the dead and with death is one of the most normal
>
> manifestations of human culture, and it presumably lies at the heart
>
> of the stuff of human existence. From the point of view of
>
> comparative anthropology, it is we [the Western cultures], not the
>
> ancient Egyptians, who are the exception. Few cultures in this
>
> world exclude death and the dead from their reality as radically as
>
> we do. (Assmann, *Death and Salvation* 1)

To assume that the ancient Egyptians' contemplations of and preparations for death reflect a morbid fascination is to miss the greater import of what they were expressing through their active and vivid relationship with the reality of death and their hoped-for afterlife, as evidenced in their literature, images, artifact, temples, and tombs.

Practices and Symbols of Renewal

In his book *Voices from Ancient Egypt*, R. B. Parkinson[16] states that the contemporary viewpoint of the ancient Egyptians as "morbid is unfounded. Preparations for death may dominate the surviving records of their culture, but these sprang from a love for life" (131). From the evidence, it appears that not death itself, but being found worthy of resurrection into eternal life was at the core of their daily thoughts. Life was the focus of their ritual activities, and it was the love of life that inspired a focus on how to perpetuate flourishing life after death.

One way they envisioned the afterlife was as a perfected replica of Egypt, where they could live on just as they always had, with the main difference being that they did not have to suffer a "second death"—provided they were "justified" in the ritual known as the Weighing of the Heart. One of the chief benefits of being justified or found "true of voice"—that is, judged as worthy of eternal life—was achieving a status that assured they would never die again. Chapter 5 explores this scene in greater detail, for it is Ma'at and her relationship to the individual heart's consciousness that shapes the outcome.

The prayers of these ancient people for life after death portray a fervent desire for mobility, for regaining use of their members, for striding forth from their tomb upon their two strong legs. A euphemism for describing someone who has died was to say the person has "fallen on his side," or become incapable of movement, rigid and still. Rituals to open the mouth and eyes, to activate all the senses and reanimate the numerous soul-parts, were performed just before the mummified body was interred. The Opening of the Mouth ritual (discussed further in chapter 4) was also the basis for other rituals performed

---

[16] Parkinson is professor of Egyptology at the University of Oxford and former curator of the Department of Ancient Egypt and Sudan at the British Museum.

to activate the statues of the gods and goddesses so they would become proper receptacles for the divine presence.

Sacred texts encouraged the deceased to wake up, roll from their left to their right side, breathe in the north wind, and live again (Kristensen 84). Ongoing offerings and speaking aloud the deceased person's name and accomplishments ensured the continuation of life after death. People envisioned being able once again to breath, see, feel, eat, drink, work, play, make love. In *Coffin Texts,* Spell 56, the deceased is urged, "O N,[17] stand up to life, for you have not died!" *Coffin Texts,* Spell 51, a hymn of resurrection, declares: "Awake to life O N, for you have not died!" In other words, *see where you are and recognize your peers, those you are joining for eternity.*

The following verse could be referencing very early burial practices or perhaps the natural process of waking up after a night's sleep, which is akin to awakening to eternal life after the ordeal of death:

> Lift up your heart and see the patricians, that praise may be given
>
> to you in the Two Conclaves. Lift yourself up from upon your left
>
> side,[18] place yourself upon your right side, and receive the breezes
>
> of the river-side; eat bread with the living and travel in peace to the
>
> beautiful West. (Faulkner 50)

It urges the deceased to breathe in "the breezes of the river-side," the refreshing, life-restoring north wind, the breath of the gods; to "eat bread with the living"—in other words, receive the offerings, share in a meal with your loved ones who do honor to your

---

[17] "N" or "NN" in the sacred literature is a placeholder for the deceased's name. It is presumed that when this was recited, the deceased person's name would be spoken here.

[18] Prehistoric finds show that one ancient burial practice involved placing the dead in a pit grave, lying in a semi-contracted position on their left side, with their head to the east and facing south (Shaw 26).

name and memory at your tomb; and to "travel in peace to the beautiful West," the land of eternal life after death.

Imagining Eternal Renewal

Ancient Egyptians had many ways of envisioning the Netherworld, but the "beautiful West" was a frequent metaphor for entrance to the underworld, the threshold between realms. The western mountains were the location of many of their burial grounds and where they built the necropolis, the city of the dead. The sun set in the West, of course, at the end of its day journey, cradled between two mountains, and there the night passage began. Two symbols—the *ankh* (the sacred symbol of the breath of life) and the *akhet*, meaning the "horizon" and "mountain of light" (two mountain peaks cradling the sun disc)—were among those most frequently used to depict renewal, resurrection, and life everlasting.

The paradox of death is underscored by the fact that a single gesture—such as the upraised arms of the goddess figures from Neolithic times forward—can be thought of as a symbol for celebration, life, and awe on the one hand, and for mourning, grief, and death on the other. In ancient Egypt, death was considered as an opportunity to move from a brief life of uncertainty, hard work, and challenges to becoming one of the Blessed Dead for all eternity. Therefore, death could be seen as a passage to an existence in the company of Re and the other Blessed Dead. As is true for many cultures, however, death was a double-edged sword; the ancient Egyptians still experienced death as an unmitigated loss for the living, with the natural feelings of grief. Again they held fast to a paradoxical perspective: that death is both the beginning of eternal life and the end of natural life.

Like birth, death was a specific, onetime event. After death, the deceased began a journey through the underworld, with the barque as the primary form of transportation. As in all their philosophical ponderings, the ancient Egyptians envisioned multiple versions of this journey, but regardless of the specifics, all who died must make their way to the Hall of Truth—the Hall of Double Ma'at—where they had to survive the necessary ordeal of the Weighing of the Heart. It was believed that if they passed through the ordeal successfully, they entered a world that, in one version, shared all the pleasant and treasured aspects of the physical world but was devoid of the hardship, suffering, and death.

The Netherworld was equated with silence, but the dead communicated with the living in dreams and other altered states of being. The living might write letters to loved ones and visit their tombs, where meals and festivals were enjoyed in their company. For the ancient Egyptians, life after death was not an empty void—provided the deceased had upheld the precepts of Ma'at during his or her lifetime.

Relationship with the Divine

One way the ancient Egyptians focused their conscious intention was in the daily acknowledgment of the reciprocal relationship between the divine, human, and ancestral realms, typically through rituals. Key to nurturing this relationship were the underlying values of self-reflection and a finely tuned spiritual awareness married to a pragmatic style of consciousness. Through the correct rituals and offerings, they continually sought to promote flourishing life and to reestablish the balance necessary to make life flourish when it was disrupted.[19]

---

[19] Other cultures, such as the Navajo—a Native American tribe with ancestral lands in northern Arizona and southern New Mexico—also believe this. The Navajo's core philosophical principle is *hózhó*, the belief

As described earlier in this chapter, the ancient Egyptians did not split spiritual and material realities. In fact, they saw all offerings placed upon the altars of their deities—bread, grain, flowers, fruit, linen, incense—as the physical representations of eternal life. These proofs of life everlasting contributed to renewal by sharing with the gods and the deceased ancestors the energy represented by the efforts of humans to propagate these gifts of the earth, in order to circulate the sacred flow of the energy of life.

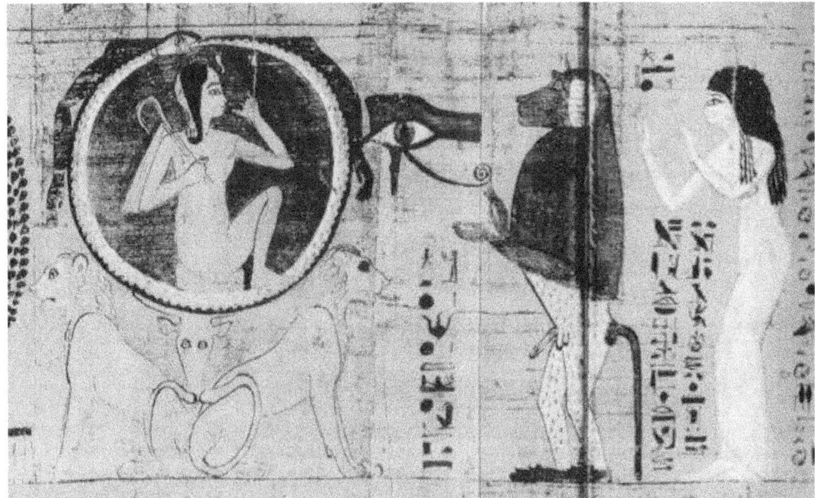

Figure 2. Renewal and resurrection scene in Papyrus #1, Her-Uben A (Piankoff and Rambova, *Mythological Papyri*). The papyrus is in the collection of the Cairo Egyptian Museum. Public domain.

The image above (fig. 2) is from the genre of literature known as the *Book of Going Forth Into Day* (or the *Book of the Dead*). This papyrus originated in the Thebes area at the beginning of the 21st Dynasty and was prepared for a priestess of the ram-headed god Amun. It illustrates the renewal of life, with Horus as the divine child sitting

---

that each individual is responsible for maintaining the balance, beauty, truth, and harmony that ensure life flourishes.

inside his solar disc. His youth is indicated by a sidelock of hair, his nudity, and his finger lifted to his mouth. The solar disc is encircled by an *ouroboros*, a serpent biting its tail—a symbol of cyclic renewal and rebirth. The goddess Nut's two black arms with breasts embrace the disc that is cradled between the horns of Hathor, the Wild Cow goddess whose origins are attested to in the earliest layers of ancient Egyptian culture. She is resting on the backs of the double lion, known as Aker. The double lion symbol, also called "Yesterday and Tomorrow," personifies two aspects of time: eternal cyclic renewal and eternal perfection or "sameness" (Pinch, *Egyptian Mythology* 197). The double lion guards the two horizons where the sun rises and sets—the eastern and the western gates—and thus refer to birth, death, and resurrection.

To the right of the central image stands a baboon—a manifestation of the god Thoth, or Djehuty as the Egyptians named him—offering the Whole (healed) Eye to the disc and Child, another symbol of resurrection. Djehuty is the lunar god of wisdom and is vizier to Re.[20] Djehuty—the god of writing, wisdom, magic, and healing, and the patron of scribes—is sometimes partnered with the goddess Seshet; together they "know the future" and inscribe the length of each king's reign on the leaves of the sacred Tree of Life, the *ished* or *persea* tree (Wilkinson, *Reading Egyptian Art* 166). In addition to these roles, Djehuty is also named as Ma'at's consort. The early Egyptologist E. A. Wallis Budge describes Djehuty and Ma'at as the masculine and feminine expressions of identical archetypal patterns.

The hieroglyphic inscription reads, "Adoration of Re. The new year of Re in the barge of Re in the sky" (Piankoff and Rambova, *Mythological Papyri* 73). The text

---

[20] Djehuty-Thoth is the Egyptian god equated with the later alchemical *Hermes Trismegistus*, the author of the Hermetic Corpus. Hermes was the ancient Greek god who was syncretized with the Egyptian god Djehuty, and Trismegistus means "thrice great."

equates the disc with the Solar Barque, and both represent constant cyclic movement.

Thus all the elements of this image combine to create a complex symbol of rebirth and

renewal. Accompanying this vignette in the so-called *Book of the Dead*, Chapter 17, is

the following text: "It is Atum, the dweller in his disk, or it is Re in the eastern horizon of

the sky. I am Yesterday, I know Tomorrow" (Roberts, *My Heart My Mother* 55). Atum is

Yesterday, the aged solar god who sets in the west at night. Re is Tomorrow, the god who

emerges from his nightly journey renewed and restored as Re-Horakhty, the newly risen

sun—and they are one.

Temporal and Spatial Orientation

As illustrated in fig. 2 above, the ancient Egyptians had two concepts of time: *nehen* and

djet, or yesterday and tomorrow. Shu and Tefnut, the first sexually differentiated couple

from the Heliopolitan cosmology (discussed in detail in chapter 5), embody these aspects.

In this image of renewal, they are depicted as Ruty—the back-to-back double lion, shown

in fig. 3 below.

The *akhet* or "horizon" symbol also illustrates the two ways of thinking about

time. James P. Allen's approach to these two forms of time is very helpful; he compares

"the Egyptian concept of time . . . to a play: its script (*dt*) is fixed and unchanging, but

each performance of the play (*nhh*) is different, with new settings and new actors" (Allen

134).[21] The solar disc symbolizes *nehen*, eternal renewal, with its continuous movement

through the cyclic patterns, ascending and descending. The two mountain peaks of the

horizon symbol are an example of *djet* time—fixed, perfected, ripened. They demark the

---

[21] Here is another example of the different ways Egyptologists work with the ancient Egyptian language; *dt*
and *nhh* are the translations of the hieroglyphic symbols (no vowels), although most scholars choose to add
vowels to make the symbols more familiar to contemporary expectations. Therefore, *dt* becomes *djet,* and
nhh becomes *nehen.*

east and west poles of the horizontal plane, as the double lion suggests the earth's

elements in the shape and placement of their back-to-back figures.

Figure 3. Ruty, the double lion (Piankoff and Rambova, *Mythological Papyri* 33, fig. 15).
Public domain.

The double lions are also known as Shu and Tefnut, the first sexually

differentiated couple from the Heliopolitan cosmology; or Aker, the name of the ancient

earth god who is often depicted as a double sphinx. Above the double lion is the *akhet*

symbol, meaning "horizon," with an *ankh* hanging off the saddle between the two

mountain peaks nestling the sun—a symbol of life engendered by the eternal cyclic

movement of sunrise and sunset. The vertical dimension that connects the above

(heavens) and the below (underworld) is referenced by the solar disc, which ascends and

descends between the mountain peaks in its daily round.

Nut and the solar disc, or barque, encircled by the *ouroboros* also point to the central axis of the vertical space, as does the primordial celestial cow goddess—all acting as means of resurrection and protection. The mythologem of the celestial cow reveals that she is the creatrix *Mehet-Weret* from prehistoric times. In her version of creation, she births her divine child (the vermillion solar disc) and affixes him between her long horns to raise him up to the stars. Originally known as the Great Flood, she saw her name change over time to the Great Swimmer: "She is the female counterpart of *Nun*, the god of the primeval ocean, and a rival for his title of 'oldest of beings'" (Pinch, *Handbook* 163).

Hours of the Day and Night

From the Egyptian perspective, the dome of the sky is divided into the twelve hours, or regions, of the day, and the night is also divided into twelve hours or regions. Each hour is related to specific gods and goddesses. A certain quality also is associated with each region. Ma'at is named as the first hour of the day and assigned to the eastern mountains, where the sun first appears. She and the goddess of the twelfth hour of the night—She Who Beholds the Beauty of Re—mark the threshold of the eastern horizon, where a joyous celebration greets the Solar Barque and its occupants each dawn. Re traverses the sky in his Day Barque, *Mandjet*, which is identified as an aspect of the feminine deity Isis.

Likewise, the western horizon is the entrance to the Netherworld. There the aged sun god, Atum, completes each day alongside his companions in the Solar Barque as Isis gives way to Nephthys as the Night Barque. They, too, are greeted with celebration and welcome by the Blessed Dead as the sun dips behind the western mountains and the sky blazes.

> [F]or the ancients the sun was the outward form of a god. As such,
> its life and being belonged to the mythical domain: the domain of
> eternal, archetypal processes that lie essentially beyond time. In
> ancient Egypt, time existed in direct relationship to the eternal.
> (Naydler, *Temple of the Cosmos* 66)

In one version of the solar god's journey, the archetypal sky goddess Nut receives the sun god Re at each sunset and swallows him (fig. 4). In this mythologem, the night journey of renewal continues through Nut's body as the solar god is rejoined with Osiris in the darkest hours of the night.[22] The journey concludes at dawn, with Nut giving birth to Re as the renewed solar disc. From sunset to sunrise Re makes his underworld passage in the Night Barque, named *Mesketet*. Nephthys is the Night Barque, and her fiery breath helps to protects Re and his companions from the threats of the Netherworld.

The Egyptologist Alison Roberts summarizes this journey as follows:

> Like the chakras in the Tantric tradition, each part of Nut's body
> becomes a place of transformation and this means that the initiate
> not only experiences death and rebirth as a process of time
> spanning the twelve night hours, but also rediscovers the renewal
> of the world within the sacred space of the female body. (*My Heart
> My Mother* 168)

---

[22] Alison Roberts' book *My Heart My Mother: Death and Rebirth in Ancient Egypt* covers the topic of the night journey through Nut's body, with original theories, ample illustrations, and in-depth scholarship.

The twelve goddesses of the night journey have names that indicate their apotropaic qualities. They defend Re and the Solar Barque from all harm they might encounter in the underworld. Taking up the tow rope to pull the barque free when the water levels sink too low and it has become lodged on a sandbar, they exemplify the active, protective, and ferocious qualities that are required to ensure the life and safety of the Solar Barque and its occupants. This quality of the fierce feminine underpins most of the feminine deities in Egyptian mythology. It is an aspect of the ancient Egyptian archetypal Solar Daughter and the Neolithic Great Goddess pattern. The goddesses who belong to this grouping share and interweave their characteristics fluidly.

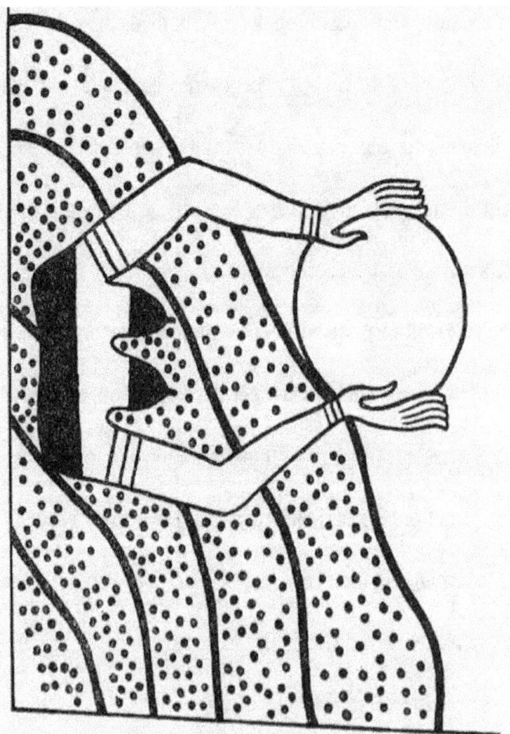

Figure 4. Nut's arms and breasts emerge from the Western Mountain to receive the sun (Piankoff and Rambova, *Mythological Papyri* 41, fig. 25). Public domain.

Concepts of Space

Understanding the overall spatial orientation of the ancient Egyptians—which was exactly the opposite of our own—is critical to reading the images and hieroglyphic inscriptions produced by these desert dwellers. Contemporary Western cultures orient with north at the top of the map and south at the bottom; it follows that the west is envisioned on the left-hand side and the east is on the right. Navigation devices follow this precedent, and the orientation seems self-evident and "correct." In truth, however, it is culturally conditioned; there is no "right way" to orient, though most people feel that their orientation is inherently correct.[23]

Geraldine Pinch is one of the few Egyptologists to introduce (in her book *Handbook of Egyptian Mythology*) a map that illustrates the ancient Egyptian perspective. Pinch states, "The Nile River flows from south to north, so Egypt's southern boundary on the First Cataract was thought of as the top of the country and the Mediterranean as the bottom" (xii). It seems quite natural that the Egyptian people would spatially orient toward the source of the river that made their lives possible, yet the maps that are used today to illustrate ancient Egypt are not oriented with south at the top. This leads to confusion and does a disservice to the Egyptian perspective by not reorienting our thinking in alignment with theirs.

To visualize Upper Egypt in the south, Lower Egypt in the north, the east and sunrise on the left, and the west and sunset on the right requires conscious effort at first. However, switching from our familiar spatial orientation to ancient Egyptian orientation aides us in visualizing their symbolism and attempting to see through their eyes.

---

[23] In a letter dating from the New Kingdom, an Egyptian emissary who traveled to Mesopotamia noted in his letter that the Euphrates River flowed the "wrong way"—namely, from northwest to southeast.

Reorienting our habitual style of consciousness also encourages the flow of archetypal symbolism and insights that slumber in our collective psyche.

To properly read ancient Egyptian imagery and symbolism, we must adopt this perspective. For example, *Gardiner's Sign List*[24] attests to this orientation, deciphering the sign for *left* as also the sign for *east* (R15), and the sign for *right* as also the sign for *west* (R13–14):

Figure 5. Glyphs for east *and* west. Credit: Illustrations by Laura Marshall. Reprinted with permission by copyright holder.

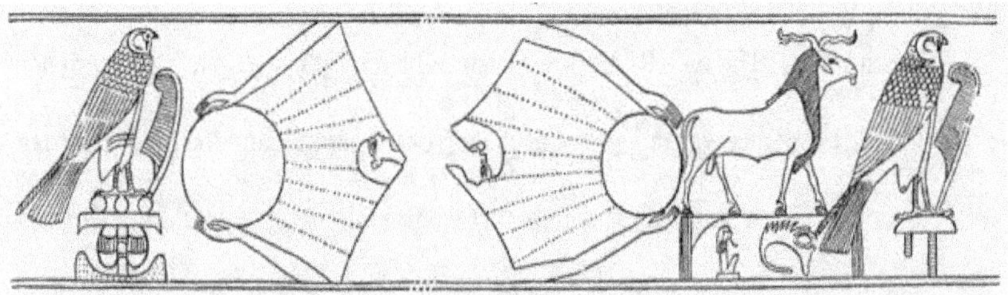

Figure 6. Sunrise and sunset. From a diagram showing versions of the hieroglyphic symbols for east (left-hand side) and west (right-hand side) (Piankoff and Rambova, *Mythological Papyri* 38, fig. 21). From the papyrus of Khonsu-mes A, #16 (Vienna). Public domain.

The map below (fig. 7) illustrates the visual difference in orientations. The map flips the orientation, putting south at the top of the map. This visual reorientation illustrates the ancient Egyptian perspective: Upper Egypt is now on top, and Lower Egypt is on the bottom of the vertical axis. This places the east on the left side and the west on

---

[24] Sir Alan Gardiner was a renowned Egyptologist, linguist, and philologist. In the early twentieth century, he compiled a detailed catalogue of common Middle Egyptian hieroglyphs that is the standard reference to this day.

the right, marking the horizontal axis—the metaphysical horizon line between life and death.

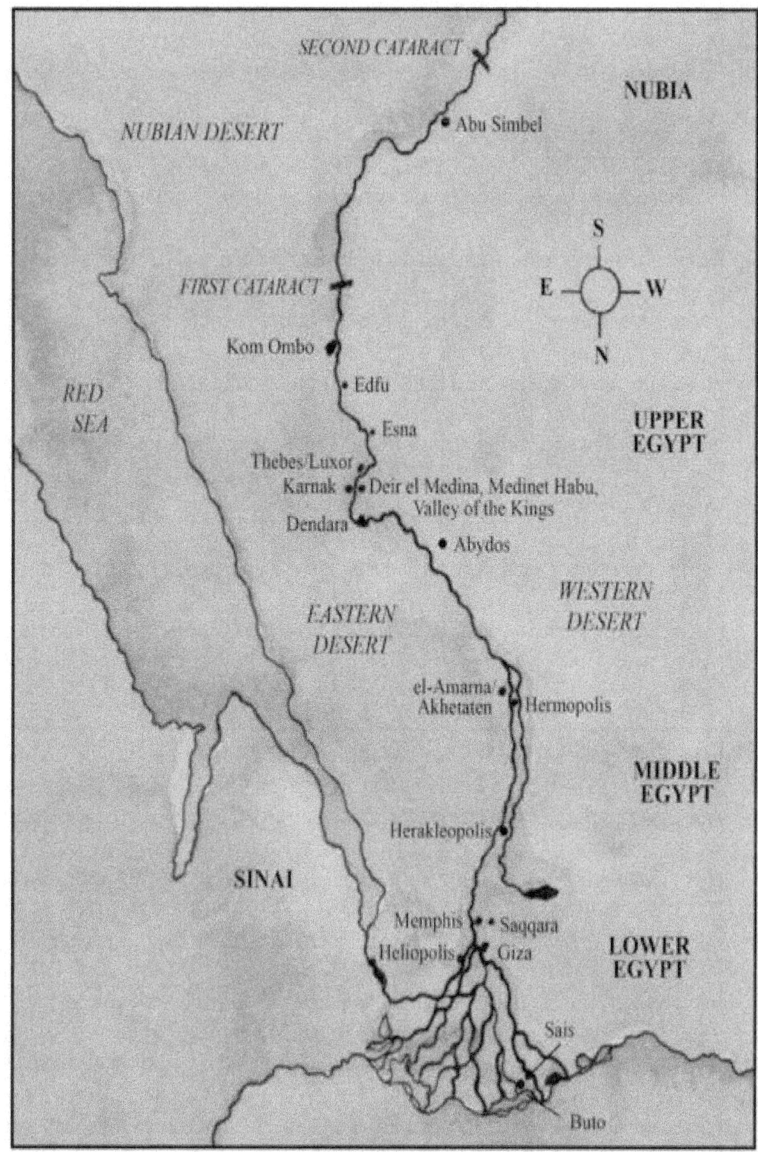

Figure 7. Map of Egypt, oriented to the Egyptian perspective, with south at the top.
Credit: Illustration by Laura Marshall. Reprinted with permission by copyright holder.

Masters of Reverie: A Meditation on Renewal and Rebirth

Key mythologems that are central to this study, such as renewal and rebirth, are not esoteric or technically specific words. They are well-known, familiar, and therefore susceptible to losing significance and liveliness. We can awaken these words, however, utilizing the phenomenological method of "reverie" articulated by the twentieth-century philosopher Gaston Bachelard, who avows, "The soul does not live on the edge of time. It finds its rest in the universe imagined by reverie" (*Poetics of Reverie* 15). In reverie, as we imagine the diurnal cycle, the images flow through the body, activating the reception centers up and down its core. Further images pour forth from this activation, this movement of psyche, bringing new insights and sparking new questions. The living waters flow.

Reverie is an action, not a concept; it is a meditation, a building of relationship between consciousness and the world—like the words describing the sacred in ancient Egypt, or the psychic energies and patterns that Jung calls "archetypes," or the warm-blooded imagination that Hillman calls "soul" (Hillman, *Dream and the Underworld* 26). According to Bachelard, "It is reverie that delineates the furthest confines of our minds" (*Psychoanalysis of Fire* 215). Thus my intention is first to free the words *renewal* and *rebirth* to move beyond the conventional boundaries of the mind, and then to align them with the more concrete material at the foundation of this scholarly pursuit.

In his writing Gaston Bachelard mingles "oases of leisure" and "organization of ideas," creating word-images that awaken the imagination and activate the heart (17). He leads his reader into the realm of experience and sensation, into relationship with word-images and the flicker of personal memories: "In the imagined, imaginary cosmic life, the different worlds often touch each other and complement each other" (*Poetics of Reverie* 205). The intermingling and overlapping of the different worlds is easily accessed through the Egyptians' holoscopic viewpoint. It appears to me that the ancient Egyptians were masters of reverie.

From the perspective of the ancient Egyptians, renewal leads to the return of the light, the dawn, the reawakening, the quickening of the heart, where consciousness soars into the heights with the rising sun. But renewal does not *begin* at the moment of the sun's dawning. Instead it begins in the darkest hour of the night, the deepest cavern of the underworld that rests upon the Lake of Fire. In the womb or egg of this cavern, the solar god joins with Osiris, the god of death and renewal.

In our reverie, the spirits lift as the dawn begins to lighten the sky behind the desert mountain peaks, which darken in reverse as the sky brightens. Earth breathes out as the night comes to a close, exhaling a coolness as the precious night's condensation activates earthly scents—memories arise of the tangy smell of creosote, which announces the coming of the infrequent rains of my homelands in the deserts of the Southwest.

As the great Solar Barque nears the threshold, all life rejoices in the rejuvenation. The Egyptians picture this with baboons standing upright, raising their arms and hooting. In the temples, the clay seals on the shrines that rest in the inner sanctum—the holy of holies—are broken, and the doors are opened so offerings can be presented to the gods and goddesses of life.

The sense of renewal is not just spiritual, but literal and physical. *Renewal* comes from the Latin *rejuvenescere*, from *re-* ("again") plus *juvenescere* ("become young") and *juvenis* ("young") ("Rejuvenescence," Etymonline.com). Rebirth, regeneration, renascence—all point to the restoration of youthfulness, to resurrection. Thus, included in this flood of renewal is the act of giving birth and being born, of begetting, of rising once more into the light.

The idea of birth invites the sacred feminine into our reverie. Mother Nut, ever-stretching above, receives the aged god as he descends the sky, having spent his life-force during the day's journey. No longer the high-flying falcon, he is the ram-headed god Amun, the one who is hidden, the one who hears—the listening god, bent over and walking with a cane, gazing downward toward the earth in his descent. His light has weakened, yet his glow is somehow more beautiful, more relational than the intensity of the blinding midday sunlight, which cannot be observed directly. The setting sun can be met with an open gaze.

My father exhaled his final breath at the very threshold between day and night, in a hospice room that looked out at the desert he loved dearly, after a seven-day vigil that gathered his family to his side. Upon his breath's departure, as its animating presence detached from the vessel of his body, we were collectively impelled to open the sliding glass door of his room and step outside. The full moon bade us farewell as it set in the west and dawn's light quickened into sunrise over the eastern mountains. The sunlight soon replaced it, a glowing radiance that blurred all hard edges of the mountains but illuminated every detail of the creosote and cacti, banishing the moon from sight. His soul had been drawn to the timing of this specific moment—the harmonious balance of the dawning sun and the descending moon.

Renewal and rebirth lead us naturally to the memory of death, and to the sense of an intimate connection between the two. The ancient Egyptians also connected life, fertility, and daily renewal with descent and death, creating a full circle that reflects the cyclic movement of the celestial bodies. How totally natural it is to contemplate life and renewal alongside the rising of death, bound together as it is with rebirth!

Is there a time—besides our own—where this is not so? The Great Goddesses of Paleolithic and Neolithic times are the womb and the tomb as one. There is comfort in this, for connecting the two is what leads to rebirth, renewal, life everlasting. A return to the mother, to be held within her embrace, her body, the coffin, the grave—this also promises her protection and our rebirth.

> Return to life is through the door of death, presaging that view of human existence which echoes right through the Greek philosophers: "we live their death and we die their life." This truth is seen by those who travel in the sun-boat through the gateways of the raging-beneficent goddess in the night. And it is seen by the ritualists in the temple when they extinguish their flames for the ancestral dead[,] . . . uttering their great prayer of trust in the returning goddess. (Roberts, *My Heart My Mother* 182)

This returning goddess is she who "brings to birth a new world at dawn. A glorious moment of cosmic unity is experienced as these worlds of the living and the dead merge and meet" (182).

Dawn is the time of Horus, the youthful vigorous falcon-headed god who flies high on powerful wings or folds them close to his body for a steep dive (fig. 8). He is the "celestial falcon whose right eye was the sun and left the moon" (Wilkinson, *Complete*

Gods and Goddess 200). He is also *Horakhty*, "Horus of the two horizons," the rising and the setting sun (201).

Figure 8. Horus as the solar falcon, with an ankh *and a* shen *symbol in each talon and the solar disc on his head.* Pectoral from the tomb of King Tutankhamun, New Kingdom, 18th Dynasty. Gold, carnelian chalcedony, glass paste. In the collection of the Cairo Egyptian Museum. Photography credit: Ayman Khoury, Art Resource, NY. Reprinted with permission by copyright holder.

Or it is Nefertem, divine golden boy and gift of the lotus, sweetest of flowers and symbol of eternal renewal (fig. 9). Its rhizome roots in the mud at pond's bottom, sending a long stem upward with leaves and blossom. The lotus, too, seeks restoration in descent, closing its petals at each day's end, withdrawing its bud below water's surface. The Night World, distinct from the Day World, bestows the rebirth and renewal necessary for life.

Figure 9. Nefertem emerging from the lotus blossom. Found at the entrance to the tomb of King Tutankhamun, in the Valley of the Kings, 18th Dynasty, New Kingdom. Wood bust, covered with stucco and painted, 30 cm height. In the collection of the Cairo Egyptian Museum, Je 60723. Photo credit: Margarete Büsing, Art Resource, NY. Reprinted with permission by copyright holder.

Re, the sun itself, recognizes the natural laws dictated by Ma'at's diurnal patterns that affect all processes of life. He willingly descends and submits to the process of renewal. He enters the underworld carried by the great feminine barque, held within his shrine-tomb-womb, in the company of his most beloved companions.

The image below (fig. 10), depicts Osiris in the Night Barque surrounded by his most devout supporters—the barque herself, containing Isis, Nephthys, Ma'at, Horus, Thoth, and Khepri, with the winged scarab above and the Two Ladies on either side. The souls of Nekhen and Pe are kneeling on along the side (3 x 3). Four goddesses support the star-filled sky, on which are resting the symbol for water and the barque. To the left the image divides into two registers on which stand the four couples, holding scepters, who make up the Hermopolitan Ogdoad. Bringing up the rear are the creatures symbolizing of the northern (upper) and southern (lower) winds.

Figure 10. The Night Barque with Osiris and his companions. From the Full Moon scene within the "Astronomical Ceiling" in Hathor's Temple at Dendera. Photo credit: kaironinfo4u, from the flickr photo album: "Dendera Temple." Photographed on 14 January 2016. Original photo has been cropped. Creative Commons, some rights reserved. Web. 9 March 2018.

Though not often emphasized in studies on the solar god, this process—above all others—illuminates how reliant upon their companions are the king and all the gods and goddesses. Re-Atum enters into the process of renewal through the acceptance of his death, borne by faith in his companions and Maʻat's natural course. All must do their part, and he must trust that the protection of his carefully chosen companions will ensure a successful journey of renewal and resurrection through the underworld.

Mysterious Khepri, whose name means "becoming one," bridges the renewal processes of night and day. In the *Litany of Re*, Piankoff explains the name as "the different stages which the *Ba* undergoes during its constant transformation in the cycle of becoming, of life and death" (19). The sacred scarab beetle (fig. 11) is an aspect of the solar god, as are all the divinities. He comes to life beneath the surface, hidden in the earth, emerging to roll his dung ball that nourishes his renewal. Originally it seems the goddess Neith, a creatrix worshipped in the Lower Egyptian cult center of Sais, was equated with the scarab beetle. In its natural habitat, the task of the scarab beetle (*Scarabaeus sacer*) is to aid in the decomposition and decay of matter, the recycling of life. The value of this service was crystal clear to the ancient Egyptians and provides one reason they chose it as an especially potent symbol of renewal.

The scarab beetle's sacred renewal process takes place in the darkest hour of the night, alongside the mysteries of the fifth and sixth hours, when Re and Osiris unite inside the womb or egg and both emerge renewed—for Re is Osiris and Osiris is Re. The birth is not a bursting forth in mature, battle-ready vigor. Instead the renewal is nascent, tender, vulnerable. In a culture so intimate with earth's processes and all life forms, naturally the birth is described in biological terms. In addition to the physical realm, the metaphysical and psychological levels are also embraced, for the depths have been visited and stirred. Renewal sparks in the deepest regions, the hidden unknowable realm that seems, to consciousness, to be utterly devoid of life—yet it is the source.

Figure 11. The scarab beetle Khepri, symbol of continuous becoming, inside the disc encircled by the ouroboros. Photo credit: kairoinfo4u, from the flickr photo album: "Temple of Seti I, Abydos." Photographed on 24 February 2014. Original photo has been cropped and the color altered to enhance details. Creative Commons, some rights reserved. Web. 9 March 2018.

In the image above (fig. 11) Seti I is on the right with the *uraeus* serpent on his brow. He is greeting the god who is Three in One. Atum is personified as the enthroned bearded god and is holding the *ankh* in his right hand and the *was* scepter of dominion in his left. Re is the solar disc encircled by the serpent, the *ouroboros*. Khepri is the scarab beetle, symbolic of continual becoming. In the upper-right corner is a solar disc encircled by the Two Ladies, who embody the unity of Upper and Lower Egypt and the Red and the White crowns—Wadjet is on the left and Nekhbet is on the right.

In the image below (fig. 12), a central paradox is given form. Apophis, the huge serpent of the depths, is both the catalyst of renewal and its greatest threat. He rises from the depths in the seventh hour of the night, after the rebirth mysteries have occurred and as the new life is ascending. His intention is to bring the journey of renewal to a standstill. He attempts to drink the river dry and strand the Solar Barque. In this hour, Isis and Seth must join in partnership on the prow of the Night Barque, which lends her fiery breath to aid them in repelling Apophis and his cadre of demons, in pinning and dismembering this urge toward unconscious stagnation. Only in the successful fending off of Apophis's unconsciousness and denial, his standstill and inertia, does the Solar Barque complete her mission of renewal and carry her companions into the Day World.

Figure 12. Apophis under the Solar Barque containing Khepri, double Hathor, double Horus. Papyrus #5, Nesi-Khonsu B (Piankoff and Rambova, *Mythological Papyri*). The papyrus is in the collection of the Cairo Egyptian Museum. Public domain.

Khepri, the winged scarab beetle, is in the Night Barque accompanied by two Hathors, a powerful apotropaic feminine deity doubled to increase her effectiveness, and two forms of Horus—a falcon on the bow with the solar disc on his head, and the anthropomorphic Horus manning the rudder, again doubled to increase Horus's protective power. The serpent of the depths, Apophis, is curled under the Solar Barque. Apophis is a paradoxical creature—both the greatest threat to the nightly and daily renewal process and its chief catalyst. His presence increases attentiveness and activates the companions; he coalesces their efforts and focuses intention.

To the right of the barque is the enthroned Osiris, with the priestess Nesi-Khonsu giving him praise and adoration and offering him three lotus blossoms in full bloom. The lotus is the symbol par excellence of resurrections and renewal. Its sweet scent brings joy, which is essential and an aspect of the breath of life. The priestess's praise and offerings, her love and intentions, are palpable (like the solar gaze in fig. 30) bestowing energy for the renewal process. Here is an image of our duty, our contribution—for her daily offerings have aided this cycle of renewal. Her papyrus, which she had created in preparation for her eventual death, envisions that in life after death she will join with these beings to continue lending her energies to this process.

Our reverie reveals powerful psychological truths about what is most threatening in life, in our own unconscious: an almost irrepressible urge to stay asleep, to resist change, growth, consciousness, and the actions that will expand our consciousness and encourage and strengthen the awakening of our heart's capacity to participate in the renewal of all life—now and after life as we know it ends. As the *Coffin Texts* urge, "Awake to life . . . for you have not died!" It comes off the page as a shout.

The ancient Egyptians noted what did and did not support life. As time progressed, these observations became more pronounced and differentiated as these people sought to maintain balance and social structure. In reflecting on natural order, they discerned an understanding of the part they played in maintaining this balance, in life and death, on earth and in the underworld. And they turned to Ma'at as the personification of cosmic patterns and natural order, looking to her as they astutely observed the workings of their world and discovered practices and behaviors that both promoted harmonious interactions and encouraged life to flourish.

Chapter Summary

The Egyptian culture had a vibrant tradition of religious speculation, ever seeking to make meaning of existence and answer humanity's perpetual questions: Where does life originate? What awaits us upon death? In *Myth and Symbol in Ancient Egypt*, the Egyptologist R. T. Rundle Clark elaborates on the ancient Egyptian style of consciousness, stating that these desert dwellers were "deeply aware that their myths and symbols expressed intuitions about the nature of God, humans, and the universe and that there could only be partial answers to the major metaphysical and spiritual problems" (29–30). They embraced a multi-perspective style of consciousness that was pervasive. Yet rather than being incomplete or fragmented, informed by partial answers, their perspective and insights were complex and fluid.

Studying the ancient Egyptian culture, literature, and art leaves one with a sense of unity, of each element contributing to a whole, of circumambulating and harvesting the mysteries of life. These people wove their insights, intuitions, and pragmatic observations into an intricate and complete cloth. In interlacing the many aspects of their multiple viewpoints, they generated a holistic milieu.

Tom Cheetham—the premier scholar on the work of Henry Corbin, who introduced the Sufi concept of "imaginal" to the Western world—has this to add to our understanding of how the ancient Egyptians' style of consciousness differs significantly from our own: "if we imagine that Imagination lies at the heart of things, we can understand the opposition between the concrete and the abstract as a contrast between two different styles of imagining. Then the entire world opens up" (143).

A holoscopic viewpoint recognizes that life is composed of innumerable interwoven facets, patterns that together create and participate in a whole system. This holoscopic wisdom belongs to the "one who watches," and his or her observations are like an arrow aiming at the heart of each experience and at the understanding of the whole. Such a perspective fosters foundational practices that transform consciousness and ensure a flourishing culture. Lastly, a holoscopic viewpoint suggests the word-image of "one whose aim is the whole," an insight that is reflected in the numerous ways ancient Egyptians envisioned unifying renewal and complementary duality as the basis of the universe.

This holoscopic, multi-perspective consciousness is evident in all the Egyptian goddesses and gods. Like a hologram, the goddesses and gods in the Egyptian pantheon share in the same elements, their patterns changing endlessly as they interact with one another. The ancients Egyptians saw the divine not as static beings, but as the underlying principles of the cosmos, expressed actively in their functions and patterns. The balancing of complementary pairs of opposites, an important symbolic element of Egyptian art and literature, is one example of their holoscopic viewpoint, often expressed in the multidimensional cosmogonic patterns and the numerous, sometimes seemingly contradictory characteristics of their *neters*.

To the ancient Egyptians these *neters*—and the wreath of archetypal symbols that express them, particularly those specific to Ma'at—would have been as essential and involuntary as the air they breathed. As the archetypal foundation of the culture, these entities permeated every aspect of life, including natural phenomena, unlike our own delimited notion of the sacred as disembodied and off-planet.

In bringing together all the pieces of this complex culture, the best method is to immerse oneself in its images and literature. Slowly a living imagination of ancient Egypt comes into focus—a system of interwoven streams that nourish the collective psyche. Emanating from ancient Egypt, a glowing web of interrelated energies and patterns touched and inspired peoples from other contemporary cultures, resonating in the collective psyche, and it continues to do so to this day.

Chapter 3. Who Is This Ma'at?

By extending our historical perspective into . . . earlier periods, we

can become aware of developments in the unfolding of human

consciousness over time that may help us to see more clearly what

is the appropriate pathway of return for today. (Naydler, *Future of*

the Ancient World 246)

Awakening the experience of Ma'at requires a continued effort to open to the imaginal as we begin to place the goddess within her mythological framework. As we weave Ma'at into her ever-renewing landscape, word-images and the sacred poetry of ancient Egypt begin to render her form and significance. Articulating Ma'at's symbolism and relationships brings into focus her essence and her place within the imagination and lives of the ancient Egyptians.

One aspect of the "pathway of return" suggested by the British philosopher Jeremy Naydler is Baring's participatory way of knowing. It is the spirit of renewal seeking to emerge, promoting a rebirth, which includes the awakening of the ethical heart, the return of the Feminine half of divinity, an ecopsychological perspective, and a lively relationship with nature and the divine.

Cosmogonically Ma'at personifies cosmic order, the natural laws, and social cohesion. She also represents the unification of Upper and Lower Egypt and the force that draws the two regions together after chaos, *isfet*, threatens to dissolve their unity. Ma'at is present in the Nun from the very beginning before the separation of earth and sky and the appearance of the first land and first light. As is relayed in the *Coffin Texts*, Spell 80 (explored in greater depth in chapter 5), it is Ma'at who triggers the raising of the primordial mound when she is placed alongside Atum's nose, bringing him joy and the breath of life.

Ma'at and the other *neters* (gods and goddesses) were seen as an integral part of the cherished land of Egypt and the skies above, experienced in both the cooling north winds that refresh life and the dry, hot southern winds that churn up destructive sandstorms. All of Egypt was imbued with their sacred numinousness, which was palpable even to visitors; Herodotus observed that "[o]f all peoples, [the Egyptians] are the most exceedingly pious" (Strassler 134).

As revealed in chapter 2, *neter* is a verb, an action, not merely a name, description, or static concept. The *neters* represented "divine processes and energies" that were "far stronger than we know" (Howell 186). Osiris (among his many attributes) was experienced as the great and mighty river with its rhythm of increase and decrease, nourishing the land, creatures, and people as well as the seeds sprouting forth from the fertile black soil. The velvety blackness of the night sky spangled with fiery stars and the shimmering blue of the day sky was the body of mother Nut. The millions upon millions of stars wheeling overhead were Re and his retinue of the Blessed Dead in the Night Barque, and the sun, of course, was the Day Barque with its warmth and bright light, and its host of ancestral souls found worthy of journeying with the solar gods and goddesses through eternity.

"Only symbols will unlock what they all have in common," Howell concludes (186). Ma'at, too, is an action, a divine energy—and the sacred texts and symbols reveal her dominion through her interactions.

The Many Faces of the Great Goddess

Ma'at shares many prominent characteristics in common with a variety of Egyptian goddesses. Archaeological evidence reveals that the archetypal patterns of the ancient Egyptian divine Feminine developed from a common notion that mythologists and depth psychologists[25] have long named the Great Mother or Great Goddess. In later historical periods, this powerful feminine energy became the active creative spark, as witnessed in Shakti in India, Inanna in Mesopotamia, Demeter in Greece, and Oshun in the Yoruba culture of West Africa. This powerful goddess also expresses destructive aspects with the potential to swing out of balance, as portrayed in the mythology by feminine Egyptian deities such as Tefnut, Sekhmet, or Hathor, who can assume the lioness-headed form when they become ferocious and out-of-balance. The remedy used to pacify the raging goddess has been passed down through the ages in the myths of these cultures, and it involves propitiating her by actively creating relationship with her. This relational mode often employs elaborate community celebrations to amplify its power and ensure its success.

In Egypt, much of the mythology and imagery of the later Dynastic Period (*c.* 3100 BCE) is rooted in a time hundreds of years earlier when the ruler or king was identified as "the Bull of His Mother." He was envisioned as both the Son and the Consort of his divine Great Mother, who might be envisioned as the Wild Cow goddess that evolved into the goddess Hathor. The image below (fig. 13) is from the New Kingdom (*c.* 1550–1069 BCE) and shows two of the earliest goddesses who maintained their primacy during the Dynastic Period. Winged Nut is on the left, kneeling and bowing

---

[25] For example, Jane Ellen Harrison (*Themis: The Study of the Social Origins of Greek Religion*); Erich Neumann (*The Great Mother*); Joseph Campbell (*The Hero with a Thousand Faces*); Anne Baring and Jules Cashford (*The Myth of the Goddess: Evolution of an Image*).

to Mehet-Weret, "the Great Flood," the celestial Wild Cow. Her body is covered with a woven cloth and a beaded net, and she is wearing a *menit* necklace with a fail, symbolic of her divine authority. Between her long horns is the vermillion solar disc. She is reclining on the hieroglyphic symbol meaning "water." A falcon in front of her most likely references one of the earliest versions of the masculine deity. She is the "personification of primeval matter" (Abt 103).

According to an early creation myth, the Wild Cow birthed the masculine solar god and then affixed him between her horns and carried him into the sky. This New Kingdom tomb image reveals the enduring quality of the ancient Egyptian iconography. The deceased, Irynefer, and his wife are at the bottom of the image, praising the sun as it rises between two sycamore trees—yet another symbol of the Great Goddess—and in this case the trees call to mind the two mountain peaks used in the *akhet* symbolism.

Many studies of ancient Egyptian history begin with the Dynastic Period and focus on the spectacular architectural and cultural achievements during this historical period of the civilization, which tends to overshadow Egypt's earlier history. This leaves one with a sense of disconnection from the deeper, more ancient source of their living traditions. The Dynastic Period saw a focused on the evolution of a new form for organizing culture—namely, a divinized king as the embodiment of the unified and imperial state. The roles and functions of the solar masculine deities reflect this changing consciousness, while the feminine deities continue to express their vital roles and functions as well. The two gendered forms coexisted and relied on the order and stability of the older androgynous form—a time before the splitting apart of the naturally

Figure 13. Mehet-Weret, the primordial Wild Cow creatrix. Nut, the winged goddess on the left, and the primordial Mehet-Weret, reclining on the symbol for water and wearing a beaded net and *menit*, alongside the falcon god. Photo credit: kairoinfo4u, from the flickr photo album: "Tomb of Irynefer, TT 290, Deir el-Medina." Photographed on 12 December 2013. Original photo cropped. Creative Commons, some rights reserved. Web. 9 March 2018.

occurring dualities—in order to build what was newly emerging from the collective living waters of the unconscious.

Of primary concern to the Great Goddess is the protection of life—in particular the divine child who is the symbol of renewal and rebirth with each dawn. She is rooted in her protective stance from the first ripple of movement in the inert waters of the great abyss. She is the irresistible life force, life continuously flowing into life (fig. 13).

The famous terracotta statue featured below left (fig. 14) is called the "bird woman" because of her bird-shaped head and upraised arms. She was found in al-

Mamoriyya at Edfu, near el-Kab, Egypt, and is from the Naqada II period, dating to approximately 3650–3300 BCE (Wickett 157)—approximately five hundred years before the rise of the Dynastic Period. (Edfu continued to be a temple site in the New Kingdom and was the cult center for Horus in the Greco-Roman period, the setting of an annual ritual celebrating the sacred marriage between Horus and Hathor.)

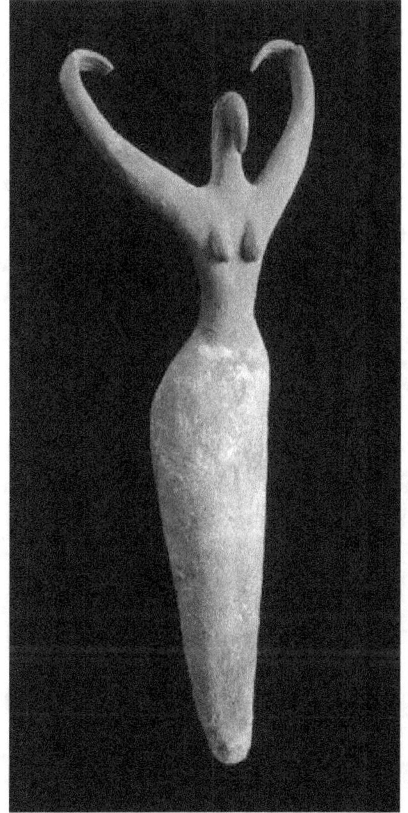

Figure 14. Terracotta female figurine, c. 3650–3300 BCE. Brooklyn Museum, New York. Creative Commons. Web. 3 February 2018.

Figure 15. Painted terracotta vessel, c. 3500–3400 BCE. Metropolitan Museum of Art, New York. Public domain. Web. 13 February 2018

Some historians[26] interpret the raised arms of the bird-headed female figurine as a

typical expression of mourning. But rather than grief, this pose is primarily a gesture of

jubilation, as seen in the papyrus of Nisti-ta-Nebet-Taui as she celebrates her justification

in Ma'at's Hall of Truth (shown in chapter 1). The terracotta vessel shown above right

(fig. 15) also shows a female figure with arms similarly upraised; another goddess in the

same pose is standing just to the right of a many-oared barque containing the four

voluptuous females. Again the gesture—common in terracotta and stone statues found in

archaeological sites surrounding the Mediterranean basin—is related to the ceremonial

expression of praise, joy, and dominion, whereas grief is most often shown with hands in

front of the face, or with the body bent forward and the arms raised up in front of the

body with a tearful face lifted up. In historical times this goddess's gesture became a

hieroglyphic symbol for "rejoice"[27] (Wilkinson, *Reading Egyptian Art* 27).

Depth psychologist Erich Neumann would identify the shared characteristics of

the divine Feminine as manifestations of what he calls the "Terrible Mother"—the

archetypal warrioress, huntress, and mistress of wild beasts, as well as fate and the Great

Round of life-death-rebirth (*Great Mother* 147–208). As a numinous, dynamic energy

she can be fierce, powerful, creative, and destructive, as reflected in the lioness-headed,

Eye of Re, and serpent aspects. In his chapter titled "The Negative Elementary

Character," Neumann clarifies attributes of this archetype: "Thus the terrible aspect of the

Feminine always includes the uroboric snake woman, the woman with the phallus, the

unity of child-bearing and begetting, of life and death" (*Great Mother* 170). What the

Great Mother gives, she takes back. As Howell points out, and as the many symbols of

---

[26] See Elizabeth Wickett's book *For the Living and the Dead: The Funerary Laments of Upper Egypt, Ancient and Modern*.
[27] "Rejoice," *hai*, A28 in Gardiner's Sign List.

Ma'at reveal, "Archetypes do not 'die' but they do change their identities, evolving and renewing their 'costume,' the specifics of their identity, to fit with the times" (186).

The One Behind the Many

Fundamental to any exploration of ancient Egyptian mythology is the insight that the multiple forms of gods and goddesses in ancient Egyptian mythology and iconography—with an array of overlapping functions and purviews—are also the multifaceted characteristics of the One God. Though often explained with masculine names and pronouns, in ancient Egypt the sole creator deity was androgynous, often referred to as "the mother of all mothers and the father of all fathers" (Clark 78, 80; Luckert 41).

As a scholar of world religions and comparative mythology, Karl Luckert identifies a dynamic within the religious speculations embedded in ancient Egyptian Heliopolitan theology that he calls the "turnaround realm" (55). He uses this phrase to describe the "creative descending emanation [that] ends in the cul-de-sac of life made manifest, as if being caught up in the curve of a U-turn" (46). This concept embraces the continual reversal in the circulation of energy between polarities that is envisioned in the mythological imagery of life, death, and resurrection. The turnaround realm connects the above and the below in continuous circulation of energy, like the infinity symbol.

Offering examples from the ancient *Pyramid Texts* and *Coffin Texts* as evidence, Luckert also states outright what the Egyptologist Geraldine Pinch suggests (*Handbook* 160): that Tefnut and Ma'at are, in fact, one and the same deity (Luckert 50). Luckert's findings corroborate the conclusion that these two feminine aspects, Ma'at and Tefnut, highlight the different functions and characteristics of a single goddess. Acceptance of this viewpoint also clarifies Ma'at's relationship with Shu and furthermore corrects the misperception that Tefnut is "colorless" or without function (Clark 45). When Ma'at and Tefnut are seen together, as different aspects of one goddess, both deities take on the more familiar dimensions normally equated with the Neolithic Great Goddess archetype.

Baring names four primary goddesses of ancient Egypt as "the image of the earlier Great Mother": Ma'at, Nut, Hathor, and Isis (75–81). She also states that "Ma'at may be the origin of the figure of Divine Wisdom in the Old Testament, for she personifies the equilibrium and harmony of the Cosmos intrinsic to all life forms" (75). Indeed Ma'at's symbolism includes many attributes of a goddess of wisdom: harmony, balance, order, justice, truth, joy. And both the relationship of daughter to creator and the role of creative spark behind the phenomenal world are evidence of Ma'at's similarity to the much later Gnostic goddess Sophia.

Exploring the complex and multifaceted symbolism of Ma'at allows us to focus on the grouping of symbols directly associated with her. Developing a visual vocabulary helps resolve some of the confusion, so prevalent in ancient Egyptian texts, over intersecting domains of influence and deity names.

Symbols Related to Ma'at

At the base of history, philosophy, religion, science, and mythology is *naming,* which begins to articulate a specific reality, to give shape through descriptions and interpretations. By consciously observing and describing a situation, object, or idea, naming defines reality and brings it into being. For most religious traditions, naming is the core mover in their cosmology—the first act of the creator.

Ancient Egyptian symbolism is a seamless visual language that communicates on many levels, and its analysis easily fills volumes. When deciphering any archetypal symbol, not all relationships can be enumerated, as their complexity is so nuanced. This chapter explores the main symbols that are directly related to Ma'at, in a reference guide or "glossary" for sorting out the complex, overlapping symbolism in ancient Egyptian mythology.

The "Sole Eye" Myth

Ma'at's cosmogonic roots are found in the Heliopolitan Ennead, a Greek word meaning "group of nine." As discussed further in chapter 5, the Heliopolitan myth of creation is the prevalent cosmology represented in the sacred texts of the ancient Egyptians and the story of Ma'at. It begins with the demiurge, Atum, amid utter blackness in the abyss of Nun. Androgynous Atum contains both mother and father within his/her being and is the embodiment of sensation and erotic excitation—waves of intense, intrinsic, creative energy. The act of creation is conveyed with word-images that describe potent physical sensations and conjure a sense of the autonomic nervous system, mentioning only body parts engaged in the birth—the hand, the penis, and the mouth, touching, arousing, spitting, and sneezing the first couple into being. In Nun, the One becomes Three.

The first couple is sexually differentiated, with Shu as the masculine and the embodiment of air and atmosphere. His sister/consort Tefnut is moisture and the active, fiery protective feminine. They embody the duality that is inherent in the phenomenal world.

Figure 16. The Eye from the tomb wall of Pashedu at Deir el-Medina. The Eye is carrying a pot, the gesture of offering, with two flaming wicks. The deceased, Pashedu, is the small figure with his hands raised in the gesture of praise. The Western Mountain is behind them, indicating that this is the Netherworld. Photo credit: kairoinfo4u, from the flickr photo album: "Tomb of Pashedu, TT3, Deir el-Medina." Photographed on 12 December 2013. Original photo has been cropped. Creative Commons, some rights reserved. Web. 9 March 2018.

Like a nascent lifeform, Atum wavers in and out of consciousness after creating the children, Shu and Tefnut. Upon awakening and realizing the children have wandered off in the darkness of Nun, Atum is filled with a sense of urgency: the children must be found. Atum detaches the Sole Eye, which marks a further shift into differentiation between masculine and feminine, with the Sole Eye becoming the feminine *uraeus* (also understood to be Ma'at) and Atum now referred to as "he" (fig. 16).

The Sole Eye is charged with a mission: find the children, the seeds of creation. She navigates the dark waters of Nun, locating Shu and Tefnut and guiding them back to Atum, who sheds tears of joy and embraces the children, sharing his *ka*[28] with them. Meanwhile, the Eye is enraged because in her absence Atum has grown another, more brilliant Eye. The Sole Eye sheds tears of rage, and these two streams of tears—joy and rage—combine to bring forth humanity.

Atum recognizes the rage of the Sole Eye and appeases her by giving her a place of honor upon his brow, declaring that henceforth she will be the most powerful of all the gods and that all will fear her. Their reunion results in a deepening of her union with Atum and reestablishes eros, the original unity, now with greater differentiation and access to higher consciousness. She circles his solar orb protectively (the *ouroboros*, situated in the center of his forehead, his seat of higher consciousness) and takes on the appearance of the *iret,* or *uraeus*, the Eye of Re.

Eye Goddess

The Eye is also named a Daughter of Re. She is the active principle of the Feminine, like the Great Goddess of prehistoric times. From her position on the brow, in the place of the third eye chakra, she is both powerfully protective as well as potentially destructive. A Daughter of Re can be personified as a solar Eye, a lioness-headed goddess, and a rearing, hooded cobra whose fiery breath protects the king and solar god.

---

[28] The ancient Egyptians differentiated nine primary parts to the soul. The primary of these are the *ka*, the vital life force; the *ba*, often depicted as a human-headed bird and closest to our own idea of the soul; the *akh*, or purified luminous light body; and the *ren*, the name. See Normandi Ellis, *Imagining the World into Existence*, for details (44).

From her prominent position upon the brow, with spread hood and direct gaze, she emerges from the center of higher consciousness.

Ma'at, as a Daughter of Re, is also imagined as the rearing, hooded cobra. In the throne name for Queen Hatshepsut, Ma'at is shown as a large, rearing cobra cradled in the arms of the *ka*, the symbol for vital life force. She is like a mother lion standing behind her cubs as they learn to master their surroundings, ever-watchful, ready to defend and protect them with an inexorable ferocity.

The Eye of Re assumes this stance with the god Re and with the worldly king as Horus, the son of Re, whose headdress is often shown as the *ouroboros* (serpent biting its tail) encircling the vermillion solar disc. She is the fiery *uraeus* worn over the king's third eye—a symbol deities and kings wore to distinguish their divinity and power, and the portal to inner realms of esoteric knowledge and insight, "a source of light, knowledge, and fertility" (Chevalier and Gheerbrant 364) that is directed both outwardly and inwardly. The Eye of Re is both motherly and a consort; in this she reflects the Great Goddesses of the Neolithic Period.

The name for this form of the goddess—*uraeus*—comes from the Greek, meaning "on its tail," the rearing cobra. One way the Egyptians referred to her was "the *Wedjat-eye*—the whole eye—meaning eye as a bodily organ" (Roberts, *Hathor Rising* 9). In this case the Eye would be drawn as a human eye with the markings of the falcon beneath and might include a hooded cobra emerging from the line describing the lower edge of the Eye (fig. 17).

Figure 17. Eye goddess. Credit: Illustration by Laura Marshall, after Lucie Lamy's illustration in *New Light On Ancient Knowledge: Egyptian Mysteries* (20). Reprinted with permission by copyright holder.

As the hieroglyphic symbol *iret*-eye, "she also acts as the agent of the god's activity, since *iret* in Egyptian means 'doer'" (Roberts, *Hathor Rising* 9). The Eye as cobra can be envisioned as wrapping around a solar orb. She can also be portrayed as the Two Ladies, Nekhbet and Wadjet, who personify the solar god-king's crowns and represent the united Upper and Lower Egypt, respectively. Whatever form her appearance takes, she indicates authority, royalty, and divinity as well as protection. She remains sovereign and potent in her own right as well: "just as Isis the throne 'made' the king and was therefore his mother, so the crown 'makes' the king-to-be a king" (Frankfort, *Kingship and the Gods* 108).

In addition to being personified as lioness-headed, the Eye of Re, or the Eye of Horus, she can also be depicted as specific goddesses, such as Hathor. One of the traits shared by these goddesses who personify the potent serpent power is the ability to be both beneficent and death-dealing. The myth known as *The Destruction of Humanity* features the lioness-headed form of a goddess (either Tefnut, Sekhmet, or Hathor) and offers an illustration of how to appease the battle rage of the destructive feminine.

Figure 18. Tefnut-Sekhmet, wearing the solar disc encircled by the ouroboros, *and Hathor*. Sekhmet is holding a papyrus staff, and Hathor is wearing her cow horns and solar disc crown and vulture headdress. From "The Temple of Haroeris-(Horus)-Sobek at Kom Ombo." Photo credit: Merlin UK. Photographed on 16 May 2010. Creative Commons, some rights reserved. Web. 19 March 2018.

The *Destruction of Humanity*, translated by Miriam Lichtheim, is the first part of a longer text named "The Book of the Cow of Heaven" (*Ancient Egyptian Literature* 2: 197). It is inscribed in five royal tombs of the New Kingdom—the tombs of Tutankhamun, Seti I, Ramesses II, Ramesses III, and Ramesses IV (197). The myth tells of a time when Re discovered that humanity was plotting rebellion against him. He convened a council of his fellow gods and goddesses—his Eye, Shu, Tefnut, Geb, Nut, Nun, and "the fathers and the mothers who were with me when I was in Nun" (198).

When all were assembled, Re asked Nun, "O eldest god in whom I came into being, and ancestor gods, look, mankind, which issued from my Eye, is plotting against me. Tell me what you would do about it, for I am searching. I would not slay them until I have heard what you might say about it" (198). Nun spoke and told Re, "Stay on your throne," and the others agreed, counseling Re to send his Eye as Hathor to smite them (198). And so he did.

The Egyptologist Alison Roberts also retells this myth in her book *Hathor Rising: The Power of the Goddess in Ancient Egypt.* Building on Lichtheim's translation, she points to the pairing of Hathor with Sekhmet (fig. 18) as an example of the "beneficent-destructive polarity" of the feminine principle (10). In this polarity the goddesses Hathor and Sekhmet are dual aspects of the feminine principle. Sekhmet is the embodiment of the duality as the fierce lioness-headed goddess, who is both a healer par excellence and the bringer of plague. Her name translates as "Powerful One."

Sekhmet strikes down the rebels with such ferociousness that Re is horrified. At the end of the day she tells Re that this slaughter is a "balm for my heart" (Lichtheim, *Ancient Egyptian Literature* 2: 198). She wades in the blood and revels in her destruction. To avert further carnage, Re must subdue her—for once engaged, her battle rage is unstoppable. He concocts an antidote and orders a vast quantity of beer dyed red to look like blood. Just before dawn he floods the fields where she will come to finish her destruction of humankind. It becomes a glistening lake of red, three palms high.

As the day dawns she comes to the lake of "blood," and it pleases her. She begins to lap up the red beer, thinking it is blood, and soon becomes so intoxicated she forgets all about her mission of murder. She returns to Re, transformed and pacified, and he welcomes her back warmly, saying, "Welcome in peace, O gracious one!" (199).

Roberts summarizes the lessons imparted by this myth and puts it into context, lest one is left with the impression that mere drunkenness was considered the cure-all. The myth portrays the time of drought and the end of the Egyptian year, when the south wind blew and all life was desiccated. This was the height of summer and the time when the inundation began. As the river swelled, it eroded its banks, turning the churning water blood-red. Eventually it breached all boundaries, overflowing and covering the fields with its red waters. This time of year was both feared and longed for (*Hathor Rising* 12), for unpredictable destruction brought renewal, and fertility followed the flood. This was a time for rituals and celebrations to keep the destructive forces within tolerable limits. The rejoicing and rituals "set the cycles in motion" and acknowledged, with bacchanal celebrations, "one's own personal attitude of respect towards the laws of nature and society that helped to contain the destructive forces" (Bonnefoy, *Greek and Egyptian* 216).

Daughter of Re

According to *Coffin Texts,* Spell 330, Ma'at, beginning in the Nun, is named a Daughter of Atum or Daughter of Re. She accompanies Re both day and night, standing either protectively behind him or (as discussed at length in chapter 5) in the prow of the Solar Barque, pointing the way. Ma'at's alter-form as Tefnut is the lioness-headed aspect of the fierce feminine or Ma'at as the Solar Barque, *Ma'aty*—double Ma'at—whose fiery breath defends Re.

Other goddesses, such as Isis (as the Day Barque) and her sister Nephthys (as the Night Barque), are also aspects of the fierce, protective mother-figure. Each night they defeat the great serpent Apophis and transport Re and his many companions along their path through the Netherworld.

The solar disc encircled by an *ouroboros*, which sits upon the heads of deities as the eye of the sky, is similar to the idea of the barque; inside the disc the renewed divine child is protectively held, transformed, and transported through the perils of the Night World. This solar symbol can also be emitting straight rays of light to indicate Ma'at and her attribute of never-ending straightness or alignment with the cosmic order.

Figure 19. Sunrise, Papyrus #16 of Khonsu-mes A (Piankoff and Rambova, *Mythological Papyri*). The original papyrus is in the collection of the Kunsthistorisches Museum, Vienna. Public domain.

In fig. 19, Ma'at stands with her arms raised in praise to the *ouroboros*-encircled sun disc and the falcon-headed god with the *was* scepter, who is holding an *ankh* symbol in his right hand and is facing Ma'at. Standing behind him is the god Heka with his arms raised in praise; over his arm are looped the *ankh* (meaning "life") and the *was* scepter (meaning "prosperity" and "dominion"). The sun is being delivered into the east, symbolized by the final two symbols: the deity holding the shining sun in his outstretched arms and looking upward, and the falcon perched upon the hieroglyphic symbol that means both "east" and "left" (Piankoff and Rambova, *Mythological Papyri* 144).

As the goddess of the sunrise, the first hour of day, Ma'at helps raise the sun. In the image above (fig. 19) she is paired with the god Heka on the left. Re of the Horizon is the hawk-headed deity in the center with the *ouroboros*-encircled disc above his head. The two *ankhs* and two *was* scepters convey the message of "life" and "prosperity" (Piankoff and Rambova *Mythological Papyri* 144).

The dynamic feminine principle is proactive and apotropaic in both realms, the Day World and the Night World. As is expressed in the ancient literature, the goddesses are essential to the renewal and resurrection of the solar principle (which is explored in greater detail in chapter 5). Tracing the differentiation of their various patterns and relationships, and the way they interact and change in relationship to one another, is helpful in developing a holoscopic perspective of one's own.

Solar Barque: Renewal and Regeneration

The Solar Barque is a vessel, like the disc and the womb, of transformation; it is the means of the regeneration of life. In ancient Egypt the barque was the primary method for movement, for passage, both in their mythology and in their daily life along the Nile. The barque offers all travelers safe passage on the otherwise dangerous waters. The holy barque is the "means of resurrection" and "the sign of resurrection" (Kristensen 96).

Contemporary thought holds human-made objects as inanimate, composed of "dead" matter. This was not so in ancient times, when everything was imbued with presence and divine life, and (more often than not) personified. The barque is the "savior of life (the 'life boat') [and] was conceived as a divine being. . . . The boat knows the mystery and has it in its power" (97). Moreover, the barque is feminine, identified from earliest times with the goddess Mehet-Weret, the celestial Wild Cow. Beginning with the *Pyramid Texts*, Nephthys is the Night Barque named *Mesketet* and Isis is the Day Barque named *Mandjet* (Pinch, *Handbook* 122). Ma'at can also be named as the barque, both day and night—called double Ma'at, or *Ma'aty*,

In *Mythological Papyri: Egyptian Religious Texts and Representations*, Vol. 3, by Alexandre Piankoff, the editor—Natacha Rambova—authors a chapter titled "The Symbolism of the Papyri." She also articulates the symbolism in each of the thirty papyri in the collection. She identifies the "root pattern" as the eternally repeating cosmic circuit of the solar god and his companions (29). The means for this journey of rebirth is the barque. Rambova's chapter begins with a lengthy quote "hitherto unpublished in English,"[29] from the Norwegian scholar of world religions W. Brede Kristensen, a professor and department head of comparative religion at Leiden University during the early part of the twentieth century. Below is a summary of Kristensen's essential distinctions (*Mythological Papyri* 29–30). Following these is an image that seems to illustrate his points. Together, words and image bring to light central mythologems informing the ancient Egyptian mysteries.

- Though life and death seem to be irreconcilable opposites, together "they form everlasting life" where neither predominates; instead they alternate and "they produce one another" (29).

---

[29] W. B. Kristensen, "De godsdienstige beteekenis van de gesloten perioden," *Jaarbericht van het vooraziatisch-egyptisch Gezelschap, "Ex Oriente Lux"* (Leiden), II (nos. 6–8, 1939–42), pp. xv–xxvi. (Translated into English by Alexander Gode von Äsch.)

- "Universal life is the totality of death and life," and in its totality hostile forces are reconciled. This is "absolute life"—life everlasting and self-regenerative (29).

- Absolute life is also called "divine life," and it is viewed as "an ever-repeated divine act of creation" (29).

- "The totality of life and death [is] the mystery at the center of all mystery religions" (29).

- The opposing aspects of light and dark engage in a "mysterious co-operation of self-renewal that takes place in a twenty-four-hour cycle" (29).

- The eastern and western horizons represent "the same mystery and are therefore regarded as points of precisely the same character" (29). The double lion (Aker) and *akhet* symbols are a reflection of this mystery.

- "Darkness is the cradle of light; in it, the sun finds the power to arise. 'The land of life' is therefore a frequent name for the nocturnal abode of the sun" (30).

- "Absolute life has its home in the realm of death" (30).

The image below (fig. 20) succinctly illustrates Kristensen's insights. The dawn is near, and with it, resurrection. In the upper register the Solar Barque is the sacred vessel of renewal, containing four passengers. Ma'at is on the far right-hand side of the image, standing in the bow of the boat with her right arm extended straight out in front of her and her left arm down at her side, holding an *ankh*, the symbol of life. She is in the position and attitude of the Opener of the Ways, the psychopomp guiding the vessel safely through all perils. Her *ankh* bestows the breath of life.

Figure 20. Solar Barque as the vessel of renewal and resurrection. Image drawn from the coffin of Hent-Taui in the Metropolitan Museum of Art (Piankoff and Rambova, *Mythological Papyri* 63, fig. 51). Public domain.

Standing behind Ma'at, back-to-back with her, is a huge baboon, most likely Thoth-Djehuty. His hands and arms are raised in the gesture of praise, and he is facing the solar disc in the center of the barque. The solar disc rests in the cradle of the two mountains symbol, known as *akhet* (see description below), denoting the east and west horizons that mark the entrance and exit points for both the Day World and the Night World. As Kristensen points out, the eastern and western horizons are identical, and when the sun sets it "reaches the hidden fountain of its life" (30). And every sunrise "occurs in and from death, which thus appears to be the potential life" (30).

Seated inside the solar disc is the divine child, identifiable by his sidelock hairstyle, the *uraeus* on his forehead, his nudity, and his finger to his mouth—all symbolizing that he is a child. At the stern of the boat a *uraeus* serpent is draped over the steering oar, the protective Eye goddess is the helmsman. Above the barque and its passengers is the solar disc between outspread falcon wings—the symbol of Horus as *Re-Horakhty*, or *Behdety* (Jackson 14), symbolizing the passage of the sun through the sky, from horizon to horizon (figs. 8, 20, and 35). Both the disc and the barque are womb-like vessels and the means for renewal and rebirth. (As described above, Ma'at is also a form of the Solar Barque—the double Ma'at or *Ma'aty* vessel.) Horus the falcon, Nefertem the child emerging from the lotus, and Khepri the scarab beetle are also ways to image the renewed solar god, akin to the divine child within the solar orb.

The underworld is often depicted as inverted. In the lower register a falcon's head is upside down, just entering the underworld; he is the source of resurrection for Osiris, father of Horus, as symbolized by the rays of light emanating from his head. On either side of the falcon's head are the tutelary crown goddesses of Upper and Lower Egypt, Nekhbet and Wadjet—the Two Ladies who personify the reconciliation of opposites: upper and lower, conscious and unconscious, life and death, day and night. Each is perched upon a *nebt*,[30] a basket that is the hieroglyphic symbol meaning "Mistress" or "Lady" and that can also be the symbol for "all, every." Therefore, these images above might be read as follows: "All life [the two *ankh* symbols] and all dominion [Nekhbet's

---

[30] This is sign V 30 in *Gardiner's Sign List*. The phonogram *nbt* means "lady" or "mistress." The masculine form is *nb*, meaning "lord" or "master." Depending on its use it could also be translated as "every, all."

flail and Wadjet's *was* scepter] are perpetuated by the unity of the Two Ladies [*sema*], the mistresses of Upper and Lower Egypt."

Lastly, the two large, five-pointed stars beneath both baskets and above Osiris's feet and head are also a visual message. The symbol for the underworld is a five-pointed star inside a circle, yet these stars are not encircled. This, combined with the other symbols, seems to suggest that resurrection has taken place—that from death, life arises. Once cyclic renewal of life is understood as the cooperation and interweaving of opposites, the complementary nature of life and death becomes clear, and seemingly contradictory aspects of ancient Egyptian symbolism are resolved.

Akhet: Horizon

The *akhet* is one way that the idea "horizon"—as in east and west—is symbolized, as shown below (fig. 21). The *akhet* is resting on the back-to-back double lion known as Aker, and also as Shu and Tefnut, the first primordial pair in the Heliopolitan cosmology. The mountains of Manu and Bakhu symbolize the western and eastern gateways to the Netherworld, the liminal thresholds marking the horizontal dimension of space, a fundamental orientation in both the inner and outer worlds. The *akhet* references the journey of resurrection the solar god and his companions undertake each day and night, as well as the journey each living creature makes in its own life—an ancient understanding that life flows into life and a critical recognition of that eternal truth.

Figure 21. Tomb of Inherkau, with Aker. The deceased kneels and offers praise to Aker—the double lion, also known as Shu and Tefnut—with the *akhet* (horizon symbol) between them and the *ankh* hanging from the saddle of the mountains. Photo credit: kairoinfo4u, from flickr photo album "Tombs of Nobles." Photographed on 7 June 2015. Creative Commons, some rights reserved. Web. 9 March 2018.

Aker: Double Lion

The double lion above (fig. 21) comprises Shu and Tefnut sitting back-to-back, flanking the sun's orb, or a lotus flower in full bloom. Neumann tells us Osiris's *djed* pillar is also flanked by Aker, "symbolizing the morning and evening sun, yesterday and today" (*Origins and History* 235). The double lion is guardian of the horizon, where the sun must pass into the Netherworld each day to make the perilous journey through the underworld and be reborn, renewed, on the opposite horizon at sunrise. It symbolizes west and east, yesterday and tomorrow, eternal sameness, as well as recurrence, renewal, rebirth, and resurrection (Pinch, *Egyptian Mythology* 197; von Franz, *Alchemy* 70–1).

Figure 22. Papyrus of Khonsu-Renep, scene of resurrection in Papyrus #11 (Piankoff and Rambova, *Mythological Papyri*). The papyrus is in the collection of the Cairo Egyptian Museum and was photographed by Hassia, Cairo. Public domain.

The image above (fig. 22) depicts the Solar Barque at sunrise. The upper register shows the Day Barque as it ferries the divine child into the day. He is sitting in the bow with Ma'at behind him, holding her *ankh*. Behind her is the *akhet* symbol. They are accompanied by five fire-spitting cobras and being towed by three jackals, deities known as Wepwawet, "Openers of the Ways"—psychopomps that lead the dead through the winding paths of the underworld. In the lower register, under the curved symbol of heaven, the solar orb is passed between two identical deities, while four baboons joyously greet it with praise as it emerges from the Netherworld. The hieroglyphic symbols above each repeat the phrase "Adoration of Re" four times. Khonsu-Renep, the deceased, is the man to the right with his hands also raised in praise.

Ankh: Breath of Life

The *ankh* (fig. 23) is probably the most common symbol in the iconography of ancient Egypt; it symbolizes the renewal of life. In tomb paintings, deities often extend the *ankh* toward the nose of the deceased, offering him or her the breath of life, or hold it as described above. As a hieroglyphic symbol it is read "life"—as in life everlasting or the breath of life. Ma'at is often depicted seated (fig. 24), her legs drawn up with an *ankh* held in her lap, or standing, one arm extended downward, holding an *ankh* in her hand. Thus we can think of the *ankh* as her specter, her insignia.

Figure 23. Wooden ankh. In the collection of the British Museum. ©Trustees of the British Museum, some rights reserved. Creative Commons.

Single Ostrich Feather: Truth

Ma'at's single ostrich feather is a symbol known as "the feather of truth." This name is related to the Weighing of the Heart ordeal, described in detail in chapter 5—the judgment that each deceased person must undergo in the afterlife.

Figure 24. Goddess Ma'at, seated. Egyptian, *c*. 664–525 BCE. Bronze. Helen M. Danforth Acquisition Fund 1989.088. Photo credit: Erik Gould, courtesy of the Museum of Art, Rhode Island School of Design, Providence. 22.9 x 5.1 x 14.6 cm (9 x 2 x 5 ¾ inches). Reprinted with permission by copyright holder.

But there is more to the symbolism of this feather, for it is also the god Shu's symbol, indicating that Ma'at and Shu are intimately related as co-characteristics of creation. *Coffin Texts*, Spell 330, identifies Shu and Ma'at as brother and sister; he is Life, the embodiment of air, atmosphere, and light (the First Light), whereas she is Order—moisture (as her alter-aspect Tefnut) and the breath of life. Ma'at establishes the cosmic order that creates the primordial mound and provides Atum both a place to stand and nourishment and renewal. She orders the natural cyclic patterns, the ever-renewing earth and the celestial wheel, and she holds the *ankh*, the breath of life.

A strictly grammatical definition of their ostrich feather headdress as the feather of truth does not explain why both are wearing the single ostrich feather as their insignia. Instead of relying just on the facts that the ostrich feather is both Ma'at's ideogram and Shu's phonogram, *šw*, the sound symbol of an exhalation or a sneeze, we must focus on the image for answers. In reading the individual facets of a symbol, it is possible to gather many related elements and add other layers of insight to create an imagining of the meaning.

The ostrich itself, for example, is a flightless bird. Imagine holding an ostrich's plume and looking closely at its structure. The soft, pliant vanes, each as complex as the individual leaves of a tree, extend from the central rachis and bend with their own weight, which makes the feather responsive to the slightest breeze or breath of air. Light gathers in its tiny hairs, giving it the appearance of radiating an inner glow. Such feathers are not designed to push the wind beneath or lift the bird into the air to ride the air currents. The ostrich is a bird that belongs to the earth, and its feathers' sensitivity to the breath of the gods reveals the presence of the divine described in light, breath, and movement.

In addition to its gorgeous plumage that is sensitive to the movements of the invisible holy breath, an ostrich has large, far-seeing eyes and powerful legs. In combination, these attributes suggest a connection to Ma'at and Shu—pattern, order, breath, air, light, fire, enlivening energies—connecting breath of life and light of creation through the symbols of earth, air, fire, and the waters of creation from which Shu and Ma'at arose.

The single ostrich feather worn by both Shu and Ma'at (figs. 24 and 25) as their identifying headdress is a cosmogonic symbol. It emphasizes both their individual contributions to creation and how those are interrelated. Ma'at establishes the cosmic order that creates the primordial mound and provides Atum nourishment and renewal. She orders the natural cyclic patterns, the ever-renewing earth and the celestial wheel, and she holds the *ankh*, the breath of life. Meanwhile, sparked by Atum's exhalation of joy when Ma'at is placed beside his nose, Shu is clothed in "the garments of life" and simultaneously lifts up Nut, the sky, separating her from her beloved, the earth, Geb. The bodies of Nut and Geb describe the boundaries that hold back the waters of Nun, and create the pocket Shu fills with atmosphere, shot through with sunbeams and the breath of life. Expanding the image with reverie and taking into account observable facts brings us closer to an ancient Egyptian holoscopic perspective and to a comprehension of Ma'at's (and Shu's) multivalent dominion.

All these actions of creation are envisioned as taking place simultaneously, when creation begins in earnest (Clark 77). These individual facets combine, and the ostrich feather becomes a symbol of both light (Shu) and breath of life (Ma'at)—images that circulate within the ordering patterns of Ma'at. Thus the ostrich feather is a symbol of the

Figure 25. Shu supporting Nut. From the coffin of Neb-Taui, Metropolitan Museum of Art, New York (Piankoff and Rambova, *Mythological Papyri* 48, fig. 31). Public domain.

sacred embrace, the sacred marriage, the circulation of primal psychic energy that is the fuel of the cosmos.

The image above (fig. 25) imagines the separation of Nut, the sky, and her beloved Geb, the earth. Shu—their father—represents the atmosphere that fills the space between Nut and Geb. This separation makes all life possible. On either side of Shu are the double recumbent Anubis jackals, who preside over the mysteries of the Netherworld. Each is wearing the crown that is a combination of the Red and the White crowns, and each is holding a flail of rulership. The doubled ram-headed god Amon, the great-*Ba* soul of the Underworld, is kneeling on either side of Nut with his hands raised in praise. Also doubled are the winged Eye and the *uraeus*. In the upper left corner is the primordial mound, and on the right side is the symbol for the Beautiful West. The deceased, the priestess Neb-Taui, is standing on the left side with a raised sistrum in one hand and the other hand making the gesture of praise. Her place directly below the primordial mound is an image of resurrection—into life everlasting.

Plinth: Foundation

The plinth is a stone foundation, offering stability and a base that supports the throne and statues of the gods and goddesses. Osiris is often depicted seated on his throne, which is placed upon the distinctive plinth of Ma'at in the Hall of Double Truth. Ma'at's plinth (fig. 26) embodies the concept of "straightness," which is the literal translation of the word *maat,* "which can signify the shaft of a spear, a staff, stalk, or rays of light" (Wilkinson, *Reading Egyptian Art* 37). Also related to Ma'at's plinth is the word *maa,* which translates variously as "true, just, and right" or "direct." Thus the plinth as the straight rule or measure is symbolic of Ma'at's foundational patterns and laws that regulate all systems of the earth and sky, including social structure and interactions. The king's throne is a symbol of the lap of Isis, indicating that all society is grounded and stabilized by the divine foundation of the feminine principle, the generative, life-giving matrix that protects and nourishes, ever-renewing.

In the image below (fig. 26) the foundation of Osiris's shrine is the plinth of Ma'at, and it is also the hieroglyphic symbol for her name. Here, the white shape with the angled end depicts the hieroglyphic symbol for Ma'at as the foundation and the source of eternal renewal. Each image in this composition reinforces this. The twelve rearing cobras that make up the roof of the shrine flank a falcon head rising up from a green primordial mound and its shroud—a symbol of resurrection and rebirth. The four sons of Horus, facing Osiris on top of the lotus, and the thirty-five rearing cobras that create the frieze below the mound also echo resurrection.

Figure 26. The Papyrus of Ani (Plate 4). Osiris is within his shrine, protected and stabilized by Isis and Nephthys, who stand behind him. ©Trustees of the British Museum, some rights reserved. Creative Commons.

Shen: Infinity and Protection

The *shen* ring is often depicted grasped in the talons of the vulture goddess Nekhbet or the falcon god Horus. Composed of a looped cord like the *ouroboros*, it reads as the words *infinity*, *eternity*, and *protection*. It combines with other symbols to create different meanings. For instance, the *renpet* symbol is a curved palm shoot or the leafless, notched stem of the palm branch. It is used as the hieroglyphic symbol for "year" and is combined with other symbols to denote different aspects of time. When the *shen* ring is placed as the base and the *renpet* symbol rests upon it, this means "eternity." Or the *shen* ring is used as the base supporting the *was* scepter, which is interpreted as "dominion" or "power"; together they are read as "eternal power" or "dominion forever and forever."

Figure 27. Winged Ma'at. In the Tomb of Nefertari, Valley of the Queens, Ma'at is protectively encircling the *shen* (symbol for infinity) and the cartouche containing the hieroglyphic throne name of Queen Nefertari—"Beloved of Mut"—with her wings. Photo credit: kairoinfo4u, from the flickr photo album: "Tomb of Nefertari, QV66, Valley of the Queens." Photographed 19 March 2017. Original photo has been cropped. Creative Commons, some rights reserved. Web. 9 March 2018.

In the New Kingdom, Ma'at is often depicted winged, like Isis and Nephthys, which indicates their ability to revive the dead by fanning them with their wings, giving the breath of life. In the tomb of Nefertari, beloved queen of Ramesses II, the *shen* ring and a cartouche that reads *Meritmut*, or "Beloved of Mut" (one of the queen's names), is protectively cradled between Ma'at's outstretched wings (fig. 27). Winged Ma'at is portrayed throughout Nefertari's tomb, flanking both doorways and painted above lintels. Clearly the goddess was important to the queen, who would have participated in selecting the imagery that covered the walls of her tomb.

Ib: **Heart**

The *awakened heart* is a term employed by this study that indicates the desired state of consciousness sought by the ancient Egyptian. For the ancient Egyptian, "the heart is the seat of creative power—the imagination" (Bonnefoy, *Mythologies* 221). The highest forms of knowing arise from the heart, which is the source of wisdom, intelligence, and the emotions.

The creator god Ptah was said to create with his heart and tongue, and even Atum spoke of creating when his heart became activated, in the *Coffin Texts*. The heart, like the breath, is "life itself" (Wilkinson, *Reading Egyptian Art* 77). Moreover, the heart is "often equated with a person's very being" (77); it informs the judgment of the deceased in the Weighing of the Heart ordeal, whose precepts are found in much of the literature of ancient Egypt (as is explored in chapter 4).

> It is the heart which carries the deeds of a lifetime. And it is the
>
> purity of the heart which determines whether a person enters the
>
> blessed company of Osiris or is condemned to an existence beyond

the glimmering of life-giving light, without water or food.

(Roberts, *My Heart My Mother* 153)

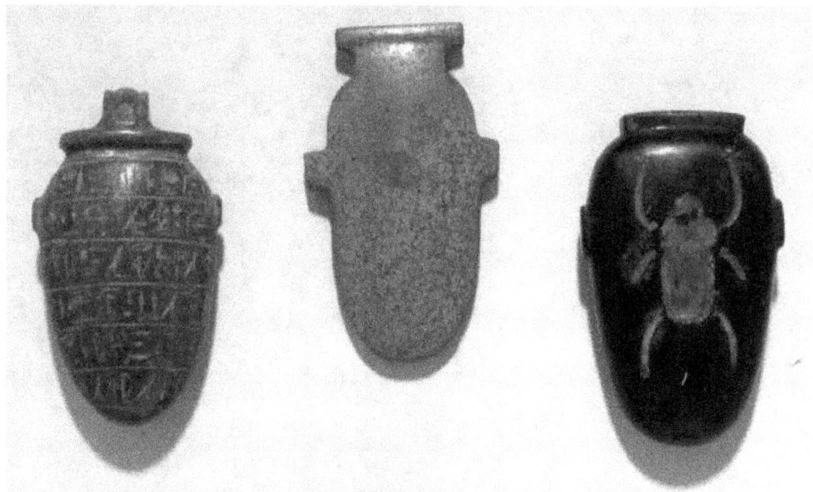

Figure 28. Ib, *the Heart—three heart amulets made of stone.* These amulets also are the hieroglyphic symbol for "heart." In the collection of the British Museum. ©Trustees of the British Museum, some rights reserved. Creative Commons.

The heart is said to belong to the mother, made from one drop of her blood at conception. In the *Book of Going Forth Into Day*, Chapter 30B, the deceased pleads with his or her heart:

O my heart which I had from my mother! O my heart which I had

from my mother! O my heart of my different ages! Do not stand up

as a witness against me, do not be opposed to me in the tribunal, do

not be hostile to me in the presence of the Keeper of the Balance,

for you are my Ka which was in my body, the protector who made

my members hale. Go forth to the happy place whereto we speed;

do not make my name stink to Entourage who make men. Do not

tell lies about me in the presence of the god; it is indeed well that

you should hear! (Faulkner, Goelet, and Wasserman, plate 3)

Figure 29. Black scarab. In the collection of the British Museum. ©Trustees of the British Museum, some rights reserved. Creative Commons.

Sacred texts might contain specific spells to protect the heart from evil influences and to encourage a favorable testimony from the heart. The plea from Chapter 30B, for example, is inscribed on the flat bottom of a heart scarab amulet (fig. 29) carved from stone, often green serpentine. This was placed over the heart of the mummified body and wrapped into the linen bandages to protect the heart. The heart was the only organ left in the body during the mummification process, because it was seen as critical to the survival of the body and the soul parts.

The image below (fig. 30) is from the Temple of Seti I, Abydos (which is the focus of chapter 6). In this powerful image the "solar gaze" is beautifully depicted and illustrates its relationship to the heart. "The solar gaze becomes an activity as the eye— the instrument of divine energy and power—is projected out into the world" (Roberts, *Hathor Rising* 9). Roberts is referencing the Eye goddess, the *iret,* which means "doer"— the Eye that is both the fiery cobra and the *Wedjat*-eye, the "whole eye," which is also a bodily organ (9).

Figure 30. The solar gaze, the nourishing look of love. In the Temple of Seti I, Abydos. On the wall between the chapel of Amun and the chapel of Osiris. New Kingdom. Photo credit: kairoinfo4u, from the flickr photo album: "Temple of Seti I Abydos." Photographed on 21 February 2014. Original photo has been cropped and the contrast increased to enhance details. Creative Commons, some rights reserved. Web. 9 March 2018.

In the figure above Seti I is portrayed as a youth sitting in the lap of his divine Mother, Isis. Isis embodies the throne and is the lap of kingship. She is tenderly raising the child's face with her left hand while her right hand gently cups the back of his head. They are gazing deeply into one another's eyes in an intimate exchange of love. The word that comes to mind is *cherishing*. This image transmits across the ages the exchange of loving energy between a mother and a child—the nourishing, life-giving force of that relationship.

Isis's crown is composed of a number of symbols—the horns of the Wild Cow cradling the solar disc, which is encircled by the rearing serpent, the *uraeus*, which in turn is supported by a platform composed of eight additional rearing cobras. Mut's vulture headdress further reinforces the Mother association, as both the goddess Mut and her vulture headdress symbolize the archetypal Great Mother.

The solar gaze is related to the feminine Eye and therefore to all aspects of the divine feminine, creative and destructive. In the image above, the gaze clearly conveys the nourishing relational energies of the divine feminine as Mother. She directs her undivided attention and care toward her beloved child. This is a representation of eros as the union between mother and child and the active, generative energy focused on promoting flourishing life. "The movement of loving is circular, and love is the real unitive force" (von Franz, *Aurora Consurgens* 181). The unity the solar gaze imparts is further underscored by the symbol upon which the child's feet rest.

Seti's feet are resting on a potent icon: *sema*, meaning "unity" (see description below). This image is symbolic of his intention to heal the fractures and reestablish Ma'at's order in ancient Egypt as being the destiny of his life. Isis is nourishing him with her solar gaze. In this image she is recognizing him as the Horus who will become the next king. Her gaze is filling the child Seti with the mana necessary to fulfill his destiny and grow into the powerful ruler that he later became. He, too, has the *uraeus* on his brow and is holding the crook of kingship, marking his divinity from his childhood. This does not reflect the literal or historical truth, for his father was an old man when Seti, already an adult, was named successor to the throne. Instead it represents a mythological truth and establishes his dynasty as a divine desire.

Sema: Unity

Though not usually equated as specific to Ma'at's iconography, the symbol *sema* embodies Ma'at's purview most eloquently. *Sema* is the binding together of opposites, of the differentiated parts—a continual reweaving of the connection between two poles, or the doubling of fecundity. As illustrated below (fig. 31), the symbol for "united" or "unity" is commonly inscribed on the side of the throne of a king or deity.

In these images (figs. 30–32), the *sema* symbol graphically depicts the unity of the Two Lands in its display of a vertical trachea terminating in two lungs. The trachea is bound by the two heraldic plants: the papyrus (representing Lower Egypt in the north) on the right, and the lotus or lily (symbolizing Upper Egypt in the south) on the left. Entwining around the trachea, their stems create a knot that resembles an infinity symbol. Both are significant elements of the *sema* symbol.

Papyrus is plentiful in the delta region, flourishing in tall stands along the river's seven branches. The papyrus clump as a symbol means "green" and includes such varied ideas as "flourish," "joy," and "youth" (Wilkinson, *Reading Egyptian Art* 123). It represents "the primeval marsh from which all life emerged" as well as the goddesses

Figure 31. Sema *symbol.* Located on the base of the throne of Sekhmet, in the Museo Egizio, Torino, Italia. Photo credit: Laurie Larsen. Photographed on 15 June 2017. Used with permission of copyright holder.

(such as Hathor, Bastet, Sekhmet, and Neith) who carry the papyrus scepter to represent flourishing life (123). The ancient Egyptians used papyrus to create many useful objects, from small skiffs to shoes to paper. This plant, like the river itself, is a symbol of life everlasting and the gift of life renewing itself.

The lotus, whose roots sink into the mud at the bottom of the pond, closes its bud at night, withdrawing below the surface of the water, and reopens with the dawn's light;

it is a symbol for resurrection and rebirth. The blue lotus was sacred and prized for its sweet scent. Its distinctive petals are pointed, and it is often shown being held to the nose—another symbol for joy.

The knot is a symbol of potent magic, representing a joining of two forces, a binding together—the unity that the *sema* symbol overall represents. The multiple expressions of this ideal of unity lent a resilience to the Egyptian people; in times of crisis, challenge, and setback they returned to the actions and values denoted by their living symbols and found a path to recreate unity.

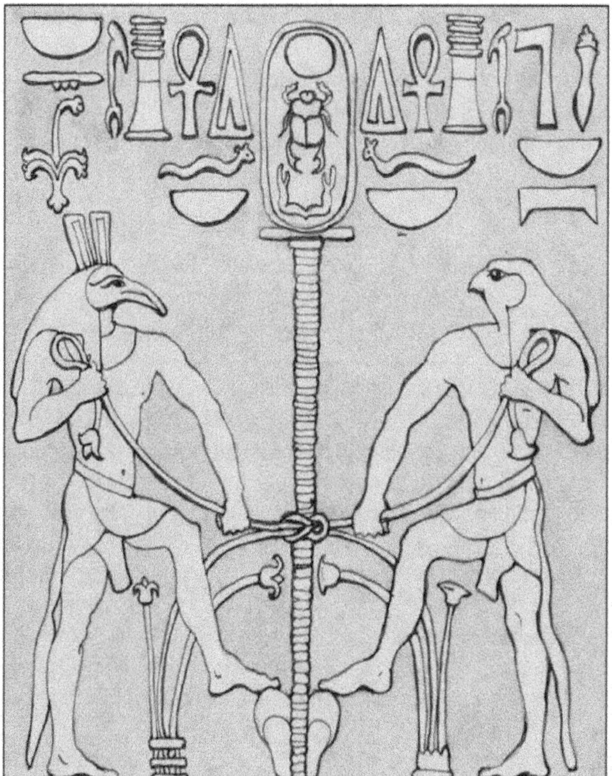

Figure 32. Sema *symbol, representing the unity of Upper and Lower Egypt.* Seth and Horus holding the lotus and papyrus stems that bind them together. Credit: Illustration by Laura Marshall. Reprinted with permission by copyright holder.

From the predynastic unification (*c.* 3100 BCE) until the demise of ancient Egypt during the Roman Period (30 BCE–395 CE), *sema* was reestablished and reimagined, renewing unity on numerous levels, many times over. It seems likely that the Egyptian civilization's final demise came when Ma'at, *sema*, and other symbols of unity no longer held the numinous power needed to reestablish their culture in the face of pressures from a changing world.

In the image above (fig. 32), Seth is on the left, with the lotus representing Upper Egypt, and Horus is on the right, holding the papyrus stem to represent Lower Egypt. As in the previous image, the lotus and papyrus stems are entwined around an upright trachea that terminates in two lungs. Seth and Horus mirror each other in every detail except for their animal heads—Seth has a mythical animal's head similar to a jackal's, and Horus is falcon-headed.

Sema is also closely related to the symbol for "beauty," *nefer*, which is composed of the trachea and the heart (Wilkinson, *Reading Egyptian Art* 79). The balance and harmony implied in the *sema* symbol reflect the ancient Egyptian commitment to put aside strife in favor of creating a thriving, harmonious country, giving rise to beauty in all its forms. This underscores the goal of harmonizing opposites rather than perpetuating a power struggle where one side is constantly trying to dominate the other, thereby creating endless war and destruction.

When we align our sense of direction to the ancient Egyptian way (as described in chapter 2), *sema* might be seen as an image of the Nile, flowing from south to north and terminating in the widespread delta region. The trachea and lungs also call to mind lungs and the exhalation of breath that indicates life and creation, which the Egyptians equated with the steady breeze that blows from north to south. The northern breeze is often mentioned in the sacred texts as a holy wind capable of bestowing the breath of life—a euphemism for Ma'at.

As the north wind, *sema* also reflects the "breath of the gods," which refreshes and fills the nose of the living and reawakens the dead. Just as the Nile is the symbol of the waters of life, Ma'at is the living symbol of the breath of life. *Sema* is a symbol of Ma'at's organizing framework, on which the cosmic patterns and natural order—and the well-being of the entire nation—relied, in this realm and the next.

Wild Cow: The Divine Feminine

The image of Ma'at as the Wild Cow goddess (fig. 33) perfectly echoes the image in my dream (relayed in chapter 1). It was carved into the living rock wall of a vestibule at the temple in Abu Simbel, Egypt, sometime between 1244 and 1224 BCE, during the reign of Ramses II (*c.* 1290–1224 BCE), as part of a relief for his beloved wife, Queen Nefertari. She is shown on the left side of this image, offering papyrus blossoms and a vessel that sits upon her altar table to Hathor as the Great Wild Cow. Emerging from a papyrus swamp in a barque, Hathor is wearing the crown of Hesat (one name for the ancient celestial sky cow goddess), just as Ma'at wore it in my dream. Another name for this Wild Cow is Mehet-Weret. She brings her barque and nourishing milk to the queen, signifying that the queen has acquired her luminous, eternal light-body form as *akh*, "the transfigured one," the purified and deified eternal soul. Hesat is coming to carry Nefertari to join the Imperishable Stars, where she will unite with the retinue of Re and participate for eternity in the continual processes of renewal.

Figure 33. Drawing of a relief from the Temple to Hathor at Abu Simbel, New Kingdom, 19th Dynasty. Queen Nefertari, the beloved chief wife of Ramesses II, is offering papyrus blossoms and pure water to Hathor as the primordial Wild Cow. Credit: Illustration by Laura Marshall. Reprinted with permission by copyright holder.

To the ancient Egyptians, the divine Feminine is the Wild Cow. She is also the starry sky, the *axis mundi*, the tree of life, the primordial mound, the foundational plinth, the protective serpent, the sacred barque, the throne, the crowns, the tomb, the womb, the temple, the sacrifices, the grain, the beer, the bread, and the breath of life—she is life itself. The Wild Cow rose from the primordial waters, gave birth to the solar god Re, placed him between her horns as the solar disc, and raised him up to the sky. She is represented in works spanning the millennia, from the iconography of predynastic artifacts to the *Pyramid Texts* of the Old Kingdom (*c.* 2686–2160 BCE).

Without the enlivening, quickening, multifaceted influence of the divine Feminine, the solar gods remain inert—unable to create form, build a throne, or raise a mound to claim dominion of the world. Without the protective, nurturing, sustaining, enduring devotion of the archetypal energies of Mother and Daughter, all life would wither and disappear, or never arise in the first place. In general, the feminine archetypal energies in ancient Egyptian mythology are proactive, apotropaic, and generative. The civilization shares these qualities with many other ancient spiritual traditions, including (as described earlier in this chapter) the Great Goddesses in Neolithic cultures around the world.

Ma'at in Relationship to the Solar God

Like Osiris, Re is considered a "universal deity" because he interacts in the three realms: divine, human, and ancestral. In his book *The Complete Gods and Goddesses of Ancient Egypt*, the Egyptologist Richard Wilkinson ascribes five roles to the primary solar god: Re in the Heavens; Re on Earth; Re in the Netherworld; Re as Creator; and Re as King and Father of the King (206–07). These distinctions provide a useful rubric for exploring Ma'at and discerning her role in each of these realms.

Ma'at in the Heavens

In the Solar Barque, Ma'at is a constant companion of Re. Day and night she accompanies him, standing either behind him protectively or in the bow to guide and open the ways before them. She also stands beside Re, delighting his heart, and her sweet scent gives life to his nostrils (Hornung, *Idea Into Image* 132). Ma'at also is named as the Solar Barque, the feminine vessel that nurtures life as it traverses the waterways of both the Day World and the Night World in the cyclic course of renewal.

Kristensen informs us that "Ma-a-t represents the fixed law and order of the world, and with this also the eternal life of the Egyptian god" (92). Re "exists through [Ma'at], and she exists through him" (59). Theirs is a mutual, reciprocal relationship that cannot be broken apart into a simple hierarchical progression. This implies that both the god and the goddess exist and perpetuate life because of their interwoven nature—similar to the relationship discerned between Shu and Ma'at (and among all the gods, for that matter). This interconnection fuels all life, including life after death (59).

Though Ma'at's position is central and critical to the stability and health of all life, she is not a stern, austere feminine entity—she is a beautiful solar daughter, and the joy she brings *is* creation. In her aspect as the first hour of dawn she initiates the celebration of the dawning solar god's beauty and youthful vigor.

Ma'at on the Earth

In her role as cosmic order Ma'at provides the organizational patterns and natural laws that inform and shape society. Her patterns and laws are also reflected in the bounty of the earth, in the agricultural produce and gifts: "Her activity was mostly perceived in the life of the earth, which underneath all changes is eternal. According to very ancient views [Ma'at] is a goddess of the earth" (Kristensen 59). Ma'at is a "force of nature" (Allen 147) and the primordial mound. Her most ancient hieroglyphic symbol is the plinth, an image related to the stepped-pyramid shape of the mound and the foundation for the throne, in the Day World and the Night World (Kristensen 59; Clark 39).

Moreover, Ma'at migrated into the mythologems that emerged in much later spiritual traditions arising from cultures that lived in proximity to the ancient Egyptians—namely, the Hebrew and early Christian peoples. In referring specifically to Ma'at,

Hornung conjures an image of Sophia, the goddess of wisdom from the much later Kabbalah and Gnostic mystical traditions that informed Judaism and early Christianity:

> Since creation she has lived among human beings. Having come to them from the gods, she has been entrusted to them, and the human act of presenting Maat returns her to the gods; in this completes the ritual circle. (*Idea Into Image* 132)

As a goddess of the natural laws of the earth, Ma'at was critical to the development of the ancient Egyptians ideas on law and the development of social justice. Judges were "priests of Ma'at," and cases were tried in the temples, the "Houses of Life," also known as "temples of Truth." To ensure his impartiality, a priest of Ma'at was required to embody personal characteristics, such as modesty and truthfulness, that would make him immune to corruption and greed. This was accomplished by putting oneself in accord with Ma'at, by saying and doing Ma'at.

Kristensen ventures to relate Ma'at to the ancient Greek goddess of justice, Themis, in her aspect of the "fixed order" of the earth (60). Indeed, Ma'at's role as a Daughter of Re can overshadow the fact that she had her own cult as well. Barbara Lesko points out the discovery of evidence supporting this in the Precinct of Montu at the Karnak Temple Complex, speculating, "Juridical matters may well have been decided in these 'temples of Truth'" (269).

Ma'at in the Netherworld

Ma'at combines "all divine might and power" in herself—"she is God's food and drink; with her he dies and rises from death" (Kristensen 92). *The Book of Gates* reveals that "even the blessed dead 'live in Maat,' just as they would be nourished by bread and beer" (Hornung, *Idea Into Image* 132). As the beer and bread of the gods, Ma'at is also the barley and wheat, the grain, the staff of life, the seed. In this she is connected to Osiris, who is also the seed—the dismembered god, once a king in the golden age of the gods, whose death ensures the cyclic, recurrent fertility of the land.

In the afterlife, the dead are judged on whether they did and spoke Ma'at throughout their lifetime. From the Old Kingdom onward, Ma'at's presence was thought to be vital to the daily regeneration of the sun god. In the genre of literature known as *Books of What's in the Underworld* she is often shown standing close to Re in the Solar Barque (both the Day Barque and the Night Barque). This, and the natural duality recognized in ancient Egypt—and symbolized by Upper and Lower Egypt united as a single kingdom—may begin to explain why Ma'at can appear as two identical goddesses, double Ma'at (Pinch, *Egyptian Mythology* 159–60).

Ma'at as the Creator

> [T]he religious life of the ancients imposed itself on all man's
>
> ways. It provided norms and ideals for the community, in art and
>
> understanding and for every noble endeavor. (Kristensen 176)

Kristensen was one of the first to recognize that Ma'at's purview includes cosmic order instead of just embracing an ethical concept (Mancini 8).[31] Although Kristensen tends to underplay Ma'at's relationship to "ethical standards" that other scholars emphasize, he broadens Ma'at's purview, saying that Ma'at is "the 'law of life, all life' including the mystery of spontaneous life—the mystery of resurrection and renewal" (59). Citing the French Egyptologist Alexandre Moret, Kristensen states that "Re created

---

[31] Jan Assmann and Philippe Derchain credit Bleeker as the person who shifted their own understanding of Ma'at toward this same recognition, and Bleeker, a student of Kristensen's at Leiden University, was undoubtedly influenced in this by Kristensen.

order and he is dependent on the same order. Re exists through [Ma'at], as she exist through him. . . . In this connection she represents cosmic law rather than ethical law" (59).

Perhaps it is not as clear-cut as a simple either/or, though this does underscore an important point: the focus of one's research and perceptions is habitually drawn to what one agrees with while discounting what one disagrees with. The holoscopic perspective takes a different approach: it seeks to bridge a connection between multiple viewpoints.

Hornung takes a broad perspective, though he does so by splitting Ma'at into two halves—a goddess and an abstract concept. He sees a clear connection between Ma'at as "the foundation of all order in the created world" as well as the cosmic (*Idea Into Image* 134). He notes that Ma'at reveals herself as both "the basis for life in a specifically social sense, and in the much broader sense of cosmic order or balance" (*Idea Into Image* 134).

Ma'at Accompanying the King and Father of the King

As a Daughter of Re, Ma'at has the task of accompanying the solar god in his journey, protectively standing behind him as a stabilizing force, or in the prow of the Solar Barque, guiding it and opening the passageways between the Day World and the Night World.

As pointed out earlier, cosmogonically Ma'at is linked to Tefnut, the first sexually differentiated feminine deity in the Heliopolitan creation mythology. Shu, her brother and mate, is the first sexually differentiated masculine deity. In the *Coffin Texts* Shu is named Life, and his sister is named Order, Ma'at. Combining these elements, and the shared emblem of their single ostrich feather headdresses, leads to the conclusion that they represent a duality that is fundamental to the manifest world, as well as the balance and harmony that are necessary to maintain the ever-renewing cycles life relies on. Light and dark, creation and destruction, life and death—the dance between the pairs of opposites is crucial to creation, to the cosmic patterns established in First Time.

Chapter Summary

A review of Ma'at's wreath of symbolic images reveals that we are exploring the multidimensional archetypal Feminine in her many aspects. Ma'at's energy can be fiery, creative, and primordial—she is the archetypal instigator of life, death, and rebirth. As an aspect of the Sole Eye, Ma'at ventures through the utter darkness of Nun and reestablishes eros so that creation is primed to continue. Ma'at's archetypal aspects connect to the divine Feminine along the spectrum of the heavens, with both solar and lunar features. Her direct link to the evolving solar consciousness is apparent in her role as the solar daughter and consort to the creator and solar gods, Atum and Re. She also represents divinity and power as the fiery *uraeus*, the protective third eye—the bright light of consciousness.

Ma'at's lunar aspect is borne out in her connection with the chthonic serpent in the watery abyss, the protective womb for the solar/lunar disc, and the endlessly renewing cycles of the moon. As an aspect of the double lion Aker, she is guardian of the west, the setting sun as it enters the Netherworld to begin its process of renewal and rebirth. In addition, she is identified as the liminal gate of the east, as the first hour of the day—the dawn, as Re reemerges renewed. Her body is linked with the building blocks of the world, the primordial mound, the first earth, and the divine water. As both earth and water she embodied the *prima materia* of creation (von Franz, *Alchemy* 66).[32] Ma'at is the creator of the celestial patterns, the one whose ordering and harmonizing are the balance and proportions of creation.

Ma'at directs her attention toward the cohesion of Egypt, uniting the children with the creator while still in the Nun, uniting with the creator as the *uraeus*, protecting and defending the king who is doing and saying Ma'at. She is both nurturing vessel and guardian, the sacred barque for Re's nightly journey through the Netherworld.

The divine Feminine in all her forms is connected to the heart, the emotional center that shapes and informs consciousness. This is key to understanding her, for eros—an archetypal principle that the ancient Egyptian culture valued most highly—is ultimately the unity and harmonizing of opposites. Eros is "the force in the universe that seeks union, not through domination, will, or control, but through connection or relation" (Odajnyk 22).

Ma'at personifies the balance that gives rise to justice, order, and truth, and seeks to harmonize opposites. When out of balance, the destructive capabilities of the divine Feminine are terrifying and immense. As Sekhmet or Tefnut she wades in blood, delighting in indiscriminate killing of men, women, and children. She relishes the chaotic watery inundation from the realm of the unconscious, as reflected in images of the annual flooding of the Nile. She experiences rage akin to the scorching, glaring heat of the summer sun, causing drought as all the moisture—all the feeling aspect—is dried up; as the fiery Eye she can wither vegetation with her gaze, and all life becomes listless, drained, or filled with hot fury. After all, "[i]n its negative expression, Eros is also behind

---

[32] *Prima materia* is an alchemical term. It seems likely that alchemy originated in Egypt and spread to the Greek, European, and Arab cultures over the centuries. Though beyond the scope of this study, the alchemical symbolism in ancient Egyptian images related to Ma'at would make for fascinating analysis.

the destructive impulse that seeks to return all forms and beings to their original undifferentiated condition" (Odajnyk 22). However, when she is approached with a Ma'atian consciousness that is seated in the heart and honoring eros, her nature is soothed and order, balance, and harmony return.

Neither the importance of the concept of Ma'at to the ancient Egyptians, nor the significance of the heart as seat of intelligence and higher principles (as is discussed in detail in chapter 7), should be underestimated. The heart is both fiery and cooling when wed to the harmony of Ma'at. The creative, imaginative power of the heart—the psyche—harnesses this fierceness and opens the path of balance; together these attributes impregnate darkness with light, consciousness with unconscious, all held fast within their unity.

The powerful symbolic images associated with Ma'at shape her form and purpose—the renewal of life—as well as her people's understanding. An exploration of these symbols reveals that opposites—fire and water, earth and air, chaos and harmony, destruction and order, life and death, the rampaging lioness and a nurturing Eye, the fire-spitting *uraeus* and Ma'at's moisture cooling the fiery rage—create unity, the framework of life, which is explored in the next chapter.

Our ability to see value in the ancient intuitive approach to naming these symbols has been undermined by the contemporary scientific model that, even though it too employs naming as the core of its traditions, rejects what can't be quantified and proven. In both religious and scientific traditions, naming identifies a potential and makes it so by describing its constitutive parts; this act in turn shapes the values and direction of the collective consciousness. From the evidence gathered, it seems the ancient Egyptians imagined the workings of a wholly mysterious, wondrous, terrifying, and terrific existence—seeking the balance and harmony that would bring order to a chaotic and unpredictable world. Their contemplation of the mysteries—and the complex rituals they developed to renew and affirm their connection to life—took them beyond the bounds of phenomena into the imaginal, weaving their holoscopic, multiple perspectives together into a coherent whole.

Chapter 4. Order and Reciprocity: Ma'at's Mighty Influence

The universe is constantly on the brink of being dislocated and its integrity

depends on the performance of rites, that is, on the intensity with which

man represents the universe for himself. Cosmogony thus becomes an

element of political and social life that belongs especially to the present

moment. (Bonnefoy, *Mythologies* 217)

From the perspective of the ancient Egyptians, to care for and preserve

community, humans must take care of the relationship between the realms, recognizing

and fostering the interdependency between the phenomenal and spiritual worlds. Spiritual

practices are needed to create the means for connecting with the realm where the deities

and ancestors dwell. Sacrifices must be offered and received.

At its very heart, ritual gives expression to the great longing for the continuity of

life. To achieve continuity and renewal, it is necessary to actively participate in creating

balance and harmony within the community and in the community's relationship with its

individual members. The key to the actions necessary for achieving life, both daily and

eternal, is reciprocity.

Reciprocity and the Keystone of Civilization

It was the duty of all Egyptians to live in accordance with Ma'at.

Only if they did so could they join the society of the dead when

they died. (Allen 149)

From the ancient Egyptians' perspective, reciprocal relationships with the divine

are foundational to social structure, ensuring that a person will be justified after death and

therefore be granted eternal life. One way humans promote their reciprocal relationship is through daily offerings. The Egyptians, like many other ancient cultures, believed that "humans must vigilantly maintain a harmonious relationship with the divine powers of the cosmos in order to prosper" (Grillo 8). They envisioned Ma'at as all the offerings—the bread and beer, the food for the gods, the incense, the cloth, the flowers—and all things placed on the altars were her essence. Like the Great Goddesses of the Neolithic cultures, Ma'at embodies both the fecund earth and the star-strewn sky, both Mother Night and Solar Daughter.

Ma'at is the coherent pattern that organizes all life, the keystone in the arch, locking all the other stones into position. Remove this wedge-shaped stone from the midpoint, and the arch collapses, for the keystone provides the structural integrity—the interconnection. Ma'at is the vital component that sustains the flow of creative impulses from the equilibrium of her pivotal point originating in First Time, while guaranteeing the circulation of the energy that renews and regenerates all life.

Ma'at's principles were the chief organizing principle that maintained the ancient Egyptian civilization and were interwoven into all aspects of life: "Ma'at was what kept the world's elements fixed in their appropriate places, the seasons following in their natural order, night giving way to day, and each generation being succeeded by the next" (Allen 148). Ma'at was the model and measure for success in maintaining "rightness" or "straightness." Her cosmic and natural order were applicable to building the necessary framework within human society for successful coexistence, where Ma'at was "the guarantor of social justice" (147).

Articulation of her natural laws gave rise to distinctions that most likely began to take form when the ancient people of Egypt still lived as hunters and gatherers. These earliest ancestors would have meticulously observed all aspects of their environment, building an intimate relationship with the natural order that sustained them, and in turn they began to discern ways to participate in its renewal. In order to survive, these predecessors had to know the characteristics and habits of the multitude of species sharing the land with them.

Yet theirs was not a cold, detached intellect that surveyed the world for their own needs only, but a pragmatic, down-to-earth approach to life—a style of consciousness that suggests a profound connection and intimacy with the natural world: the earth, stars, sun, and moon. In this fertile land, life arose from a sacred wellspring of living waters. These prehistoric people translated the living waters into wisdom that enabled them to discover the right proportions in their interactions—and eventually hieroglyphic symbols evolved that further expressed their understandings and discoveries in a transparent literary record of the natural world and the inner world, the above and the below.

Creating a Relationship with the Divine

In the ancient Egyptian culture, the focus of religious expression is its daily rituals, which are the physical manifestation of a dynamic, ongoing relationship—a conversation of sorts—between deities, ancestors, spirits within nature, and humanity. As discussed above, these interactions are based on reciprocity, a continual flow of energy that must be diligently, intentionally cared for. This is accomplished through both the offerings and the main way that the offerings are transmitted—the rituals, which are sacrifices in and of themselves.

The ancient Egyptian religious traditions are based in a dynamic enactment of their beliefs and myths. Their myths exist in a living, vibrant flow of celebration and ritual actions. The essential aspects in the dynamic enactment of beliefs and myths break down into four basic elements. Firstly, in a ritual symbolism is an activity, an engagement of the worshiper with a specific reality. Secondly, in the ritual action one's experience of the world is refashioned and reoriented. Thirdly, in the ritual process one receives by *doing*; meaning becomes known as one performs the effective action. Lastly, sacrifice is essential, an effecting act; offerings are a recognition and honoring of the continual flow between life and death, divine and earthly (Pemberton 24).

The Opening of the Mouth ceremony formed the basic framework for many rituals. It was performed to animate statues of deities and ancestral personages, to give them the breath of life and the use of all their senses. With the performance of this ritual the statuary would become a divine image, a suitable vessel that created the link between the unseen and the seen. Naydler remarks, "Through a combination of skilled craftsmanship and the performance of certain specific rites, the statue could become the physical vehicle through which the goddess [or god] manifested as a tangible presence on the material plane" (*Temple of the Cosmos* 135–36).

The Opening of the Mouth ritual symbolized rebirth and can be visualized as the opening of an egg, or the breaking open of the dung ball that births the golden scarab beetle, Khepri. It is the baby being born, or the divine child birthing each dawn as the glorious sun. Sculptors, who were priests of the creator god Ptah—patron of artisans— also birthed their sculptures when they broke open the clay mold after their casting had cooled. All of these acts have their symbolic roots in the Opening of the Mouth ritual.

The ceremony was also performed just before the mummified body inside its coffin was to be interred in its tomb, with the exact same intention. No representation was merely a characterization, including the mummified body; "all physical images could become vehicles of an indwelling divine presence" (Naydler, *Temple of the Cosmos* 134).

Through rituals, reciprocity was embodied in the sacred acts and offerings, and it was this that fostered the continuation of life. Through the performative acts of rituals, the harmonious balance required to keep Ma'at's cosmic patterns whole and healthy was maintained. The ritual of presenting Ma'at to the main gods and goddesses of the temple was the enactment of the reality that the gods receive sustenance from Ma'at. According to the Egyptologist Emily Teeter, the scenes of offering Ma'at "were placed in the realm of the deities, in temples and tombs, because the scenes were considered to be for the gods' consumption and were to be viewed from the gods' perspective" (78).

Presentation of Ma'at Ritual

> [T]he thinker of the Old Kingdom envisaged the order of human
>
> society as the mirror image of the order that governed the universe.
>
> As the sun-god through his never failing daily circuit ruled the
>
> world, so the divine king guaranteed the human order. (Lichtheim,
>
> *Ancient Egyptian Literature* 1:5)

Throughout Egypt's Dynastic Period, the king was divinized and therefore the conduit for connection between the divine and human realms. It was the king's first and foremost duty to mediate and maintain this relationship, and he accomplished this through his relationships to Ma'at, in all his sayings and doings. The daily ritual of presenting Ma'at to the main deities took place in temples throughout the land. Its goal was to nurture the reciprocal relationship between the king, his land and subjects, and the gods and goddesses who made life possible—including the Blessed Dead, the ancestors. The king appointed the highest priests to represent him in these daily ceremonies.

As has been established, Ma'at was considered the food and drink of the gods, the embodiment of all the offering. All were sustained, including the ancestors, the social structures, and cohesion in the human realm, through the king's ritual offering of her. Below is an example of what the priest presiding over this ritual might have recited:

> O Re, Lord of Ma'at! O Re, who lives in Ma'at! O Re, who rejoices over Ma'at! O Re, who loves Ma'at! O Re, who unites with Ma'at! I have come to you. I bring you Ma'at. You live in her. You rejoice over her. You feed on her. You are strong through her. You endure through her. You are healthy through her. You adorn yourself with her. She casts your foes to the ground. Your heart is glad when you see her! Your fellow gods rejoice when they see Ma'at in your retinue.[33] (Hornung, *Idea Into Image* 131–32)

Egyptologist Jan Assmann's study of sun hymns and the solar mysteries highlights the role of the king as the sole sun priest because of his unique divinized position (*Egyptian Solar Religion* 36). The daily ritual cycle maintained by the king (as the premier sun priest) and his representatives aided the gods in perpetuating the solar journey, and thus the cosmic order and the life of humankind was maintained. Humans participated, lending their energy focused in rituals, prayers, chants, and offerings. The

---

[33] Hornung's translation does not cite the source of this ancient Egyptian *Hymn to Re*, but identifies it as being used for both the Presentation of Ma'at and the Opening of the Mouth rituals—an interesting juxtaposition.

gods and goddesses actually performed the acts necessary to keep the Solar Barque

moving through the rounds of day and night.

A cult theological treatise that Assmann highlights in his book *Egyptian Solar*

Religion in the New Kingdom succinctly brings to light the king's duties in the Egyptians'

own words: "to give law to the people | to satisfy the gods | to realize Ma'at | to destroy

Isfet | to make offerings to the gods and the dead" (30).

In the Presentation of Ma'at scene below (fig. 34), the small figure of Ma'at is

seated in a basket that is the hieroglyphic symbol *nebet*, meaning "mistress" or "all." The

Figure 34. The Presentation of Ma'at to the gods of the Temple of Seti I at Abydos. New
Kingdom. Bas-relief on the north wall in the 2nd Hypostyle Hall in the Temple of Seti I,
Abydos (Calverley and Broome, "Plate 10"). Credit: Courtesy of the Oriental Institute of
the University of Chicago. Reprinted with permission by copyright holder.

king, Seti I, carries her on his cupped hand, extended in front of him, and is slightly stooped—gestures that indicate his respect and deference before the gods and goddesses within the shrine and to whom he is presenting her. Ma'at holds her essential symbol—an *ankh*, the breath of life—in her lap and extends it toward Osiris, Isis, and Horus. Seti I is wearing the blue crown (a war crown denoting his military affiliation) with a *uraeus* serpent coiled upon his brow, a sign of his divinity and kingship.

Thirty-six *uraei* with solar discs upon their heads create the roof. Osiris's throne rests upon the plinth. Both are Ma'at's primordial symbols. Three deities are shown within the shrine: Osiris, Isis, and an aspect of Horus, here identified as Harsiēsi (Porter and Moss 8). Isis, standing protectively behind Osiris, is greeting Seti I with upraised right hand, while her left arm encircles Osiris in a gesture of intimacy that shows her relationship to Osiris. Behind Isis is their falcon-headed son. This trinity plays a central role throughout the history of ancient Egypt.

In the upper right-hand corner, just above Seti I's head, is a falcon whose wings create the symbol for protection. Its talons grasp a *shen* ring, symbolizing infinity, and the "[d]eterminative in *šnw* 'circuit' (of the sun)" (Allen 501). Below the *shen* ideogram are two symbols, a combination of an alabaster basin symbolizing "feast" (W3 in Gardiner's Sign List) and the hieroglyphic symbols that combine the ideas of "counsel, advice" with "tent, booth" (O22 in Gardiner's Sign List) (Allen 502, 490). Reading these images suggests that the sacred feast, which Seti I devotedly offers daily in front of the shrine enclosure, demonstrates the high value he places on the guidance and counsel he receives in return from the deities within. In front of Seti, on a small altar table that is resting on another plinth, are lotus in full bloom, the symbol of resurrection and the

initiation of cosmic order established through Ma'at in First Time.

These daily ritual actions signaled that the king upheld Ma'at's tenets and was in

alignment with Ma'at's order. This enabled the energy contained in all the offerings to

circulate between the human and divine realms. The ritual enacting the Presentation of

Ma'at also validated the king's right to rule. The energies inherent in the food, drink, and

other gifts placed on the altar were what nourished the gods. The images and actual

objects were akin to vessels that carried the numinous energies of life. These energies

were the source of the endless, constant regeneration that had the capacity to reanimate

all the body's, and soul's, functions after death.

The Building Blocks of Life

> Consciousness and recognition of the initiation occurring at death
>
> was reproduced in act, in a sacrament—a sacred cult act.
>
> (Kristensen 177)

The daily rituals performed by the king and his assigned representatives, directed

toward the maintenance of order, unity, harmony, and balance, indicate that Ma'at was

foundational for ancient Egypt. Enacting the Presentation of Ma'at to the primary deities

of the main temples was essential to perpetuating the reciprocal relationship between the

human and the divine realms. And this reciprocity was key to a flourishing life. The gods

provided the bounty of the earth that nurtured all life, and recognition and gratitude for

this bounty were returned to them through the daily offerings made by the people.

The gifts placed upon the altars symbolized not only the physical goods but also

the energy required to produce these offerings. Imagine the many steps involved in making a simple loaf of bread: planting the wheat and barley seeds, tending the fields day by day, harvesting the produce, winnowing the chaff, grinding the seed into flour, creating the batter, baking the bread. Each item on the altar was an acknowledgment of the building blocks of life—the many complex steps involved in the production of that item, beginning with the cycles of nature and the gift of life that flowed from the divine into all material existence to make life possible.

Normandi Ellis likens this understanding to the recognition of an "ecological spirituality" based on the premise of divine order that suggests "the whole world is the body of the divine. Neter is nature" (259). The cosmic patterns, the natural order, the balanced scales, and even the harmonizing of opposition—day and night, life and death, light and dark—are Ma'at's purview, her essence.

Ma'at's multifaceted characteristics reveal her role within Egyptian cosmology as a carrier and harbinger of the active feminine creative impulse. As such, she embodies *eros*, a word that can identify "the force in the universe that seeks union, not through domination, will, or control but through connection or relation" (Odajnyk 22). In the daily tending to their relationship with Ma'at, Egyptians partook of and contributed to the circulation of Ma'at and of eros, both individually and collectively.

Ma'at shaped the Egyptian culture and gave structure to their consciousness, encouraging the evolution of principles seated in the ethical heart. Gestures of relationship, such as turning toward the gods and goddesses daily, created a framework that enabled the people to be aware of and actively engaged with renewing their relationship with the divine, in all their sayings and doings. This courting ritual gave rise to practices, both pragmatic and metaphysical, that encouraged the culture to flourish.

Uniting Opposites in Ma'at

As described throughout this study, the ancient Egyptian view marries life and death, celebrating how they are interwoven and necessary for the flow of all life. This wisdom holds that within a pair of opposites, one does not exist without the other.

> [I]n a relationship of any kind, opposites can attract, war, or
>
> polarize; they can dismiss, discount, or diminish each other; or
>
> they can differentiate, strengthen, and cohabitate, and of course
>
> genuinely marry. (Wikman 71)

Ma'at's purview includes order and chaos, harmony and imbalance, truth and injustice, joy and sadness. She is the embodiment of natural order, the cosmic pattern established in First Time. As in a number of creation myths, the world was created in balance and harmony, but this harmony must be diligently attended to. One of the seminal myths of the ancient Egyptian culture offers an overview of the mythological history, with the gods Horus and Seth contending in an ongoing dispute over who is the rightful heir to the throne of Osiris. In this articulation of Ma'at's guidelines (explored later in this chapter), discord and chaos naturally arise.

Chaos is an opposite expression of Ma'at—that which disrupts the balance she established at First Time and goes against the order of life's patterns.

> Even the best organized of worlds contained its reserves of chaos
>
> that could never be totally reduced; the best one could do was to
>
> keep destructive forces within tolerable limits by fighting against
>
> them every day, every year, and with every flood that one rejoiced
>
> to see return. (Bonnefoy, *Greek and Egyptian* 216)

The concept of chaos is sometimes captured in the hieroglyphic symbol *isfet*, which (like *Ma'at*) is difficult to translate with just a word or two. *Isfet*—often translated as "chaos"—is in contrast to many of Ma'at's attributes. In fact, no god or goddess embodies *isfet*, which can mean "wrong," "incorrect or antisocial behavior," "disorder," "injustice," or "falsehood" (Allen 148). Instead *isfet* is merely a single trait or attribute of a specific god or goddess; for instance, Apophis or Seth can be seen as embodying *isfet* characteristics.

To the list of characteristics (above), Hornung adds "unreasonableness"; *gereg*, which means "lie" or "deceit"; and *khab*, meaning "the crooked" (*Idea Into Image* 136). As the analysis of *The Eloquent Peasant* reveals later in this chapter, *isfet* includes such personal failings as being unreasonable or greedy, lying or being deceitful, and causing harm. In short, what was deemed as contrary to Ma'at's harmonizing, ordering, and balancing was disruptive to the flow of *sema*, or "unity" (as described in chapter 3), and was articulated in the different literary genres as undesirable and requiring correction.

The unity of opposites is key to understanding Ma'at, who personifies order and justice through balance and harmony. Indeed, the divine Feminine's essence always embraces the paradoxical. She delights in the passionate expression of life, whether she is celebrating life in dancing, feasting, imbibing intoxicants at Hathor's feasts, dealing out death and destruction, or leaving in a stormy passion after a fight with Re. As Odajnyk reminds us, "connections and relationships can be either positive or negative, for conflict is also a connection" (22).

Texts as Offerings and Instructions

The earliest hieroglyphic writings were inscribed on columns in the stone vestibule and sarcophagus hall of the pyramid of King Unas at the necropolis (burial grounds) of Sakkara, near Memphis in northern or Lower Egypt (Hart, *Egyptian Myths* 9). King Unas, also spelled Wenis or Unis (*c.* 2350 BCE), was the last ruler of the 5th Dynasty, during the Old Kingdom (*c.* 2686–2160 BCE). These writings continued to be inscribed in the tombs of kings and later of queens and high-ranking officials, until they became what are now referred to as the *Pyramid Texts*. From these sacred texts evolved, during the Middle Kingdom (*c.* 2055–1650 BCE), the *Coffin Texts*; rather than being reserved only for the upper echelons of society, they were available to anyone who could afford to commission a wooden coffin, mummification, and the rituals and burial expenses.

Outlining the earliest recorded religious speculations, the *Pyramid Texts* and the later *Coffin Texts* have provided scholars with invaluable information and insights into the spiritual and philosophical reflections of ancient Egyptians, as well as their rituals and practices.

The classicist and linguist Susan Brind Morrow has translated the *Pyramid Texts* with poetic sensibilities she shares in common with her mentor Henry Fischer, the former curator of the Egyptian collections at New York's Metropolitan Museum of Art. Bringing a literariness to her translations, she explains that hieroglyphic inscriptions are "writing as it first was, a mirror of life. Eliminating the dimensions of time and place and decay, it was a holy thing" (7). The ancient Egyptians referred to their hieroglyphic symbols as "the *medu netcher*: 'the god's words'—a meaning preserved in the word *hieroglyphs* that the Greeks coined for the carved Egyptian temple reliefs and inscriptions" (Wilkinson, *Reading Egyptian Art* 9). This does not imply that the hieroglyphs themselves were a secret script. Once correctly understood, hieroglyphs become "instruments of absolute clarity" that offer a poetic, metaphor-rich feel in their expression of the natural world (Brind Marrow 7).

Both the experience of the world and the knowledge the ancient Egyptians gleaned from it are reflected in the forms and shapes they gave their *neters*, and these forms are reflected in the hieroglyphic symbols themselves. When a god or goddess is depicted with certain physical characteristics, this references the specific functions and essence of that particular deity. The hieroglyphic symbols and images communicate a universe of knowledge about the beings portrayed, and this "backstory" tells the viewer a multivalence of stories.

The practice of saying and doing Ma'at was taught using engaging storytelling in this manner. Throughout Egypt's history the people held to the belief in "the teachability and perfectibility of man" (Lichtheim, *Ancient Egyptian Literature* 1: 5). Behavior that adhered to Ma'at's tenets could be learned, and to that end the people gave instructions for living "an exemplary life . . . through the realization of *Ma'at*" (Hornung, *Idea Into Image* 138).

From the Old Kingdom onward, as well-educated individuals continually did their part to perpetuate Ma'at, their spiritual feelings (reflected in their cosmologies, philosophical ponderings, and rituals) combined with their pragmatism to create certain codes of behavior. These codes were laid out in a genre of literary works they called

Instructions, which we now refer to as *Wisdom Literature.*[34] Their pragmatic thoughts on these matters were shaped by their astute observations of what did, and did not, promote social cohesion and balance. Their literature "reflected the ethical standards of the society" and illustrated that it was important to "practice the precepts" (Lichtheim, *Ancient Egyptian Literature* 1: 5) in order to live in harmony with Ma'at's divine order. Moreover, their concern for fostering social order and cohesion was intimately intertwined with their personal quest for eternal life, and both inspired their literary outpouring.

Autobiography

The 6th Dynasty (*c.* 2360–2195 BCE) saw a transformation of the *Autobiography* genre that had begun during the 5th Dynasty. Autobiographies were in epitaph form and would be inscribed on the walls of a private tomb or on a stela—a hard stone tablet similar in shape to a massive tombstone. As "a self-portrait" of the deceased that "highlighted the person's admirable qualities" (Lichtheim, *Ancient Egyptian Literature* 1: 4), they were intended to characterize the individual as having lived an exemplary life of positive worth. This ensured that the individual would be well remembered and, upon death, would be deserving of transfiguration, resurrection, and eternal life. In other words, the autobiography developed "in the quest for immortality" (Lichtheim, *Ancient Egyptian Literature* 1: 4).

As a literary genre, the autobiography documented Ma'at's principles and illustrated how the individual had upheld these during his or her lifetime. Lichtheim names this type of inscription a "catalogue of virtues" and outlines its two main

---

[34] Scholars refer to this genre using a variety of terms, such as "*Instructions in Wisdom,*" "*Instruction,*" or "Didactic Literature" (Lichtheim); "the Instruction" (Hornung); and "*Wisdom Literature*" (Roberts).

components: "first, that it reflected the ethical standards of the society; second, that it affirmed, in the form of a monumental inscription, [that the deceased] practiced the precepts" that the *Instructions* enshrined (Lichtheim, *Ancient Egyptian Literature* 1: 5). Though often disparaged in modern scholarship as tools of self-aggrandizement, these stelae are a testament to the values of the people. They were also an effective way to reinforce the ethical basis of the culture and thus to foster and perpetuate these values in future generations.

An early example of this genre comes from the 6th Dynasty and is called *The Autobiography of Harkhuf*. It describes an official who had served two kings and become governor of Upper Egypt, a powerful position that speaks to his values and trustworthiness. Harkhuf's inscription follows the format of tomb autobiographies—opening with offering prayers and prayers for a good burial and continuing with "the catalogue of virtues" (Lichtheim, *Ancient Egyptian* 1: 23):

> I gave bread to the hungry, | Clothing to the naked, | I brought the boatless to land. | O you who live upon earth, | [...] | I was one who spoke fairly, who repeated what was liked, | I never spoke evilly against any man to his superior, | For I wished to stand well with the great god. | Never did I judge between two [contenders] | In a manner which deprived a son of his father's legacy. (Lichtheim, *Ancient Egyptian Literature* 1: 24)

Harkhuf's list of virtues specifically reflects Ma'at's principles as they are recorded in the so-called 42 Negative Confessions that compose Chapter 125 of the *Book of Going Forth Into Day*. These virtues illustrate the essential component of compassion and care for one's fellow human beings, traits these ancient people recognized as leading to the flourishing of culture. The description of feeding the hungry, clothing the naked, and providing boat fees for those who can't afford them recommends the precept that those who have prosperity and well-being should help those who lack the basic necessities.

In the 6th Dynasty, the autobiography attained fuller form, becoming capable of capturing "the formless experiences of life in the enduring formulation of the written word" (Lichtheim, *Ancient Egyptian Literature* 1: 5). These autobiographies were the primary source of the literary exploration that would emerge from the non-royal tombs of the Old Kingdom and would evolve into new formats during the Middle Kingdom.

Wisdom Literature: The Teachings

A significant transformation in the ancient Egyptian culture came at the end of the 6th Dynasty (*c.* 2300–2150 BCE), which coincides with the transition of the Old Kingdom to the Middle Kingdom—generally agreed upon as a period that ended in the breakdown of society, when societal chaos and disorder turned the orderly Egyptian world upside down. According to Clark, the societal structure "crashed in ruins" around 2250 BCE, after the last "effective pharaoh" of the 6th Dynasty died (124).

In assessing what had caused this collapse, the people realized upholding Ma'at was the answer. No longer could Ma'at be taken for granted or upheld by the king alone. Ma'at—and thus world order—must be maintained through the diligent efforts of many people, for "only through proper behavior and active engagement is world order achieved" (Hornung, *Idea Into Image* 135). As their texts reveal, they recognized that sustaining Ma'at was not a passive pursuit, but an activity, involving *doing* and *speaking*.

Egyptologists are not in agreement about the nature of the civil unrest, but most agree that the First Intermediate Period experienced an upheaval that led to significant transformation and lasting memories of this period's trauma. Many placed blame for the catastrophic changes at the end of the Old Kingdom on a series of weak kings and corrupt officials. Lichtheim stoutly argues against the view that there was civil war, however, proposing that the numerous literary references to societal upheavals, where "the master becomes the servant and the servant the master," are merely a "literary style" rather than mirroring an actual breakdown in social structure (*Ancient Egyptian* 1: 5). What seems evident in the Middle Kingdom literature is that a major upheaval in society caused collective trauma, which in turn increased individual consciousness and conscience. It is possible that later authors used the collective memory of the trauma as inspiration for reflection and contemplation—similar to a cautionary tale. Over the centuries, both the literature and the public celebration of spiritual rituals and reenactments of these mythologems handed down through the ages educated the population and expanded their consciousness.

One result of this change was the evolution of literary genres that put forth the principles of Ma'at, concentrating on educating all levels of society in how to uphold Ma'at through their own actions and the practice of self-reflection. *Wisdom Literature,* which contains life instructions that were written down between the late 5th Dynasty (*c.* 2520–2360 BCE) and the start of the Roman Period (30 CE) (Hornung, *Idea Into Image* 187–88), was "the repository of the nation's distilled wisdom" (Lichtheim, *Ancient Egyptian Literature* 1: 5).

The formulaic catalogue of virtues prevalent in autobiographies blended with the prose of a narrative style to create the new genre called *Wisdom Literature*. It "reflected the ethical standards of the society" by providing a model of valuable virtues while enhancing its entertainment value and literary appeal (Lichtheim, *Ancient Egyptian Literature* 1: 5). This genre operated from the premise that the order of the universe, Ma'at, could be taught to people and thus mirrored in human society. This natural order required conscious attention and knowledge to be present in the individual, for—as Ptahhotep states in the opening remarks of his *Instructions*—"no one is born wise" (Lichtheim, *Ancient Egyptian Literature* 1: 63).[35]

The *Wisdom Literature* genre continued to evolve over the centuries. Though its text was written approximately four thousand years ago and has been called a "purely literary working of the theme 'national distress'" (Lichtheim, *Ancient Egyptian Literature* 1: 145), *The Complaints of Khakheperre-Sonb*—from the reign of Sesostris II (*c.* 1897– 1978 BCE), in the Middle Kingdom—rings with laments we might make today:

> I meditate on what has happened, | The events that occur
>
> throughout the land: | Changes take place, it is not like last year, |
>
> One year is more irksome than the other. | The land breaks up, is
>
> destroyed, | Becomes [a wasteland]. | Order is cast out, | Chaos is
>
> in the council hall; | The ways of the gods are violated, | Their
>
> provisions neglected. | The land is in turmoil, | There is mourning
>
> everywhere; | Towns, districts are grieving, | All alike are burdened

---

[35] *The Instructions of Ptahhotep* includes thirty-seven maxims presented as lessons he wished to convey to his son, who would one day become a vizier like his father. The focus is on imparting the "code of behavior befitting the gentleman of the Old Kingdom" (Lichtheim, *Ancient Egyptian Literature* 1: 7).

by wrongs. | One turns one's back on dignity, | The lords of silence are disturbed; | As dawn comes every day, | The face recoils from events. | I cry out about it, | My limbs are weighed down, | I grieve in my heart. | It is hard to keep silent about it, | Another heart would bend; | But a heart strong in distress: | It is a comrade to its lord. (Lichtheim, *Ancient Egyptian Literature* 1: 145)

Wisdom Literature portrayed the belief that an individual was capable of actively perpetuating the ethical values and principles related to Ma'at, provided he or she received the training in consciousness: "[T]he Egyptians discovered the sources of their selfhood: the heart (*ib*) and the character (*qd*) were the forces that raised, shaped, and channeled man's thoughts, desires, inclinations, and actions" (Lichtheim, *Maat in Autobiographies* 23). Their pragmatic thoughts on these matters were shaped by their astute observations of what did and did not make life flourish, especially recognizing the importance of social cohesion. It appears they refined these systems of thought over the centuries, using each period of decline and setback as an opportunity to return to what they knew to be the ways that promoted social cohesion—the natural laws and cosmic order of Ma'at, their wellspring.

The Eloquent Peasant explicates Ma'at.

An outstanding literary work in the *Wisdom Literature* genre, *The Eloquent Peasant* provides an excellent example of the typical state of mind in the Middle Kingdom.[36] This fictional text illuminates the depth of thought and conscious reflection on the social unrest and disorder caused by internal discord spurred on by greed, violence, and avarice. It paints a graphic image of both a significant social justice issue

---

[36] Toward the end of 12th Dynasty, in the reign of Sesostris III (*c.* 1878–1839 BCE).

and the appropriate response. Based on a narrative frame, it comprises nine poetic speeches or "petitions" delivered by an impassioned peasant to the high steward of the king. Lichtheim translates this story in its entirety in *Ancient Egyptian Literature: The Old and Middle Kingdom* Vol. 1 (169–184), and hers is the primary source this study relies on for its retelling.

The Eloquent Peasant makes three main points that are critical in their illustration of how Ma'at's energies are circulated throughout society in all that we say and do, despite our differences in social standing. It instructs us in the essential need for justice at all levels of society; in the efficacy of eloquent speech; and in the necessity for determination and persistence in pursuing justice for oneself, regardless of social status. The takeaway message: if one understands Ma'at's primary principles, one can apply them in every situation.

Synopsis of The Eloquent Peasant.

The main character is the peasant Khun-Anup, a simple man, "unlearned" but wise and well-spoken—a value equated to Ma'atian consciousness. On his way to market, Khun-Anup is robbed by a wealthy man who contrives a reason for confiscating his donkeys and goods, depriving him of all he owns. When the peasant repeatedly protests, refusing to leave the estate where the theft took place, the wealthy man has him beaten.

Despite this maltreatment, the peasant Khun-Anup will not back down. He spends ten days appealing to the wealthy man's higher instincts, with no success. Then he goes to the high steward and makes his complaint. Other magistrates with the high steward dismiss the wealthy man's actions and blame the peasant, casting him in a poor light by implying that he is crooked and dishonest. The high steward falls silent at this denigration and responds to neither the wealthy man and his allies nor the peasant.

The peasant persists, returning to the high steward the following day to state his case. He begins with a greeting of praise and then proceeds to articulate the natural order of Ma'at's justice. The high steward maintains an impartial silence in order to draw out the man's speech and records every word.

After Khun-Anup leaves, the high steward reports to the king, who tells him to encourage the peasant's testifying and to anonymously provide him with bread and beer. The king also instructs the high steward to arrange for the peasant's family to be cared for throughout the duration of the testimony. All actions in the story highlight examples of Ma'at's justice—or the lack of it.

At the close of nine days, after listening every day to Khun-Anup give his views on justice, truth, and social order, the high steward rules in the peasant's favor and gives him all the wealthy man's property. In the end, the peasant's beautiful words prevail, yet his persistence in presenting his case contributes just as much to his success. Despite receiving no encouragement from the high steward, the peasant never gives up and goes home in poverty and defeat. His meticulous arguments are a catalogue of Ma'at's spheres of influence, but it is his diligent actions—Ma'at's *saying* and *doing*, her natural laws— that are upheld. The greed of the wealthy man is punished, and justice is served.

Exploration of **The Eloquent Peasant.**

The peasant's statements illustrate that in the temporal world, Ma'at's natural laws must be modeled, sustained, and enforced by the king and his wise administrators. It is their duty. Khun-Anup also reminds his listeners that "in keeping with Egyptian ethics,

Ma'at is a norm that should not become an overly rigid standard or model of behavior"
(Hornung, *Idea Into Image* 136). Balance and harmony have a danger of swinging over
into rigidity and literal one-sidedness, which is not Ma'at, and this too should be avoided.

The peasant points out that for the sake of everlasting life as well as the
preservation of the everyday world, Ma'at's laws must be upheld. Otherwise the gods
will depart. This calls to mind the hieroglyphic symbol of the wick that is part of Heka's
name—three loops of a thick string that holds the fire, the light of illumination. The three
loops may signify the three realms: divine, ancestral, and human. The luminosity aspect
can be equated to the energy that flows between the three realms, perpetuating life
everlasting and illuminating the world.

Each of the eloquent peasant's petitions to the high steward underscores natural
laws, with metaphors taken from observations of nature and life that would have been
familiar to all the people of the time, especially those living close to nature and working
the earth. The following is a brief outline of the nine laments, which readily reveals how
even the simplest of folks would have understood Ma'at and her natural laws. (Except
where noted, all cited page numbers in the remainder of this subsection are from
Lichtheim, *Ancient Egyptian Literature* vol. 2.)

1st petition. The overarching metaphor used in the first petition is the image of
sailing on "the sea of justice" with "a fair wind" (172). The peasant names the qualities of
Ma'at-like behavior that originated in the *Autobiography* genre and ascribes them to the
high steward in his opening praise statement about the responsibilities of "a father to the
orphan, husband to the widow, brother to the rejected woman" (172). He concludes this
list with a unique metaphor—"apron to the motherless"—which, by forgoing the more

common "mother to the motherless," alerts the listener or reader to Khun-Anup's creative, fluid use of language.

The peasant then outlines the characteristics of a good ruler, who must be free from greed and baseness, a destroyer of falsehood and creator of rightness. In addition, the peasant cites the quality of hearing and responding to pleas for justice. He concludes, "Remove my grief, I am burdened, | Examine me, I am in need!" (172). The high steward remains silent.

2nd petition. Again the peasant comes before the high steward with praise, comparing him to a "[r]udder of heaven, beam of the earth, | Plumb-line that carries the weight" (173)—pointing to Ma'at's attributes by directly invoking the image of the scales of justice in the Hall of Double Ma'at. Khun-Anup then subtly describes the crimes against him by posing them as a series of questions that point out injustice: "Is it not wrong, a balance that tilts, | A plummet that strays, | The straight becoming crooked?" (173). Ma'at's straightness is contrasted with the crookedness of the actions perpetrated by the wealthy lord who stole the peasant's donkeys and goods. The peasant goes on to underscore the insight that no matter their station in life, all people are mortal and, in death, equally subject to impartial justice in Ma'at's Hall. He asks of the high steward, "Shall you be a man of eternity?" (173).

The high steward now responds, questioning the peasant, which inspires another flood of examples of crookedness couched in the form of questions about right behavior. This clever method of monologue inspires thoughtfulness and engages the audience in considering what they believe—a useful teaching tool. As his monologue continues, the peasant becomes more passionate, seeming to accuse the high steward of being in league with the criminal. Here the peasant introduces the metaphor of the dread crocodile and the "Lady of Pestilence"—Sekhmet in her destructive aspect (174). Like the crocodile or the plague, his examples represent the unseen dangers that lurk beneath the surface, ready to swiftly take their prey in their powerful jaws—or that lurk in one's very own body and can extinguish life just as swiftly. With these comparisons, the peasant offers guidance: attention and care are necessary at all times, to guard against the waiting dangers.

Khun-Anup winds down his fervent speech with a plea for mercy, reminding the high steward of his appointed task by identifying more of Ma'at's precepts: The wealthy should be merciful. Violence reveals a criminal. Greed motivates one who has enough but wants more and is willing to steal what others have to satiate his appetite (174). He ends with a moving metaphoric plea: "Guider to port of all who founder: | Rescue the drowning!"

3rd petition. In the third interview with the high steward, the peasant explains that Ma'at is as necessary for life as the air we breathe. "Doing justice is breath for the nose" suggests how vital Ma'at was to her culture—the very breath of life, as explored in chapter 3 (Lichtheim, *Ancient Egyptian Literature* 1: 175; Hornung, *Idea Into Image* 135). Again, the peasant's appeal calls upon the common knowledge of the justice of eternity, employing the balance beam metaphor and recalling how Thoth records the deeds of each person's lifetime. The peasant reveals his understanding of the high steward's duty: "Earth's rightness lies in justice! . . . Do not swerve—you are the norm! . . . Do not drift, steer, hold the helm-rope!" (176).

4th petition. The peasant seeks to activate the high steward's consciousness by invoking the heart's wisdom: "Let the eyes see, let the heart take notice" (178). The heart is autonomous from the personality; it records all thoughts, words, and deeds. This line encourages recognition of that fact, implying the higher authority that will have consequences in the final Weighing of the Heart ordeal.

From this we can deduce that the qualities of the heart were well-differentiated in the minds of the ancient Egyptians. Clearly, with a model of excellence available to all, such an important distinction would not be left to innuendos. This is further illustrated by the following: "Pass over the matter, it becomes two" (178). This warning—that each overlooked, unresolved wrongdoing multiplies and thus weakens the entire system—is one we might take notice of in our own times.

5th petition. By now the peasant, who has returned many times to seek justice, is frustrated. He begins his speech by accusing the high steward of being unjust and corrupt, telling him, "You were placed as a dam for the poor lest he drown, but you have become a swift current to him!" (178).

6th and 7th petitions. The peasant persists, contrasting the right order of Ma'at's precepts with the opposites: "He who lessens falsehood fosters truth." He then flips his tactic, again accusing the high steward of wrongdoing, this time using imbalance as a contrast to right behavior. The sixth petition calls up a metaphor that also appears in the *Books of the Underworld* texts from the New Kingdom (*c.* 1550–1069 BCE): "The sounding pole is in your hands; sound! | The water is shallow! If the boat enters and is grounded, its cargo perishes on the shore" (179). This condition reflects the seventh hour of the night journey, when the gigantic serpent of the depths, Apophis, seeks to stall the Solar Barque. Yet the peasant adds a layer of caution to what is at stake: the cargo will perish. Psychologically this can be interpreted as the warning: when one adheres to unconscious urges, what is most precious is threatened with being wasted. Being consciously attentive, on the other hand—"The sounding pole is in your hands; sound!"—is the path to right action, right proportion, and expanded consciousness.

Through these down-to-earth examples, the eloquent peasant imparts his culture's treasured wisdom, subtly reinforcing Ma'at's precepts through the guise of an entertaining story.

8th petition. The peasant tells the high steward that the sun god himself dictates that humans should "[s]peak Maat and practice Maat, for she is great, mighty, and lasting." The lament continues as the peasant states that Ma'at "remains until eternity. She accompanies the person who practices Maat down into the realm of death. He is placed in a coffin and buried with her; his name shall not be erased from the earth" (Hornung, *Idea Into Image* 136). This emphasizes Ma'at's multiple domains of influence; she is the eternal fixed order of cosmic dimension. The challenge for the human realm was putting oneself into alignment with her perfected order, and this required daily conscious effort and care.

9th petition. The peasant comes to the high steward on the ninth day in a reserved mood and gets straight to his point, addressing Ma'at's precept of balance and comparing a man's tongue—his ability to speak—to the balance beam. The phrase "When falsehood walks it goes astray" couldn't be clearer in its simple elegance (181). Khun-Anup implores: "Be not heavy, nor yet light, | Do not tarry, nor yet hurry, | Be not partial, nor listen to desire. | Do not avert your face from one you know, | Be not blind to one you have seen | . . . | Let your speech be heard" (181–82). The peasant is calling for a decision, reminding the high steward one last time to fulfill his duties as a lord of Ma'at, an impartial judge—to uphold Ma'at's harmonizing balance between the opposites. The peasant signals to the high steward that, having reached the end of his discourse, if he cannot find justice in the high steward's court, he is ready to plead his case to Anubis, the god who attends to the balance of the scales in the underworld. He refers here to his own death, for he likely is ruined without his donkeys and produce.

In the petitions detailed above, the peasant offers everyday examples that clearly outline Ma'at's precepts. These metaphors pull on the ever-present river and the dangers encountered there, underscoring the paradoxical nature of the mighty Nile (as discussed in chapter 2), and come from the judgment scene in the afterlife, which awaits each person upon death and equalizes all people through the testimony of the heart. The word-images associated with the heart imply a sense of a collective standard, a wisdom encoded in the heart that is impersonal and immutable. The heart of each person is poignantly aware of each thought, word, and deed. It is into this silent, personal realm that Ma'at seeks to reach and work her influence, nurturing the heart's wisdom, which was laid down at the dawn of creation and is renewed with the dawn of each day.

The Contendings of Horus and Seth reveals Ma'at's principles.

A central mythological theme is woven around Horus, Osiris, and Seth. The main action ensures that the dead king, Osiris, assumes the throne of the Netherworld, and Horus ascends to the throne of the Day World. In *The Contendings of Horus and Seth,* the god Horus is depicted as the son of Isis and Osiris, while Osiris's and Isis's brother[37] is Horus the Elder—Harwer or Haroeris. The outcome of this story establishes the younger

---

[37] In a variation on the Heliopolitan multigenerational "family of deities," the fourth generation can also include another god: Horus the Elder. He is considered the second child born to Nut and Geb. The firstborn is Osiris, and Seth becomes the third son. The brothers are then followed by their sisters, Isis and Nephthys.

Horus as Har-mau, "Horus the Uniter" (Wilkinson, *Complete Gods* 202). "Uniter" has the root *mau*—indicating a relationship to Ma'at.

Discovering life in death.

The final phrase in the *Autobiography of Harkhuf* states, "Never did I judge between two contenders in a manner which deprived a son of his father's legacy." (Lichtheim, *Ancient Egyptian Literature* 1: 24). This calls to mind the central mytheme of *The Contendings of Horus and Seth* and thus reflects the underlying importance of this mythological story. It is not dissimilar to the Judeo-Christian mytheme of Cain and Abel, and both have shaped their respective cultures. One brother kills the other in an impulsive, jealous rage, and future generations are marked by this single act. In ancient Egypt, however, the myth became a teaching story that raised consciousness and shaped an ethical outlook. It also determined the dynastic legacy of the right to rule being passed from father to son. In contemporary Western culture, meanwhile, it continues to be acted out relentlessly.

Coffin Texts, Spell 74 is a moving lament that was most likely performed annually at Abydos during the annual rituals commemorating Osiris's murder, dismemberment, and resurrection. The myth portrayed in the ritual lament begins when Isis and Nephthys hear Osiris's call for help and rush to his side, saying, "Ah Helpless One Asleep! Ah Helpless One in this place which you know not—yet I know it!" (Clark 125). They assure Osiris of their presence and their desire to guide him through his transformation.

These actions are seen as taking place in the prehistoric Golden Time when the gods and goddesses still lived upon the earth. In murdering Osiris, Seth inaugurates death, and Isis and Nephthys invent the mortuary rituals necessary to ensure the continuation of life by preventing Osiris's body from decaying. By assuring Osiris that they "know" where he is, they express their support in guiding his soul toward eternal life in the underworld. Isis, using her profoundly powerful magic, *heka*,[38] animates Osiris's body, which enables her to conceive their child, Horus.

In a different flow of events Horus is also said to come to his father Osiris and awaken him, telling him to throw off his weariness and inertia so that he can recognize his new status as a denizen of the underworld and its destined lord. Many gods and goddesses participate in the renewal process, for as this fertility aspect of the solar god is rebirthed and renewed, so too is all life, all creation.

Those interested in ancient Egyptian mythology will be readily familiar with the falcon-headed god Horus. The Egyptologist Richard Wilkinson created a list of the domains where Horus presides, noting that he is one of the oldest Egyptian gods and that his roles encompass sky god, solar god, god of kingship, and son of Isis (*Complete Gods* 200). To this list we can add *son of Osiris,* and thus Horus's relationship to Osiris includes his duty as the newly ascended king to establish his father's kingdom in the underworld. Horus's role as the divine child who emerges from the underworld at each dawn, bringing renewal and regeneration to all life, is an underlying theme in the popular and instructive *The Contendings of Horus and Seth.*

Horus is the living king who is seen as uniting Upper and Lower Egypt. Yet this, like so many other mythical events, is never a onetime event; instead it is ever-renewing

---

[38] Although "magic" is the translation in our contemporary language, "power" (as in the power of the spoken word to make manifest, to create) is a more accurate translation. The difficulty arises because our culture (and thus our language) has split up so much of what the ancient Egyptians considered paired together. For example, magic has the ability to impact and transform, yet in our own language the word *magic* is often associated with trickery, deception, or evil.

and therefore inspires the ongoing astute attention and actions necessary to promulgate Ma'at's principles. In upholding Ma'at's balancing, harmonizing, and ordering, Horus—in his many forms—ensures the renewal of all life in Egypt. One of the most common symbols of Horus is depicted below (fig. 35): Horakhty, "Horus of the two horizons."

Figure 35. Winged falcon symbol with solar disc surrounded by two uraei. The frieze above comprises rearing cobras with solar disc headdress. This is from the Temple of Hathor at Dendera, built in the 1st century BCE. Photo credit: Richard Mortel, from the flickr photo album: "Dendera." Photographed on 14 January 2016. Creative Commons, some rights reserved. Web. 9 March 2018.

Over time Horus coalesced with other gods, yet he also maintained his own symbolism. This very brief overview of Horus's characteristics illustrates how the interwoven characteristics flowed within the ancient Egyptian mythological structures. But these facts alone do not make the gods and goddesses come alive. This is simply a necessary step in familiarizing ourselves with the ancient Egyptian viewpoint.

Most often, the god Seth was acknowledged as the embodiment of raw strength and instinctual energies. He is often portrayed as out-of-balance, ignoring all sense of proportion, and thus causing chaos and discord due to his unrestrained appetites and greed. He is the embodiment of the "Red Lands"—the wild, uninhabited desert—as contrasted with the fertile, settled agricultural lands along the Nile, known as the "Black Lands" and embodied by Osiris.

Seth is the guardian of the desert and the brother of Osiris, Isis, and Nephthys, all children of Geb and Nut, and the fourth generation of the Heliopolitan Ennead. His raw strength and instinctual energies must be harnessed and harmonized to be beneficial to society; otherwise he runs amok and produces the opposite of Ma'at's harmony, balance, and order.

Though often disruptive of the social order and harmony, Seth's energy and raw strength were also seen as necessary—just as all opposite pairs (life and death, light and dark, order and disorder) were essential, for the existence of one without the other is not possible. Cavalli states, "We cannot simply consider the importance of light without speaking of it in terms of darkness" (101). As explained earlier in the chapter, Ma'at's ability to harmonize and balance these opposites is the core of her symbolism—and is essential to successfully living within her cosmic patterns.

Moreover, "Seth is a *limiting agent* necessary for the transformation Osiris is to suffer (undergo)" (Cavalli 101). Seth is a powerful catalyst for change, though he seems to wield these transformational effects unconsciously, for his actions do not guarantee his own goals and he is his own worst enemy. In this he appears to be similar to the Greek god of war, Ares, often portrayed sowing discord and violence that work against his own best interests. Yet Seth's belligerence and outrageous behavior do stir up others, awakening them so they can shed the complacent energies that keep them from taking right action. As an unintentional, unconscious agent of change, Seth is the opposite of Ma'at, the embodiment of intentionality and conscious transformation.

In *The Contendings of Horus and Seth*, Seth's right to the throne of Osiris is questioned. A council of the gods convenes to help determine who will be best suited for the role of king. The council hears the testimony and claims of both Horus and Seth, and the lines of support are demarked: Thoth, the wise vizier—the "tongue and heart" of the gods—is clearly in favor of Horus's succession. Isis, as Horus's mother and Osiris's widow, sees Seth as a poor replacement for his brother Osiris; she actively works on behalf of Horus, despite the fact that Seth is her own brother.

The fact that Seth is directly responsible for murdering Osiris is never enunciated as a reason that Seth is unfit for the throne. Most scholars suggest that the Egyptians were loath to depict anything negative, as hieroglyphic symbols are sacred, powerful magic, even to the point of being alive. Yet the reason for this omission may go beyond this standard explanation. Ever pragmatic (after all, the deed was done), the Egyptians may have accepted that the ruling king—Osiris—was worn out and needed to be replaced. Furthermore, his death transformed the afterlife into a kingdom, and introduced death as necessary for life to flourish—a reality witnessed in any natural habitat or environment. Again it comes down to this: all must be balanced with its opposite.

The Eye of Horus and the wholeness of death.

After the murder, Horus seeks to vindicate his father's death and to establish Osiris's kingdom in the underworld. This will be granted, provided Horus receives his father's throne. Once that is accomplished, Horus goes to his father (or sends an emissary) and presents him with the healed and whole Eye of Horus, the one with inner vision (including the 1/64th that remains hidden). As wholeness embodied, the Eye of Horus activates Osiris's Netherworld kingdom and establishes the throne of Osiris there. Once again, the symbols of the feminine—throne, crown, Eye—are the creative spark that catalyze necessary action.

In the contemplation of death, the ego's everyday consciousness and literal interpretations are transcended. In *Anatomy of the Psyche*, Edward Edinger states:

> The outstanding example of death as the genesis of religion and consciousness is the elaborate mortuary symbolism of ancient Egypt. This is also clearly the origin of alchemy. The embalming of the dead king transformed him into Osiris, an eternal, incorruptible body. This is the prototype of the alchemical opus, which attempts to create the incorruptible Philosopher's Stone. The alchemical vessel has been equated with the sealed tomb of Osiris, containing all the limbs of the god. The psyche cannot come into existence as a separate entity until the death of the literal, the concrete, and the physical. (168–69)

Seth is indispensable, then and now, for he is the one who models the darkness within each person and within the culture as a whole. He holds up a mirror to the rampant corruption and degradation in the old system, and to the unconsciousness in each individual. The repugnance of his actions and his speech—in clear opposition to Ma'at— render him a potent catalyst for change. Redeeming him through exposing and then containing his effect in each of us enables his vital energies to be harnessed and put in service of the transformation of consciousness. Recognition of his influences is a much-needed remedy for the Sethian energies now embodied and revealed in so many quarters of our culture and personal lives today.

In the end, Seth's wrongdoings are recognized, and he is guided to a constructive use of his powerful, instinctual drives. Ma'at is reestablished and upheld, embodying assurance that the world will continue to exist as it has from the beginning. To appreciate the essential significance of *The Contendings of Horus and Seth*, we turn once again to a maxim from the Old Kingdom's *Instructions of Ptahhotep*:

> "Maat is effective, lasting, and sharp; | it is undisturbed since the
>
> time of him who made it. | He who bypasses its customs is
>
> punished: | it is the path even in the face of the ignorant. . . . | In the
>
> end it is Maat that lasts: | a man says: 'It is the legacy of my
>
> father'." (Allen 147–48)

"Democratization" of Ma'at in the New Kingdom.

By the New Kingdom, upholding Ma'at was the responsibility not just of the king or the upper echelons, but of all those who hoped for eternal life—each and every man and woman. Self-reflection was a critical skill for success in this undertaking—one that could be learned, though it required diligence. Texts belonging to the *Wisdom Literature* genre continued to be written and revised, which gives testimony to the significance of this responsibility. The vignettes in many of the *Underworld Books* from the New Kingdom and the Third Intermediate Period show Ma'at standing directly behind Re or in the prow of his vessel, pointing the way (Pinch, *Egyptian Mythology* 159–60). These images reveal what was required of the people in their efforts to interact with the divine.

According to Lichtheim, *Wisdom Literature* reached its culmination in the New Kingdom with *The Instructions of Amenemope* (Lichtheim, *Ancient Egyptian Literature* 2: 146). When compared with the 6th Dynasty text *The Instructions of Ptahhotep*, the evolution in standards and values over approximately eight hundred years becomes obvious. Lichtheim summarizes her observations of the cultural transformation by stating that the "new ideal man" is inward, modest, "self-controlled, quiet, and kind towards people, and he is humble before God. This ideal man is indeed not a perfect man, for perfection is now viewed as belonging only to God" (146). This text is believed to have originated in the Ramesside period and continued to be copied into the Late Period. Parts of this text can even be found in the Hebrew *Book of Proverbs* (Lichtheim, *Ancient Egyptian Literature* 2: 147).

Afterlife Literature

The ancient Egyptians, in the literature that addresses the afterlife—the *Pyramid Texts*, *Coffin Texts*, and the *Book of Going Forth Into Day*[39]—speak of life everlasting and resurrection. The words and images of these sacred texts celebrate joining with the gods and goddesses, living in a world filled with what these people loved most: nature in its infinite display of diversity and abundance, their beloved family members, and the celestial stars. These ancient people recognized that the world is created in the harmonious balance of the natural order—Ma'at's order—and that each person must do his or her daily part in promoting and promulgating this order so that all life may flourish.

The demise of the Old Kingdom gave way to a time of transition that appeared to be ancient Egypt's darkest hour.

---

[39] As discussed earlier, this literal translation of the ancient Egyptian name is preferable to the misleading *Book of the Dead*, the misnomer assigned to this genre of sacred texts by an early Egyptologist.

> The collapse of the ordered society of the Pyramid Age shook
> confidence in everything. Doubts were expressed not only about
> the justice of the social order but about the possibility of survival
> after death, the nature of the gods and of the worshipper's relation
> to them. (Clark 125)

In the long run, however, the destruction of the old systems had a positive outcome, for the Middle Kingdom was "one of the great ages of the liberation of the human spirit" (125). It birthed an explosion of sacred literature that modern historians have named the *Coffin Texts*. Whereas the *Pyramid Texts* had evolved for the sole use of the king and a very select group of his own choosing, the afterlife journey communicated in the *Coffin Texts* was available to a much wider portion of the population.

The Coffin Texts: A "new inquiring spirit."

Apparently the scribal and military classes wished to "share in the Osiris fate after death but without the materialist trappings of tomb endowments and funeral estates" (Clark 124). Coffins, wooden and usually made in pairs so one fit inside the other, were painted with the scenes of tomb and ceremony, offerings, furniture, and the inscriptions recited on behalf of the deceased, formerly reserved for kings and the select privileged few of their circle. Making the sacred texts available to more people, instead of limiting them to use only by the king and his select few, enabled a large number of people to engage in the Osirian mysteries directly.

However, access to the eternal afterlife was not granted without the hard work of self-reflection and self-growth. No longer just the elite, but every deceased person, regardless of social standing, had to undergo the Weighing of the Heart ordeal in Ma'at's

Hall of Truth. This requirement inspired an "intense intellectual ferment. . . . Fundamental problems about the nature of man and God, the problem of evil and—most insistently—the nature of the individual soul were raised for the first time in recorded history" (Clark 125). As the people began to explore these topics, literary activity increased exponentially. This "new inquiring spirit," as Clark puts it, is reflected in the *Coffin Texts*, which also give us a window into the rituals and ceremonies that would have incorporated many of these texts (125).

The tone of the *Coffin Texts* is more personal and reflective—contemplative yet oriented toward the actions and attitudes, the values and ethical stance, that are required for everlasting life to be realized. The Osirian drama is at the center of the emerging ideas: "The rites are no longer the business of the kings or even of society as a collective unit; they reflect the inward feelings of ordinary men and women" (Clark 125).

As discussed in chapter 3, in both religious and scientific traditions, naming identifies a certain potential and makes it so by describing its constitutive parts; this in turn shapes and forms the values and direction of the collective consciousness. Observe how, in *Coffin Texts*, Spell 330, the author has named specific aspects of the Osirian myth and Osiris's relationship to Ma'at's chief characteristic, "Order":

> Whether I live or die I am Osiris,
>
> I enter in and reappear through you,
>
> I decay in you, I grow in you,
>
> I fall down in you, I fall upon my side.
>
> The gods are living in me for I live and grow in the corn
>
> that sustains the Honoured Ones.

> I cover the earth,
>
> whether I live or die I am Barley,
>
> I am not destroyed.
>
> I have entered the Order [Ma'at],
>
> I rely upon the Order,
>
> I become Master of the Order,
>
> I emerge in the Order,
>
> I make my form distinct,
>
> I am the Lord of the Chennet[40]
>
> I have entered into the Order,
>
> I have reached its limits…
>
> (Clark 142)

R. T. Rundle Clark tells us that Spell 330 is the "clearest identification of the soul with nature that the ancients have left us" (143). Yet when Osiris speaks of becoming "Master of the Order," he is not emphasizing his mastery over the goddess Ma'at, but instead stating that he has mastered his *connection to Ma'at*. It is not a power-over relationship. As specifically indicated by the lines "I have entered the Order, | I rely upon the Order," he has put himself *in accord with Ma'at*. And as shown in the lines "I emerge in the Order, | I make my form distinct," he has learned to *speak and do* Ma'at. Osiris and Ma'at share a reciprocal relationship wherein each maintains a separate identity and authority, yet they interact and are mutually reliant. By association, for each deceased person became "an Osiris" upon death, this alignment with Ma'at's order applied to all.

---

[40] Clark suggest this is possibly a reference to the Granary of Memphis.

Maintaining the connection to the divine order required daily ritual actions that in turn permeated every interaction. In Spell 330, Osiris says that he has reached the "limits" of the cosmic order, of all creation. Beyond its limits—Ma'at's limits—is the ocean of Nun, formlessness, the abyss "containing the potential for all creation" (Bonnefoy, *Greek and Egyptian* 216). Osiris and all the deities arise within the order of creation. This is what Ma'at embodies: order, woven in activities from the most mundane to the most significant.

Ma'at's natural laws and order created a sense of harmony and balance that pervaded the ancient Egyptian consciousness. To refer to this impulse as "values" or "ethics" is too restrictive; it is so much more than an intellectual concept or a moral code of behavior imposed from without by some external authority. The recognition and enactment of Ma'at's laws made the whole land holy and sustained the civilization for more than three thousand years, through all the challenges and upheavals this culture faced.

Evolution of the journey into the afterlife.

Ma'at travels with Ra in the Solar Barque (as explored in chapters 2 and 3), delighting his heart and giving "life to his nostrils." The "life" she imparts requires self-mastery, which is necessary for the transformation of consciousness that encourages actions that promote social order. For best results, a standard model of excellence is necessary to illustrate various ways to apply the wisdom. With poetic metaphors that invoke the Great Goddess herself—in the forms of Hathor, the barque, and Nut—*Coffin Texts*, Spell 44 describes the rewards of a lifetime spent pursuing Ma'at, received in the afterlife:

> [T]he doors of the sky are opened because of your goodness, may
> you ascend and see Hathor, may your complaint be removed, may
> your sin be erased by those who weigh in the balance on the day of
> reckoning characters, may it be granted that you join those who are
> in the Bark by those who are in the Suite, … Hathor has provided
> clothing for you; betake yourself to me, draw near to me, be not far
> from me [in] your tomb; turn to me, for I am your son Horus, and I
> enclose you within the arms of your mother Nut—may you live for
> ever! (Faulkner 36–37)

Faulkner believes the grammar and word use reveal that this text is of great antiquity. This accounts for the transformation of the deceased into Horus—in later texts, the deceased becomes Osiris.

Three points exemplify the critical importance and influence of Ma'at in these responsibilities. Firstly, initially it was the primary duty of the king to champion Ma'at. When conditions deteriorated, the king's failure to uphold Ma'at was seen as the cause. With the passage of time, a wider and wider portion of the population was given access to the religious insights necessary to begin the transformation of consciousness that would embody Ma'at's teachings. By the time of the New Kingdom, personal piety (which will be explored in chapter 6) became the standard for all who hoped to achieve eternal life.

Secondly, the dead were judged solely on whether they had done Ma'at more often than not. It was their own heart that gave testimony to their veracity, during the Weighing of the Heart rite. Lastly, from the Old Kingdom onward, Ma'at's presence was seen as vital to the daily regeneration of the sun god. The success of these efforts was gauged on whether or not life flourished.

Each dawn, as the Night Barque becomes the Day Barque, Re is renewed, as are all his companions. It isn't just the solar god, the king, the gods, or the rich and powerful who receive the benefit of this renewal. All life benefits. It is the nature of First Time that this rite is enacted with each dawn—and that death gives birth to life.

In the Old Kingdom (*c.* 2686–2160 BCE), the journey into the afterlife was first inscribed on the tomb walls of the last king of the 5th Dynasty. The afterlife literature of this period was directed toward the king's afterlife and his identification with the solar god, Re. Before then, the inscriptions in the private tombs of lesser royalty and nobles consisted solely of the names and titles of the deceased and other family members, prayers for a safe journey and a good reception in the "beautiful West," and requests for offerings—the autobiographical inscriptions.

By the Middle Kingdom (*c.* 2055–1650 BCE), as revealed in the *Coffin Texts*, those eligible for eternal life included all who were wealthy enough to afford the preparations. The *Coffin Texts* were painted on the coffins, sarcophagi, and funerary accoutrements of all who could afford to employ the artists and craftsmen.

From the New Kingdom (*c.* 1550–1069 BCE) onward, the *Book of the Dead* and the *Books of What's in the Underworld*[41] reveal that all people could achieve eternal life, provided they upheld Ma'at in their lifetime and successfully passed the judgment of the dead on their personal journey into life everlasting. During this period, and throughout

---

[41] Underworld, *Amduat*, *Duat*, and Netherworld all refer to the afterlife and are used interchangeably in this study.

the transformations initiated by the Amarna period,[42] many new texts describing the afterlife were written on papyri scrolls. These and the so-called *Book of the Dead* texts were placed within the coffin or tomb of deceased individuals from many levels of society. *Book of Going Forth Into Day*, Chapter 125 comprises the 42 Negative Confessions that the deceased must be able to declare. The Negative Confessions outline the ethical values that were held to be most critical for a personal life to be lived in accord with Ma'at's principles and for the smooth functioning of society.

The literary genres and these specific beliefs model the cultural values of the ancient Egyptians and are imparted through rich metaphors and word-images embedded in nature. The themes and narratives describe the direct benefits to the individual, as well as society as a whole, when these values are applied to everyday practices. Greediness, lying, crookedness, and gluttony are specifically cited as characteristics that disrupt well-being—for both the individual and the culture as a whole—and are contrary to the natural laws that ensure that all life flourishes.

Chapter Summary

Against these terms of opposition, [Ma'at] may be interpreted as truth, justice, authenticity, correctness, order, and straightness. It is the norm that should govern all actions, the standard by which all deeds should be measured or judged. (Hornung, *Idea Into Image* 136)

The natural order of the world is based on renewal and can be observed in the sun's daily circuit; the moon's regular waxing and waning; the orderly procession of the

---

[42] The Amarna period spanned approximately fifteen years during the New Kingdom when a new king decided to utterly transform the religious focus and practices, closing down and defunding the cults of the ancient gods and goddesses. His reign, and its negative impact on the lives of many, is a focus of chapter 6.

stars in the heavens; the annual inundation of the river's waters; and the fertility of the land and the animals, insects, and birds. The cosmic laws that rule the forces of nature also were applicable to human society, but to recognize this interdependence required education, for "no one is born wise." It was recognized that humans must learn what is required to live in accord with the cosmic principles, with Ma'at.

Ma'at was considered the food and drink of the gods, the organizing principle underlying the social structure. Initially, this structure—and the relationship with the gods and goddesses—was maintained through the king's ability to mediate Ma'at. The Presentation of Ma'at to the divine, in rituals conducted each morning by the king or his representatives, was the king's number one priority.

Due to a combination of spirituality and pragmatism, beginning at the end of the Old Kingdom it was taken for granted that the well-educated individual—and not just the king—would perpetuate Ma'at's laws and thus promote social cohesion. Upholding these cosmic laws was the only insurance that eternal life would be possible for those who were not the king. Over the centuries the precepts of Ma'at spread into the entire population, as upholding her order was the only means for achieving eternal life.

Some scholars—such as Anna Mancini in *Maat Revealed*—stress the aspects of Ma'at best described as circulation, the flow of energies that sustains the reciprocal relationship between the three realms: divine, human, and ancestral. Other scholars see Ma'at mainly as the foundation of the cosmos and its basic natural laws that govern the functioning of nature and society. Indeed she is all these aspects and more. To relate to her as an abstract concept is to keep her unnecessarily at arm's length. She is the beautiful, powerful, joyous goddess who brings both delight and the measure of a well-lived life. She patiently teaches each individual, and society at large, how to do and say Ma'at—and she does not expect or praise perfection. Instead her quest is to balance the contrary pulls and inclinations, to harmonize conflict. To swing from discord into righteousness would perpetuate imbalance, disharmony. Therefore, as Ptahhotep wisely warns, "Adhere to [Ma'at], but do not exaggerate" (Hornung, *Idea Into Image* 136).

Ma'at's teaching should be used to inform each action and to offer a model of excellence by which we may judge our actions as upholding Ma'at—or not. Ma'at is worthy of our keenest attention, for—as the ancient Egyptians discovered when their social order collapsed and the flowering of Old Kingdom culture came to an end—Ma'at is precious, and her place in our consciousness and actions promotes life. Here is a goddess and a critical organizing principle for many centuries of ancient Egyptian civilization, a framework that allowed the people to reestablish order after a societal breakdown.

Chapter 5. Ma'at: The Framework for Stability and Renewal

As the embodiment of cosmic order, the goddess Maat is also the
guarantor of social justice, that is, the wisdom of the ordered
creation that exists in the immanent world and that extends, in the
Amduat, into the netherworld. (Schweizer 36)

To be in accord with Ma'at is crucial for sustaining life. Ma'at is the natural balance and order of the world, "a force of nature—in fact, the most fundamental of such forces" (Allen 147). Walter Burkert, a historian of ancient religions, calls the organizing principle of a culture the "framework for stability," which includes "order and morality within its purview" (Burkert ix). Indeed, Ma'at is a guide for the people of ancient Egypt as they move through the inevitable cycles of creation and destruction. Her natural laws are based on life-sustaining participatory practices that promoted right proportion, harmony, and the balance necessary to create a flourishing culture through recognition that all of the actions, thoughts, and words of her people influenced the overall quality of life. Surviving examples from ancient Egyptian literature indicate a belief that the rigor with which Ma'at was attended to determined whether or not the civilization flourished.

Ma'at is circulated into the world through words and deeds, referred to in the Egyptian literature as "saying" and "doing" Ma'at. It is through the actions of the people that Ma'at's presence is most apparent—or most glaringly askew. Ma'at's model of balance and harmony clearly draws attention to what is out of balance and incongruent. Ma'at is "the yardstick against which the Egyptians measured their important experiences: their society's values, their relationships with one another, and even their own perception of reality" (Allen 148).

Multifaceted Ma'at

There is no precise equivalent in our language for the idea of Ma'at. She is a goddess who embodies the cosmic order, natural laws based on right proportion, sacred order, and social cohesion that lead to renewal and thus the flourishing of life. The author R. Athens, in *Die Maat des Echnaton Amarna*, published in 1952, succinctly summarizes Ma'at's multidimensional importance during the Amarna period in the middle of the New Kingdom (*c*. 1550–1069 BCE):

> Ma'at holds this small world together and makes it into a
>
> constitutive part of world order. She is the bringing home of the
>
> harvest; she is human integrity in thought, word, and deed; she is
>
> the loyal leadership of government; she is the prayer and offering
>
> of the king to the god; she permeates the economy, the
>
> administration, religious services, the law. All flows together in a
>
> single point of convergence: the king. He lives in Ma'at and passes
>
> her on, not only to the sun god but also to his subjects below.
>
> (Hornung, *Idea Into Image* 138)

Athens portrays Ma'at as essential to maintaining the reciprocal relationship described in the previous chapter—the circulation of energy—between the human and divine realms. It is essential to recognize the intimate relationship between the two spheres, with Ma'at providing for the physical needs of the people ("the bringing home of the harvest") and for their spiritual needs ("human integrity in thought, word, and deed") (Hornung, *Idea Into Image* 138). The former represents the roots of survival for any people, and yet a successful harvest was seen by the Egyptians as reliant on a number of dynamics, both physical and spiritual. Therefore, a successful harvest was directly related to fostering a dynamic, reciprocal relationship with the divine, and to growing a reciprocal relationship with Ma'at in particular.

Daily practices that honored the *neters* were a recognition that the gift of life flows into the world from a divine source. In turn, these practices fostered a religious attitude of uprightness in thoughts, words, and actions, which was as foundational to human integrity as were Ma'at's principles of right proportion and harmonized balance. The rituals, as imagined in the image below (fig. 36), were not hollow actions performed in a perfunctory way; rather, "they refer to things other than themselves, and this reference is always to something in the world of the gods. In Egyptian religion there is a theology wound around the ritual, so that one cannot be considered without the other" (Clark 27).

The uprightness of Ma'at's teachings is not rigid moralism with laws that are set in stone, dictating right and wrong. This is *not* Ma'at—she is much richer. Ma'at's way is based in the wisdom of the ethical, awakened heart, and begins in the reciprocal field, the dialectic between divine and human realms. In the presence of Ma'at the human heart awakens and establishes a communion between the personal and the archetypal, transcendent energies, the flow of energy between the two nurtures this communion. As Clark points out in the quote above, ritual is the expression of their theology. It is the relationship between what Jung named "the Self" and the other and includes subtle body practices. This relationship grows the attention and actions, and this is what creates culture. The goal is to grow Ma'at, which in turn grows the presence of the transcendent in the culture. The rituals are offered with the intention of producing a change of consciousness—in individuals and in the culture at large.

Figure 36. Nefertari offering two nemset *jars to three goddesses.* On the east wall of the descending corridor in Nefertari's tomb in the Valley of the Queens are three goddesses, from left to right: Ma'at, Serket, and Hathor. A photo from the same album, depicting Nefertari facing the goddesses with her offerings, has been added to complete the images on this wall. Photo credit: kairoinfo4u, from the flickr photo album: "Tomb of Nefertari, QV66, Valley of the Queens." Photographed 19 March 2017. Original photos have been cropped. Creative Commons, some rights reserved. Web. 9 March 2018.

Persistent Renewal

As discussed at length in chapter 2, renewal in ancient Egypt was well imagined and pervasive. Renewal was essential in their landscape, their religious beliefs, their life and afterlife practices, their political and social institutions. For the Egyptians, every single element of life partook of the phenomenon of renewal. Each sunrise was a return to the first sunrise, when Atum-Re arose from the nun and creation began. Ma'at symbolized what was essential for this paradigm of renewal to perpetuate. That is why she was ritually presented to the main deities by the king or his high priests—as the first ritual act of each day. This ritual cycle recognized the king's primary responsibility of maintaining the reciprocity at the foundation of the cosmogonic cycle.

The renewal these people sought was a result of maintaining right relationship to the cosmic patterns and natural laws as well as nurturing social cohesion. This appears to have been accomplished in part by putting oneself into accord with the precepts of Ma'at. Each individual was responsible for harmonizing and balancing his or her thoughts, words, and deeds. The right proportion wasn't possible without an effort, which included actively nurturing one's personal relationship to Ma'at on a daily basis. They believe that when the culture experienced a major breakdown of social systems, the order and balance had been violated to such a degree, it resulted in disharmony and imbalance. Ordering, harmonizing, and balancing were essential to Ma'at's spheres of influence; therefore the people directed their attention toward reestablishing Ma'at's principles daily.

Historical periods of disruption and societal breakdown provided the impetus for developing precepts, arrived at by refining their social-emotional intelligence, which led to greater self-reflection and assuming responsibility for one's own thoughts, words, and deeds.[43] This circulation of energy brought constant renewal to all aspects of life—and the ancient Egyptians saw this renewal as critical to maintaining the natural, harmonious balance of the cosmos.

In the day-to-day world, Ma'at's principles inform wise and measured leadership, beginning with the king. Athens tells us that "she is the prayer and offering of the king to the god" and that "she permeates the economy, the administration, religious services, the law." Ma'at is the personification of social order as well as "the embodiment of cosmic

---

[43] The significant breakdowns of societal structure are identified by Egyptologists as the First, Second, and Third Intermediate Periods.

order" (Schweizer 36). Cosmic order is witnessed in eternally recurrent patterns: the sun's daily circuit, the moon's regular waxing and waning, the orderly procession of the stars in the heavens, the annual transition of their three seasons. Renewal of the natural order is also reflected in the annual inundation of the Nile that promoted the fertility of all life in their world. Thus, as the breath of life, the *ankh*, Ma'at is the cyclic renewal that permeates nature, where she is "the wisdom of the ordered creation that exists in the immanent world" (Allen 147).

Balance and Stability

As the plinth that supports both the king's and Osiris's throne, Ma'at provides foundational stability, thus she is related to kingship and dominion. Yet Ma'at's ideal order did not encourage the elimination of what was considered "bad," or its replacement with what was considered "good"; instead "the concept of Ma'at was one in which all parts of nature lived in balance and harmony" (Allen 148). This included the understanding that life gives way to death, just as day gives way to night; each side of any pair of opposites is necessary. What matters most is harmonizing and balancing the opposite aspects. Essential to the balancing and harmonizing is proportion. Right proportion can even be discerned in the harmonious visual aesthetics so prevalent in all manifestations of ancient Egyptian art forms—architecture, design, hieroglyphic inscriptions, and so on.

In addition to Ma'at's influence in the manifest world, Ma'at's percepts are critical to attaining life after death. After a lifetime accumulating the forces of both Ma'at and *isfet*, the Weighing of the Heart determines whether or not the deceased individual has achieved eternal life. Ma'at's wisdom is not based in fixed and rigidly enforced human laws or by self-righteously imposing dogmas and viewpoints; this is *not* Ma'at.

Rather, she encourages the balancing of conflicts and the harmonizing of relationships,

the right proportion in all one's doing and saying. Ancient Egypt did not develop codified

morals determined by religious conventions; instead the culture nurtured "distinctions

determined by practical experience: behavior that promoted balanced, harmonious

relationships between people was *maa*, 'right, correct, orderly, just, true'; that which did

not do so was a manifestation of *jzft*"[44] (Allen 148).

Ma'at's Spheres of Influence

The Egyptologist Alison Roberts states Ma'at's essential nature forcefully: "Maat

is no empty abstraction. She is vitally real and alive, the very bread of life, sustaining

those in the circuit of the sun" (*Hathor Rising* 34). Relationship to and with Ma'at is

fostered through conscious, intentional saying and doing that was seen as leading to a

prosperous life worthy of remembrance. As described above, Ma'at's symbols include

the *ankh*, the plinth, and *sema*, and she is foundational for ancient Egypt in three

fundamental areas of concern: creation, kingship, and the afterlife.

Creation

Even during periods of occupation and rule by foreigners, the indigenous

pharaonic culture of historical Egypt managed to endure and dominate for more than

three thousand years, all while maintaining its recognizable features and ideologies. Over

its long history, the Egyptian mythopoetic imagination gave rise to numerous myths

about creation and the multiple gods and goddesses that populated the landscapes.

As revealed in chapter 2, for this ancient culture the goal of exploring the

ineffable mysteries of life's abundance was never the articulation of one definitive truth.

---

[44] *Jzft* is also translated as *isfet*, most often translated as "chaos," "disorder," "dishonesty."

Instead observations and intuitions revealed themselves to the human imagination in a myriad of shapes and forms:

> The Egyptians knew that their answers could not be definitive, and this flexible and pluralistic approach is the essence of their philosophical position. The idea that there is no single answer, that everything is flow and every answer provisional, is worth investigating today, in an age that has focused attention on fragmentation while continuing to cling to a history of absolutes.
>
> (Hornung, *Idea Into Image* 13–14)

It comes as no surprise, then, that the people developed at least six main accounts of creation, with different deities assuming the lead role.[45]

Due to the ancient Egyptians' holoscopic viewpoint, this dynamism did not fragment and polarize their culture; instead it gave them the flexibility and freedom to explore vast metaphysical questions and envision multiple possibilities. This multiplicity seems to have unified Egyptian culture from prehistoric times until the demise of ancient Egypt and its mythological systems, which coincided with the advent of Christianity. As described below, it is in the Heliopolitan cosmology or grouping of deities that Ma'at's mythological origins are delineated.

The essentialism of joy.

As shall be revealed in chapter 7, the *Hymn to Ma'at* recognizes her as a divine Feminine co-creator who actively participates in the manifestation of the world, and as a dynamic cosmological pattern. Ma'at is also envisioned as promoting joy, which may

---

[45] It is outside the scope of this dissertation to outline each cosmology. See the works of Alison Roberts, Geraldine Pinch, Eric Hornung, and Jan Assmann, listed in the Works Cited section, for more information on this interesting topic.

seem incongruent to her role in cosmic patterns and natural order. In explaining Ma'at's relationship with Re (as her father), however, Hornung illustrates the essentialism of joy, describing Ma'at's role in "making the creator happy she gives pleasure to the entire world" (*Idea Into Image* 134). This is a critical distinction, and one contemporary cultures might do well to take note of. In contemporary culture there is a split—a polarization between the notion of serious pursuit (i.e., meaningful, financially rewarding) and joyous expression (i.e., frivolous, capricious)—and this often short-circuits the renewal so necessary to a healthy, balanced, and meaning-filled life.

In creation, even before the primordial mound was raised, Ma'at was with Atum in the inert waters of Nun. In *Coffin Texts,* Spell 80, line 35, Atum complains to Nun that he is "very weary" because, with no land or throne yet created in the watery abyss, he has no place to sit or stand. Nun counsels him, "Kiss your daughter Mā'et, put her at your nose, that your heart may live, for she will not be far from you" (Faulkner 84). The act of placing Ma'at near his nose is a gesture of joy (Wilkinson, *Reading Egyptian Art* 27), a breathing in of the essence of Ma'at, whose sweet smell is comparable to the precious, fragrant blue lotus—a flower sacred to ancient Egyptians that (as mentioned in chapter 2) symbolizes eternal life. Her essence brings his heart alive, awakening feelings of love and joy that spark the raising of the primordial mound—and so creation begins.

In a different translation of this same text, by R. T. Rundle Clark, Atum is "still alone in the waters in a state of inertness" (45). It is the time before time, before creation, "before a perch had been formed for me to sit on." Again he is complaining of inertia to Nun, the Abyss, who instructs him on how to remedy his weariness:

> *And the Abyss said to Atum:* | Kiss your daughter Order, put her to
>
> your nose, | so will your heart live. | Never let her leave you, let
>
> Order, who is your daughter, | be with your son Shu, whose name
>
> is Life. | You will eat with your daughter Order, | while your son
>
> Shu will lift you up. (Clark 45–6)

Ancient Egyptians urged that the pleasure and enjoyment of life not be taken lightly or dismissed as superfluous, an unnecessary luxury. In a culture where the average life expectancy was short, about thirty-five years, life was seen as a precious gift from the divine. It was meant to be enjoyed and used well, not spent in nonstop work, squandered in ineffectual laziness, or bemoaned as a burden. As Nun counsels Atum, the consequence of experiencing joy is that your heart will live. For the Egyptians, the heart was symbolic of one's "spiritual identity" and "always essentially pure. It lives on *maat*" (Naydler, *Temple of the Cosmos* 250). Quoting the *Book of Going Forth Into Day* (Chapter 29b), Naydler expands on the connection between the heart and Ma'at:

> I live on Truth [Ma'at], | and I have my being in Truth. | I am
>
> Horus, who dwells in the heart, | who dwells in the center of the
>
> body. | I live by saying what is in my heart, | and it shall not be
>
> taken from me. | My heart is mine, and it shall not be wounded. |
>
> No terror shall subdue me…. | I have committed no sin against the
>
> gods; | I shall not suffer defeat; | I shall be victorious. (*Temple* 250)

Literary genres such as the *Hymns*, the *Harpers' Songs*, and the *Wisdom Literature* give voice to these values and also encourage taking pleasure in being alive, whether by participating in festivals and celebrations, enjoying sitting in one's garden, or simply promoting the flourishing life that sustained them. For the ancient Egyptians, just as inertia and laziness were anathema, debauchery to excess and greed were frowned upon. Enjoyment of life came from balance, right proportion, and served to harmonize hardships—also one of Ma'at's principles.

Generally, the *Harpers' Songs* exude a sense of happiness in life that a deceased person will continue to enjoy. These are not ritual texts, though they were inscribed on the walls of the tombs as well as on papyri, to be enjoyed as literature. Instead their function is assumed to be a "reassurance of the owner of the tomb about his fate" (Lichtheim, *Ancient Egyptian Literature* 1: 193). This poetry is meant to be sung or recited to the accompaniment of a harp: "O Tomb, you were built for festivity, | You were founded for happiness!" (Lichtheim, *Ancient Egyptian Literature* 1: 194). Images of the harper are painted on the tomb walls along with other pleasures of life, family, and the beauty of the earth.

The continuous flow of creation.

> Creation is continuous: it is a flow of living manifestations towards
> extinction—death. But out of death a new Re is to be born,
> sprouting new life. Two gods personify the cycle of life and death:
> Re, who with his living manifestation moves towards death, and
> Osiris, the dead god, who represents the process of rebirth.
>
> (Piankoff vii)

This succinct observation inspires with its twist: "creation is continuous" in its movement toward death, which in turn is a movement toward renewal. Piankoff reframes the customary flow, reversing the stream of images to quiet the primacy of the ego's perspective, its solo "I." The mystery of creation deepens into life *and* death, as a continuous flow from one to the other and back again, with Re as its visible, solar aspect, in movement toward death, and Osiris as the hidden, chthonic aspect, in movement toward life.

If *solar* is imagined as consciousness (or the potential for it), the chthonic realm represents the unconscious, the hairy roots of renewal. From this hidden realm comes the rebirth that refreshes and regenerates the "dayworld,"[46] which Hillman describes as "the literal view of any world where things seem as they appear, where we have not seen through into their darkness, . . . literal realities, natural comparisons, contrary opposites, processional steps" (*Dream and the Underworld* 13). In contrast, a "nightworld" style of thinking enters the realm of imagination and dreams, and "thinking moves in images, resemblances, correspondences" (13). Like Piankoff, Hillman encourages an alternative approach to the flow of creation, "foregoing all ideas that originate [in the dayworld]— translation, reclamation, compensation"—and crossing the bridge into the other world, the underworld (13).

An exploration of the dynamic between Re and Osiris quickly reveals that they are not alone in their roles and functions. They are continuously accompanied by companions, masculine and feminine deities who array themselves around the principle deity—Re or Osiris—and work on behalf of all creation to ensure the successful outcome of the continuous, ever-flowing process of renewal.

Re is the shining solar disc with its precise, repetitive movement through the Day World sky. By the end of the day he becomes Atum, the aged solar god, and then is fixed

---

[46] Hillman, in *The Dream and the Underworld*, makes the distinction between "dayworld" and "nightworld" styles of thinking. This study uses the similar terms *Day World* and *Night World*.

and inert in his underworld journey as the regenerating solar principle in the Night

World, the midnight sun. His presence remains illuminating, casting a softer lunar glow

that awakens and enlivens the deceased in each of the twelve "hours" through which he

passes. He must rely upon a whole cadre of deities to move his barque through the

Netherworld and protect him from the obstacles and dangers that would destroy him.

The Heliopolitan cosmology.

Heliopolis was the Greek name for the ancient Egyptian "cult center of Junu,

named *On* in the Hebrew Bible" (Luckert 41). Located not far from Memphis,[47] which

was the first capital of the united Upper and Lower Egypt, Heliopolis was one of the most

ancient and renowned of Egypt's sacred religious centers. It was here—near where the

Nile split into the seven branches that created the delta region before it emptied into the

Mediterranean Sea—that the *Pyramid Texts* were first inscribed in the pyramid tomb of

King Unas.

The sophistication of these sacred texts and of the *Coffin Texts* they spawned

suggests there was a well-formulated "cosmogony to explain the vital elements of their

universe" by the time of the unification of Upper (southern) and Lower (northern) Egypt

(Hart, *Egyptian Myths* 11). The *Pyramid Texts* give evidence of complex concepts that

have clearly influenced the development of other, later cultures in the region, including

the Minoan, the Greek, and the Semitic people who laid the groundwork for the

monotheistic religions of the modern world. For instance, Ptah—the demiurge of the

Memphite cosmology—creates "through his heart and his tongue," meaning he uses

intuitive thought and creative speech to create the cosmos (see chapter 7 for more on

---

[47] Located in Lower Egypt, Memphis remained the city where rulers often set up their main residence. The king who is credited with the initial unification of Upper and Lower Egypt was named Narmer, or Menes. He was a human model of the supreme, as Moses was for the much later Hebrew culture.

this). This is "the earliest known example of the so-called 'logos' doctrine in which the world is formed through a god's creative speech" (Wilkinson, *Complete Gods* 18). The logos mytheme "lies before, and in line with, the philosophical concepts found in the Hebrew Bible . . . and the Christian scriptures" (19). But unlike the deity of these two descendant religions, Ptah was also viewed as combining masculine and feminine elements within himself and was never seen a monotheistic deity. The same is true of Atum, the Heliopolitan creator.

One becomes three.

Chapter 3 described the Heliopolitan creation myth in some detail, starting with the black abyss of Nun, inert dark waters without end or measure, that existed before there was a cosmos. Nun is the primeval stillness that has no likeness; it is simply "nonexistence." Here the myth varies: Arising from Nun, the sweet-smelling blue lotus flower opens to reveal a golden child, the young solar god Nefertem. Or, from Nun emerges a primordial mound, the *benben*, from which the androgynous creator, Atum, emerges, heralded by the *benu* bird arriving from the Isle of Flame. This bird, the phoenix, is linked to the morning star, as *benu* means "to rise in brilliance" and "to shine" (Hart, *Egyptian Myths* 16; Pinch, *Egyptian Mythology* 117).

Within the Heliopolis Ennead, Atum is the primordial demiurge whose name means simultaneously "not to be" and "to be perfect" (Bonnefoy, *Greek and Egyptian* 215). As described earlier, an erotic excitation that Atum carries within him-/herself suddenly moves him/her to draw out his/her phallus; Atum "makes a mate of his fist," and thus the world is born from his/her masturbation. Atum takes his/her own semen into his/her mouth, sneezing out Shu, the first masculine deity (the atmosphere that divides earth and sky) and spitting out Tefnut, the first feminine deity (moisture and the female creative principle). They are the first divine couple (216).

The following verse from the *Coffin Texts*, Spell 77 gives a succinct rendition of the creation of the first generation. In these sacred texts Shu is to be understood as both the deity and the deceased:

> I am this soul of Shu which is in the flame of the fiery blast which
> Atum kindled with his own hand. He created orgasm and fluid fell
> from his mouth. He spat me out as Shu together with Tefnut, who
> came forth after me as the Great Ennead, the daughter of Atum,
> who shines on the gods. I was set in it as son and daughter of Nut,
> she with the braided hair who bore the gods. Such am I. (Faulkner
> 80)

The third and fourth generations complete the Ennead.

Tefnut gives birth to the twins Geb and Nut, the male earth and the female sky; like their parents, Shu and Tefnut, they are sibling consorts. They are born in a passionate embrace, until their father Shu, the atmosphere filled with sunbeams, separates them—creating the pocket in the nun needed to bring forth the first sunrise and allow all life to emerge. This separation—which can also be thought of as the process of differentiation on a cosmic scale—also allows Nut to birth the children she had already conceived, by withdrawing Geb's phallus from her vagina.

Later interpretations offer Shu's "sexual jealousy" as the motivating factor behind his act of separating his children, but this sidetracks from the deeper metaphysical meaning. Shu's gesture is quite clearly the symbol for Shu sharing his *ka*, his vital life force. The space he creates between Nut, as the sky, and Geb, as the earth, is the manifest world, and he fills this cavity with his elemental air, the atmosphere, and light. In raising up and supporting Nut, he continually shares his vital life force with her and all of creation.

The children of Geb and Nut are the fourth generation. Listed in their birth order they are as follows: Osiris, Seth, Isis, and Nephthys. In some versions, where there are five children in the fourth generation, Horus the Elder is named as the second child and Seth becomes the third child, with Isis as the fourth and Nephthys as the fifth. Horus the Elder is distinct from the more familiar Horus the Younger. Horus the Elder seems to share lunar aspects with the deities Djehuty and Khons—son of Amun and Mut. Horus the Younger belongs to the fifth generation—the only child of Isis and Osiris, a falcon-headed solar deity. Other gods and goddesses, such as Hathor, Sekhmet, Nefertem, Ptah, Amon, Mut, Anubis, Thoth, Khepri, and the solar god Re (whose name is synonymous with the sun) are all aspects of the one god and are included in the rites, celebrations, and myths.

Ma'at's place in creation myth.

The Egyptologist Geraldine Pinch tells us that "the role of a deity is often defined by the pair or group of which he or she forms a part" (*Egyptian Mythology* 95n13). Atum establishes the standard of creation based on duality in creating the first sexually differentiated generation, and then Atum becomes differentiated into masculine and feminine with the separation of the Sole Eye as well. Each successive generation procreates and thus populates the Ennead of Heliopolis, which consists of four generations of deities, or nine main gods and goddesses. The Egyptian name for this grouping of nine deities is *Pesedjet*;[48] it implies the formula *3 x 3* and indicates the concept of "many" (Wilkinson, *Complete Gods* 79), and indeed there are many more deities just as vital as the nine named *neters*—including Ma'at, as the alternative aspect of Tefnut.

In addition to her role as the embodiment of moisture, Tefnut is often envisioned as a protective, fiery, lioness-headed female or the fire-spitting *uraeus*, whereas Ma'at is named the "most beloved daughter" and personified as an anthropomorphic female divinity. In addition, Ma'at is also depicted as a rearing cobra. For example, in Queen Hatshepsut's throne name—Maatkare, or "Ma'at-is-the-*ka*-of-Re"—a rebus presents Ma'at as a giant rearing cobra, resting between the upraised arms of the *ka* symbol, and wearing the solar disc of Re upon her head.

Osiris and Isis appear in the *Pyramid Texts* and continue on throughout the history of ancient Egypt as the first couple to rule on earth—though this, too, has a number of variations. For instance, the gods lived among the humans in the Golden Time, until humans became quarrelsome and the gods withdrew. Or Re ruled until he became old and weary of humans and the great Wild Cow came to carry him between her horns into the heavens. In yet another version, Ma'at lived among the humans as their ruler, until she too grew weary of the discord and the disregard of the sacred patterns and natural order that she had established in First Time. In each version, as the gods withdraw from earth because of human discord and disregard of the sacred order, societal collapse ensues.

In the Golden Time, when Osiris and Isis ruled, Osiris traveled throughout the land teaching humans the arts of civilization—agriculture, wine making, wise governance, arts and crafts—while Isis tended to the duties of the throne, and all life

---

[48] An alternative spelling is *psdt*.

flourished. Their brother Seth was apparently jealous, and he plotted to kill Osiris. The most prevalent version of the Isis and Osiris myth that has come down to modern times was retold by the Greek Plutarch (46–120 CE). He supposedly gathered versions of the myth during his travels through Egypt and compiled them into the narrative recognized today in modern mythology. Though Plutarch's version titled *De Iside et Osiride*, is certainly the most familiar version, numerous aspects of this most important Egyptian mythologem can be discovered in their own sacred texts and images, beginning with the *Pyramid Texts*.

The murder of Osiris was not as specifically articulated as it is in Plutarch's version; in the Egyptian sacred texts the murder of Osiris was commemorated during the annual ritual at Abydos, with the followers of Horus and the companions of Seth engaging in mock battles. The *Coffin Texts*, Spell 74 preserves a soulful hymn of lamentation that young women (chosen to represent Isis and Nephthys) sang as they ritualistically recovered Osiris's dismembered body and rejoined his members. This mythological event marked the creation of funerary rites, embalming, and the establishment of the Netherworld. One can't help but see the early glimmer of the later alchemical teachings in the symbolism of these works.

Isis is Horus's mother, and Osiris is Horus's father. Images in the New Kingdom tomb and temples, of Seti I in particular, preserve the mystery of the conception of Horus after Osiris has been murdered. In these mysteries Horus symbolizes the living king and his father Osiris is the recently deceased king. It is Horus's duty to see to the burial and ancestor rites of his father, Osiris, the deceased king. The king is also equated with Re, the solar god. *The Contendings of Horus and Seth* sets out the details of Horus's and Isis's efforts to ensure that Osiris was vindicated and the throne went to his son.

Ma'at, though not specifically featured in the story, is present through the actions and intentions of the mytheme. These rituals portray parts of the myth discussed in *The Contendings of Horus and Seth* (as described in chapter 4), which gives words and images to the constitutive elements necessary for the health and well-being of the culture. In harmonizing and balancing Horus's and Seth's competing claims to the throne, the myth's long narrative illustrates, articulates, and envisions Ma'at's traditions.

Kingship

Ma'at was the highest priority and the main concern of the king and the religious rituals he enacted—the underlying framework informing all aspects of the culture. It was the duty of the king "to make the country flourish as in primeval times by means of the designs of Maat" (Frankfort, *Ancient Egyptian Religion* 51). As Athens's describes, the king's attention to the reciprocal relationship with the divine impacted the harvest (Hornung *Idea Into Image* 138). By enacting the ritual that offered Ma'at to the primary deities of the main temples, the king and his high priests were perpetuating the reciprocal relationship between the human and the divine realms. In this capacity, Ma'at was known as the food and drink of the gods, the embodiment of all the offerings; bread, beer, wine, fruits, vegetables, cloth, incense, flowers, and all the other things placed upon the altars were her essence.

Figure 37. Seti I presenting an abundant offering and lighting the incense. In this bas-relief Seti I is offering incense and an abundance of other offerings, placed upon four altar tables and under the platform supporting the barque within the shrine. This image is in the Amun Chapel, accessed through the 2nd Hypostyle Hall in the Temple of Seti I, Abydos. New Kingdom, 19th Dynasty. Photo credit: kairoinfo4u, from the flickr photo album: "Abydos reloaded 2013." Photographed on 9 February 2013. Contrast enhanced to bring out details. Creative Commons, some rights reserved. Web. 9 March 2018.

The ritual as a motif "epitomizes all worship activities" (Hornung, *Idea Into Image* 136). The gesture of making an offering to a god or goddess is similar regardless of the ritual, for all offerings are seen as Ma'at. A particularly moving verse comes from the Presentation of Ma'at ceremony (discussed in detail in chapter 4): "Presenting Maat | I have come to you, my arms full of Maat | With Maat spread out on my fingers" (Assmann, *Egyptian Solar Religion* 33). These simple words convey an image that evokes the love underlying the offering, which is an act of worship. What is offered is loved, and the recipient is loved. Offering is a gesture of love, not a hollow, rote act.

All papyri of the *Book of Going Forth Into Day* genre show altar tables and mats piled high with the produce of the earth, and all are considered Ma'at. The inscriptions carved and painted in temples, tombs, and coffins from the Middle Kingdom (*c.* 2055–1650 BCE) to the end of this Egyptian culture also give rich testimony to this (see figs. 36 and 37). In fact, the entire temple and tomb can be seen as an offering to the divine, in stone, and meant to permanently resound with the prayers, chants, scents of incense and flowers, and rituals performed there over the ensuing millennia.

In ancient Egypt, agricultural success relied on the same physical factors that impact farmers today: weather, crop pests and disease, quality of the soil and seeds, appropriate levels of moisture and sunlight, and the care and attention of the farmer. Yet beyond these physical factors, it was also considered essential to attend to spiritual influences in order to promote fertility and abundance. Life was a balancing of spiritual practices alongside pragmatic concerns.

> As a guiding principle *maat* is a point of orientation or a standard of measurement; it is the "ought" against which the "is" of life is ruthlessly and repeatedly measured and almost always found lacking. The scene of the offering of Maat shows the constant exertion required to increase the amount of *maat* throughout the world. (Hornung, *Idea Into Image* 143)

As fig. 37 reflects, Ma'at is the focus of daily rituals performed by the king and his high priests, directed toward the maintenance of unity, harmony, and balance. Ma'at represents "immanent lawfulness" in the natural order, the social order, and the sacred order. By maintaining alignment to Ma'at's principles in his own actions, the king models behavior for others that support the flow of reciprocity between the human and divine realms. It is understood that alignment of the king's thoughts, words, and deeds with Ma'at's natural order would be reflected in the world as harmony and balance. It is recognized that "passively adapting to a pre-existing order, following it and respecting it, will not suffice; rather, this order must be established and actively realized time and again" (Hornung, *Idea Into Image* 135). This is the king's number one responsibility.

As articulated in the chapter 4 section on *The Eloquent Peasant*, the health of the land and its people was reliant on the integrity of the king and his administrators. Ma'at provided the structure, and the king's adherence to her precepts supplied the model of excellence, the embodiment of her principles—dispensing justice, living with authenticity, and ensuring truthfulness, straightness, and correctness. Upholding her ideals and tending to her precepts taught people what it meant to be wise and just. The king was the foremost promoter of Ma'at's actions, and this translated into what was expected of others as well.

The sixth petition sums up this commonly held belief succinctly:

> Whoever decreases lying promotes Maat,
>
> Whoever supports good reduces evil to nothing,
>
> As satiety drives away hunger,
>
> Clothing covers nakedness.
>
> As the sky becomes clear after a violent storm,
>
> … as fire cooks raw food,

>> As water slakes thirst.
>>
>> (Hornung, *Idea Into Image* 143)

Greed and lying are recognized as the main sources of disorder and are very disruptive to the well-being of the individual and culture. All the literary genres that evolved over the millennia attest to this and were designed to impart the social expectations for people at all levels of society. Injustice, greed, deceit, lying, and crookedness represent a primary failing of humans and a threat that creates chaos at all levels of society.

Afterlife

>> Ma'at could still be thought of as living with an individual like his or her good angel and accompanying that person into the afterlife. Eventually "joining Ma'at" became a euphemism for dying. (Pinch, *Egyptian Mythology* 159)

As explored at length in chapter 4 and elsewhere, upholding Ma'at came to be the crucial responsibility of each man and woman, and, as always, was the primary responsibility of the king. Moral and ethical education was considered necessary for an individual to develop the awareness of Ma'at's cosmic laws that included right proportion, balance, harmony, justice, truth, and beauty—and to be held in esteem by one's family and community during one's lifetime. It was necessary to live in accordance with Ma'at's cosmic principles and with the natural order, which was observable. One's actions and words either helped life flourish, or it didn't; the saying and the doing of Ma'at were critical.

"The same Maat that guarantees success and continuance in life is also the standard of the Judgment of the Dead and leads to immortality" (Assmann, *Death and*

Salvation 413). Upon reaching the final judgment in the Hall of Double Ma'at, only a deceased individual who had followed Ma'at's principles in life was considered worthy of eternal life. In Ma'at's Hall the deceased declared their innocence and displayed their knowledge of Ma'at's precepts through the so-called Negative Confession, forty-two declarations that began "I have not . . ." Found in Chapter 125 of the *Book of the Dead*,[49] this declaration of innocence begins by addressing Osiris as "great God, Lord of the Two Truths!" (Lichtheim *Ancient Egyptian Literature* 2: 124). The final five lines of the greeting equate Osiris and Ma'at: "Lo, your name is 'He-of-Two-Daughters,' | (And) 'He-of-Maat's-Two-Eyes.' | Lo I come before you, | Bringing Maat to you, | Having repelled evil for you" (125).

The Hall of Double Ma'at.

> The Egyptians recognized a divine order, established at the time of
> creation; this order is manifest in nature in the normalcy of
> phenomena; it is manifest in society as justice; and it is manifest in
> an individual's life as truth. Maat is this order, the essence of
> existence, whether we recognize it or not. (Frankfort, *Ancient*
> *Egyptian Religion* 63)

Ma'at plays an exceptionally central role in the afterlife. The afterlife was "the place where absolute Truth [Ma'at] dwelled" (Parkinson, *Voices* 132). Her council chamber, the Hall of Double Ma'at—also known as the Hall of Double Truth—is the place where each person journeys upon death. There Osiris, Isis, Nephthys, Anubis, Thoth, and Ammit—plus forty-two assessors (or councilors) from the underworld—

---

[49] As noted earlier, this study prefers the ancient Egyptian literal translation of the title—*The Book of Going Forth Into Day*—but occasionally references the commonly ascribed name for clarity's sake.

assemble on either side of Ma'at's great golden scale to witness the weighing of the deceased's heart. This ordeal determines whether or not the individual will be justified and thus invited to enter the eternal afterlife. Ma'at's feather of truth, or a tiny figure of Ma'at, is placed in one pan of the scales, and the deceased's heart is placed in the other. For a favorable judgment, the two must balance. An unfavorable finding results in the heart being devoured by Ammit, the goddess who waits by the scales to enact this consequence; this "second death" was considered more dreadful than the actual experience of death.

Depictions of the Weighing of the Heart scene, which is central to the *Book of Going Forth Into Day* (Chapter 125), are plentiful and rich with symbols, including the heart scarab and its text, as noted in chapter 3. In ancient Egypt, "death was regarded as the interface between the ideal and the actual world" (132). The images that follow (figs. 38 and 39) epitomize key aspects of Ma'at's dominion in the afterlife and her role of presiding over the council of forty-two deities.

Ma'at's essence is contained in the hall where the truth is discerned, the scale that weighs the heart, and the counterweight on the scale. Ma'at's precepts are the measure of the saying and the doing throughout a lifetime, as is indicated by the epithets ascribed to Osiris in the greeting above. Ma'at lives in each person's heart, and it is in the individual's heart that Ma'at's weight can be measured. The heart, which belongs to the mother, is the testifier, having recorded a lifetime of the thoughts, words, and deeds. The forty-two councilors, also interpreted as "judges" in many translations of the sacred texts, are the witnesses to the deceased's declarations that she or he has upheld Ma'at's teachings. Their witnessing lends veracity to the final result—joining the Blessed Dead, or suffering the second, eternal, death.

The basic question each person must answer is: *Have you done and said Ma'at more often than not?* "The conception of Maat expresses the Egyptian belief that the universe is changeless and that all apparent opposites must, therefore, hold each other in equilibrium" (Frankfort, *Ancient Egyptian Religion* 64). Misdeeds are not sins, as in Judeo-Christian traditions. They are "aberrations" that create disequilibrium and disharmony and are thus undesirable (73). In the *Instructions* of Ptahhotep (from the 6th Dynasty), the person who violates Ma'at's balance is "not a sinner but a fool," and therefore a more thorough understanding of Ma'at's precepts, "not repentance" (73), is called for. When people are dishonest, they "sever [their] heart from [their] tongue," and the "doomed man is deaf to the teachings of the sages"—he is the "one that hears not" (75).

The greedy dissembler is destroyed by a cosmic force. His or her destruction is a result of not attempting to be in harmony with Ma'at, for Ma'at is the universal order, and every one of the gods and goddesses requires "right conduct" (76). If the accumulated actions of a lifetime measure up to the lightness of Ma'at's feather of truth—that is, the heart weighs no more and no less than the feather, and thus is in balanced harmony with Ma'at—then the deceased is found to be "true of voice." Thoth records and reports the outcome to Osiris, who then extends a welcome to eternal life.

The following is a short list of some "I have not . . ." statements from the "Declaration of Innocence to the Forty-two Gods" (*Book of the Dead*, Chapter 125):

I have not done crimes against people | . . . mistreated cattle | . . .

sinned in the Place of Truth | . . . robbed the poor | . . . caused pain |

. . . made anyone to suffer | . . . cheated in the fields | . . . added to

the weight of the balance | . . . taken milk from the mouths of

children | . . . held back water in its season | . . . stopped a god in

his procession. (Lichtheim, *Ancient Egyptian Literature* 2: 125)

The journey to the Hall of Double Maʻat is a requirement from which none are exempt.

Every single deceased person has to be able to declare the statements above in order to be

justified and granted eternal life after death. Only when one has actively sought to

harmonize and balance one's appetites and instincts during one's lifetime will the heart of

the deceased be as light as Maʻat and her feather. Maʻat and the heart are intimately

intertwined.

The image below (fig. 38) is sparse in its details but especially rich in its depiction

of two ordeals that potentially await the deceased. The "Greenfield Papyrus" belongs to a

priestess named Nestanebetisheru. Her titles identify her as "First Leader-in-Chief of

Musicians of Amonrasonther," "Priestess of Amun-Ra Lord of Iurud," "Priestess of

Inheret-Shu Son of Ra," "Servant of the Archive of Amonrasonther," and "True of voice"

(British Museum online description of EA 10554,80, *The Greenfield Papyrus*, sheet 80).

True of voice indicates that Nestanebetisheru has been justified.

Figure 38. Double Ma'at and the Weighing of the Heart scene from the Greenfield Papyrus, Sheet #80. In the collection of the British Museum. From the Thebes area, the late 21st Dynasty (*c.* 950–930 BCE). ©Trustees of the British Museum, some rights reserved. Creative Commons.

Double Ma'at.

On the right-hand side of the scene above is the doubled image of Ma'at. Standing side by side the two images are identical; each holds an *ankh*, symbolizing the "breath of life," and a papyrus scepter, which means "flourishing, greening." Anubis, the jackal-headed deity adjusting the plumb and steadying the scale, is directly in front of double Ma'at. Sitting on the pans of the scale are a small vessel containing Nestanebetisheru's heart (on the left), and a small figure of Ma'at with her distinctive feather of truth headdress on the right. A small baboon sits atop the balance beam of the scale, facing

Anubis and the doubled Ma'at. To the left of the scale, kneeling on a stepped platform (primordial mound), is the deceased priestess.

Ammit, the Devouress.

The goddess Ammit, "the Devouress,"—an essential deity in the Weighing of the Heart process—on the first step behind the deceased Nestanebetisheru, wears an attentive expression. Ammit's symbolism is rich and deserves further explanation, instead of simply judging her appearance as hideous and moving on. She stands ready to consume the heart of anyone who is not aligned with Ma'at's measure and thus is found unworthy of eternal life. This is a vital role, and her composite nature recognizes what is required to inflict the "second death." Energy can't be destroyed but only transformed, and Ammit's combination of qualities underscores this understanding. Displaying a crocodile's head; a lioness's chest, heart, and forelegs; and the back side (digestive and reproductive organs) of a hippopotamus, Ammit comprises the three top predators in ancient Egypt.

Each animal lends its specific attributes to this combination. The crocodile uses cunning, stealth, and surprise to hunt, bursting forth from the murky waters of the river to grab its prey in its powerful jaws. There is no escape as it drags down its victim. The lioness hunts by coordinating her efforts with her pride's. Employing keen vision, speed, sharp claws, and teeth, she brings down her prey. She embodies the solar qualities of creativity, expansive heart, and intelligence. The hippopotamus has a powerful digestive system and regenerative capacities. A mother hippo is aggressive and extremely protective of her young. She spends much of her time in the water and even gives birth to her babies there, where the newborn instinctively knows to swim to the surface to take its first breath. The hippo is symbolically linked with the water and the earth.

Clearly this combination was held in high regard and was necessary for Ammit to execute her responsibilities in managing the portals between life and death. In *An Encyclopaedia of Traditional Symbols*, J. C. Cooper points out that the hippopotamus also "represents the Great Mother *Amenti*, the 'bringer-forth of the waters'; [and] Taueret,[50] the hippopotamus goddess" (83). Taweret shares Ammit's physical characteristics—crocodile head, lioness forelegs, hippopotamus body—and is the midwife and goddess of birth.

Like the double lion (figs. 3 and 21), Ammit and Taweret are guardians of the threshold between this world and the next. Female hippopotami were held in high esteem in ancient Egypt, while the masculine of their species was equated with aggressive, deadly behavior. For instance, Seth is often depicted as a dangerous red hippo in his typhonic aspect (Cooper 83).

The Lake of Fire.

In the upper left-hand corner of the Weighing of the Heart scene is the Lake of Fire (fig. 39). The Lake of Fire is surrounded by four lamps, pouring forth watery fire, and four baboons, an aspect of Djehuty (Thoth), the god of wisdom. The zigzag lines that fill the lake denote water, but here they are drawn in red to indicate the mercurial waters of transformation (Abraham 77). These are the living waters—the fiery water, watery fire.

The Lake of Fire is related to the Isle of Fire—Re's origin—a place of dazzling light, or a subterranean body of water in the lowest depths of the Underworld. However it is envisioned, it symbolizes the refinement and purification of the soul. When one turns

---

[50] Also spelled *Taweret*.

toward it and submits oneself to its burning, "the Lake of Fire loses its destructive aspect and becomes the essential means of inner transformation" (Naydler, *Temple of the Cosmos* 243). Its waters purify and establish the *akh* body, the luminous body of light.

This ordeal burns off the last dross of a lifetime; the fiery water is refreshing, renewing, and invigorating for the person properly prepared. The luminous light body allows the deceased to ascend and take his or her place in the Boat of Millions. For one properly prepared, this would be the ultimate goal upon crossing the threshold of death.

On the other hand, there is a risk. If the deceased enters the watery fire but has not prepared for this test, he or she suffers a horrendous death by incineration. Naydler envisions it in psychological terms: "if a person enters it wholly identified with those aspects of themselves that are unregenerated and unable to transmit the life-giving light of Ra, then they will suffer a torment similar to being hacked to pieces" (242–43). From this "second death," there is no return.

In the image below, the 21st Dynasty priestess of Amon and chantress Nisti-ta-Nebet-Taui is doubled; her two aspects face one another, each mirroring the other as she pours fiery water from a sacred vessel. The four baboons guarding the four corners and the continuous renewal process of the Lake of Fire are, because of their number, "symbolic of earth, of terrestrial space, of the human situation" (Cirlot 232). The number four indicates the stability equated with manifestation. It represents the four cardinal points and symbolizes the ordering and interconnection between the separate parts. There are four main points of transformation in the daily cyclic, transformative journey of the Solar Barque: the two gates of the horizon (east and west) as well as the vertical points of midday and midnight (zenith and nadir). The lake itself—a square—reiterates the

Figure 39. Lake of Fire scene from the Papyrus of Nisti-ta-Nebet-Taui (Piankoff and Rambova, *Mythological Papyri* 52, fig. 36). Public domain.

symbolism, and reminds us that "a great many material and spiritual forms are modelled after the quaternary" (232).

In the *Book of Going Forth Into Day* (the so-called *Book of the Dead*), this vignette accompanies Chapter 126, a prayer to the four baboons.

> Homage to you, you four baboons | who sit upon the bow of the
>
> boat of Ra | who make the truth of God advance | who apportion to
>
> me both my strength and my weakness | who pacify the gods with
>
> the flame that issues from your nostrils | who give holy offerings to
>
> the gods | and invocation offerings to the Shining Ones | who live

> on *maat*, who gulp down *maat* | whose hearts harbour no lies, | who detest falsehood | Purge the evil that is in me! | Destroy all falsehood that is in me! | Heal the wounds which I had on earth! | Purge away all evil that clings to me! (Naydler, *Temple of the Cosmos* 243)

Baboons are often depicted in the afterlife texts as greeting the Solar Barque at dawn, celebrating and jubilating. Here they are guardians of the sacred, purifying Lake of Fire; they are said to "live on *maat*" and possess pure hearts. Indeed the god Djehuty, often represented as a baboon, is witness to the Weighing of the Heart, a creator god, and the consort of Ma'at.

Like the alchemists in their work, the four baboons attend to this continuous process of renewal with diligent focus. Here the perfected spiritual essence is once again subjected to the fiery solution to multiply its strength and capacity to flow into the world, where "the flame of life is extinguished in the body [so the fire of life] burns more brightly in the soul" (Naydler, *Temple of the Cosmos* 243).

As introduced in chapter 2, this transformation can be envisioned as taking place during the sixth hour of the night, when the Solar Barque reaches the depths of the Amduat. There, above the Lake of Fire, sits a womb- or egg-shaped cavern in which dwells the god Sokar (an ancient chthonic god related to Osiris). In the darkest hour of the night journey, Re and Osiris enact the greatest mystery: merging and becoming one, thus renewing all. This imagery weaves together the final purification of the soul in the fiery water and the mysteries of the renewal of all life. The ultimate processes of transformation rely on the paradoxical combination of these opposites—water and fire, Osiris and Re.

As in alchemy, fire and water are the ultimate agents of transformation. They combine in a continuous process of separation and coagulation that purifies the *prima materia,* the raw material into gold, the Philosopher's Stone, the treasure, the shining soul, the light body. As water pours down from the heavens, fire leaps up from the earth, and the two opposites create the final processes of transformation, calling to mind the word-images offered by the depth psychologist Helen Luke: "There comes a time when it is no longer a question of tending fires, of finding fuel, but of becoming our self the fuel, walking open-eyed into the flames" (*Woman, Earth and Spirit* 49–50).

Through a lifetime of tending to the fires with their devotion, of nurturing the reciprocal relationship between the human and the divine realm, these ancient people felt prepared for the ordeal of entering the fiery water. "Walking open-eyed into the flames" burned away the last remnants of their personal life, and they emerged renewed; the *akh* body, the shining body of light, was the reward. Their devotional practices and beliefs revealed their greatest treasure, the pure gold of spirit. This, too, was realized in the world as the psyche's living waters flowed and circulated between the conscious and the unconscious realms.

The Book of Gates: The Twelfth Gate.

The Twelfth Gate is the final hieroglyphic image in *The Book of Gates*, and a part of the genre of literature known as the *Books of What's in the Amduat.* The image below (fig. 40) shows the final passage of the Solar Barque as it issues from the underworld on its journey to deliver the transformed solar deity Khepri-Re, the dawn, into the Day

World. Khepri symbolizes "eternally becoming." Of particular interest are the deities

accompanying the solar god in his final phase of renewal during the nightly underworld

journey, the companions in the barque.[51]

Starting on the left and moving to the right, three gatekeepers stand in the prow of

the barque, right arms raised with their fists placed over their hearts—a universal pledge

of devotion, praise, and allegiance. The next grouping also comprises three deities: Isis,

Khepri, and Nephthys. Isis and her sister Nephthys face one another, lending their

considerable energies to raising the scarab beetle, Khepri, as he rolls his solar ball

upward. The sisters are identifiable by their headdresses—Isis's throne and Nephthys's

sacred enclosure topped with a basket. Behind Nephthys are five additional masculine

figures. The three directly behind Nephthys mirror the gatekeepers in the prow, with their

right arms bent—fists to their hearts. They are Geb, Shu, and Heka. The last two are Hu

and Sia, steering the barque.

Geb is the earth, the masculine half of the Heliopolitan third generation and Nut's

consort-brother. Shu is Geb and Nut's father, and one half of the second generation, with

Tefnut as his consort-sister. Heka (Magic), Hu (Utterance), and Sia (Perception) are

named as constant companions of both the creator god and Ma'at. Together they embody

the power of the spoken word, "insightful planning," and right action that came into

being in the beginning (Hornung, *Idea Into Image* 44).

---

[51] In an image of this scene not published here, hieroglyphic symbols name each of the companions
(Hornung and Abt 452).

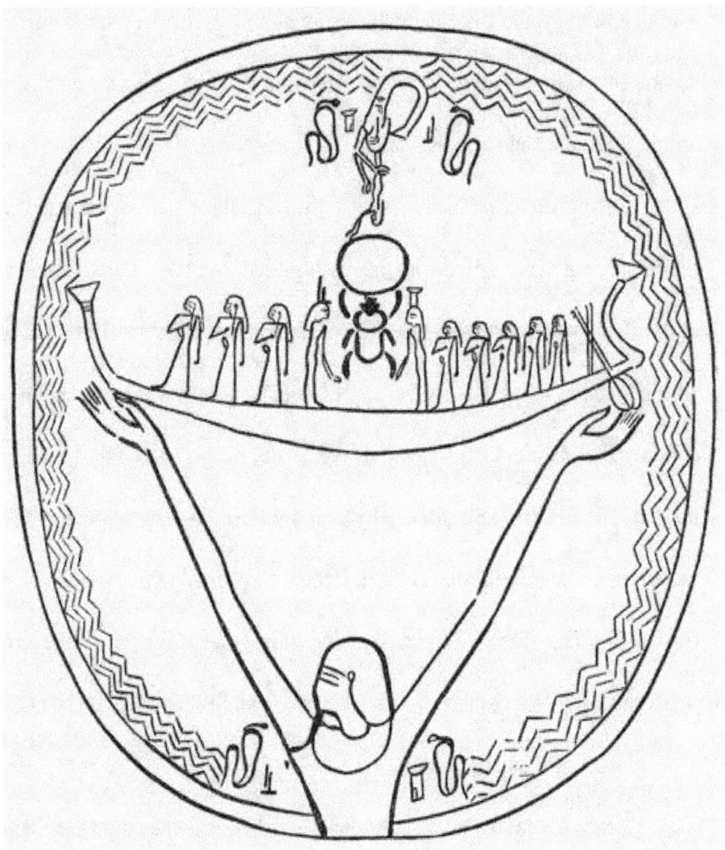

Figure 40. The Twelfth Gate. Drawn from Papyrus #30, Khonsu-mes, now in the collection of the Bibliothèque Nationale (Piankoff and Rambova, *Mythological Papyri* 49, fig. 33). Public domain.

Above the Solar Barque are two more figures, inverted: Nut and Osiris. Nut is standing on Osiris's head, and his body is curled in a backbend, like the *ouroboros* encircling the Netherworld. His arms reach up to stabilize Nut, who is reaching out to receive the solar disc. On either side of Osiris are the rearing cobras—with Nephthys on the left and Isis on the right (just the opposite of the anthropomorphic figures of Isis and Nephthys below). The largest figure by far in the image, rising up from below and supporting the Solar Barque with his upraised arms, is Nun, the personification of the watery abyss and the source of the living waters of creation. On either side of him are, once again, the rearing cobras identified as Isis and Nephthys—also the guardians of the Twelfth Gate. The zigzagging lines represent the waters of the Nun that surround creation—the formlessness from which all form arises, the undifferentiated source of creation.

All are the companions of Re, the forces aiding the sun god's rebirth. They make possible the transformation of consciousness that regenerates the world with each dawn, in part by faithfully attending to the solar deity. Each god and goddess has specific characteristics that, when understood symbolically, illuminate the processes of renewal. Their relationships with one another and with the solar god denote a critical aspect of the constant renewal process—namely, that it takes a focused community effort to ensure the renewal of all life.

Here the cosmic order and balance that Ma'at established in First Time is recreated, renewed with each sunset and each dawn. As Atum-Re-Osiris is renewed, so are his companions. Re and his companions receive this renewal and radiate it into the human realm. With graphic clarity, the image models the devoted group of beings who lend their energies to ensure renewal. Ma'at's presence is evoked through the actions represented in this scene. Renewal is rooted in the cooperative actions—a viewpoint in sharp contrast with the fierce individualism of contemporary culture.

Upholding Ma'at's "divine order" is action oriented; it is the saying and the doing in one's daily life. For this reason, Ma'at is often in the company of the three gods who best represent the power in spoken and written words: Heka, who represents the act of speaking or "saying Ma'at"; Hu, who stands for authoritative utterance and creative statement; and Sia, or wisdom, perception, and "doing Ma'at." The *Admonition of Ipuwer* in the First Intermediate Period speak of Ma'at as spending time with the creator god and the two creative powers Hu and Sia, accompanying the god on his nocturnal travels through the underworld.

Hornung points out the numerous cosmogonic deities who use the spoken word in their version of creation—beginning with Neith, whose "close ties to the primeval cow Mehetweret link her with the early image of the celestial cow" (*Idea Into Image* 44). In the prehistoric era Neith was also the beetle, a role superseded by Khepri the scarab beetle (44). Ptah is also associated with Hu, Sia, and Heka as a creator who calls upon both the naming and the physical shaping of creation—as the patron of artisans and a master craftsman himself. Khnum is the ram-headed god whose cult center is in Esna, and he, too, actively shapes the forms of creation forming both the physical body and the *ka* on his potter's wheel.

Chapter Summary

Ma'at's symbolism, images, and ancient texts attest to her central and essential roles in shaping the ancient Egyptian civilization, particularly in the areas of creation, kingship, and the afterlife. To bring Ma'at alive is for the sake of awakening her mysteries. Her living waters have the ability to awaken our hearts, refresh our atrophied consciousness, and unite the three realms—human, ancestral, and divine—so the energy of the awakened heart's consciousness might flow once again, bestowing healing waters from the spirit of the depths through Ma'at's mysteries.

This culture was not built, as has been taught in history courses, biblical renditions, and media portrayals, on static adherence to tradition and archaic magical practices. Instead its layers were built up over time, a reflection of the natural processes of the river and land of Egypt herself. Each successive generation strove to interweave the Golden Time and the wisdom gained with new reflections and insights gathered. This is the nature of a holoscopic perspective that fosters resilience and creativity—the conservation of best practices in combination with ever-evolving perceptions.

Ma'at is both the balance and the counterbalance on the scale of life. Ma'at embodies the impartial cosmic and natural laws, which determine the quality of each person's heart. Ma'at embodies the form of time known as *djet*, which represents eternal perfection and is comparable to a perfectly ripe fruit. When *djet* is wed with its opposite, *nehen*, the psychic energy is circulated from the living waters of the depths into the Day World, and back again. Ma'at is the reconciliation and cohesion that bestows the energy and *theoria*—the practice—that frees the living waters (Wikman xxi).

The reciprocity that underlies these movements was the central focus of the king, the priests and sages, and eventually the population at large. The recognition of the part each person played in perpetuating renewal enabled ancient Egypt to survive its periods of destruction and regain its momentum of creativity.

Henri Frankfort points out that "we lack words for conceptions which, like Maat, have ethical as well as metaphysical implications" (*Ancient Egyptian Religion* 55). Fortunately, the ancient Egyptians themselves have provided us with not only words, but rich imaginings that cover the whole gamut of human concerns. Through the framework of Ma'at, their imaginings provide an example of a culture that had a model for an ethical stance in life. Ma'at's natural laws offered both the potential and the path for the civilization to achieve impressive stability and perpetual renewal.

Chapter 6. Restoring Balance: Seti I's Temple at Abydos

Every extreme provokes the opposites since nature does not

tolerate any one-sidedness. The more wholly we think and live and

the more aware we are of the laws of day *and* night—taking into

consideration the symbol of Aker, the double sphinx that unites the

opposites—the more likely we are to partake of the regeneration

emanating from the innermost center. (Schweizer 113–14

[emphasis added])

During the 18th Dynasty, in the middle of the New Kingdom (*c.* 1550–1069 BCE),

a king ascended to the throne of Egypt who was to have an impact, both negative and

positive, in reshaping the culture. He was the son of the very successful and long-lived

king Amenhotep III and his Great Wife, Queen Tiye. Taking the throne name Amenhotep

IV, he began his reign (*c.* 1349–1334 BCE) after his father's death. In year five of his

reign he began construction of his new capital, Akhetaten, meaning "Horizon (or, Place

of the Light) of Aten," and renamed himself Akhenaten, meaning "Effective for Aten"

(Hornung, *Akhenaten* 63). The changes that followed, to both the physical and psychic

infrastructure and the established practices of ancient Egypt, signified a break with

centuries of religious, political, and social tradition. It would take a new dynasty to

recover the polytheistic culture from the brink of collapse—and to recreate it through

healing and balance in Ma'at.

Breakdown Fuels a Transformation

Akhenaten is notorious for defunding and closing down cults and temples of the

primary gods and goddesses, and in particular Amun and Osiris. In their stead, he disseminated a solar religion focused on a God-image called "the Aten." Visually he represented the Aten with a sun disc emanating rays that ended in little hands holding *ankhs*. He composed poetry to glorify the Aten, referring to himself and his Great Wife, Queen Nefertiti, as Shu and Tefnut, the firstborn children in the Heliopolitan cosmology. He was the sole priest of his religion, representing a will to power and control that seems unprecedented.

Akhenaten's religion had no place for the rituals that celebrated the solar god's nightly journey into the underworld, nor for the veneration of Osiris, Lord of the Underworld, or of Amun, the Hidden, as an aspect of the solar god (95). As the Egyptologist Alexandre Piankoff explains, Akhenaten's theology "accentuated the visible life-giving aspect of the solar divinity" (*Shrines of Tut-Ankh-Amon* 12). He focused on the Day World, the solar aspect of his God-image, and the Night World was simply ignored, darkness split off from the divine. The feminine half of divinity was also depotentiated.

One of Akhenaten's epithets is "He who lives on Truth" (13). The "love for truth" that manifested during Akhenaten's reign as a spirit of "reformation" was especially seen in the art of the period (13). "Egyptian phenomenalism—an expression of a quite sensual catlike enjoyment of life and of the life-giving sun—was obviously conceived as Truth by Akhenaten and his court" (13). Ma'at is the goddess Truth, Daughter of Re, and "one of the manifestations of the solar deity" (13).

However, Ma'at was not represented as a goddess; instead her hieroglyphic symbol of a single feather referred to Ma'at's many principles (Hornung, *Akhenaten* 74). Ma'at—Truth—was still the measure for eligibility in the afterlife, but it was through the king's grace and mercy that those loyal to him would receive this boon. "Without this loyalty, there was no life after death, for Akhenaten was the 'god of fate (Shai), who grants every lifetime and a burial (after) old age in his favor'" (102).

After his death Akhenaten's city was abandoned, and during the 19th Dynasty he was branded a heretic. Akhenaten's approximately seventeen-year reign is now referred to as the Amarna period, a modern name taken from the archaeological site *Tell el-Amarna*. Immediately after his death an intentional turnaround began, intent on renewing the age-old traditions. Eventually the name of Akhenaten was stricken from inscriptions, and his statues were destroyed; his city was demolished, and his memory all but erased.

Taking a somewhat less positive perspective than Piankoff's, the Egyptologist Jan Assmann describes Akhenaten's theological attempts to impose his religious viewpoints a "revolution from above" and points out that Akhenaten's determination to "change all aspects of Egyptian culture and to adopt the doctrine of One God by the forcible removal of traditional polytheism" was ultimately unsuccessful (*Egyptian Solar Religion* 2). Yet he, too, agrees that it added fuel to a transformation already well under way during the New Kingdom.

After the death of Akhenaten, the boy Tutankhamun became king. It has recently been established that he was Akhenaten's son (Abt 21). He may have been as young as ten years old when he ascended to the throne with Akhenaten's daughter, Ankesenamun, as his queen. No doubt under the guidance of official advisers, the royal pair abandoned the city of Akhetaten, reestablishing the capital of Egypt at Thebes, which had been the cult center for Amun, the primary solar god of the New Kingdom. Tutankhamun began his reign by reversing the ban on the cult of Amun and restoring the shrines that were in a terrible state of disrepair and disfigurement. He died approximately ten years later without producing an heir.[52]

The two men who had been Tutankhamun's closest advisers—Ay, his vizier, and Horemheb, his commander-in-chief—succeeded to the throne, one after the other, but (like their predecessor) neither produced a living heir. Horemheb instituted a vigorous campaign to restore the cults of ancient Egypt's gods and goddesses and to repair the desecration of the temples. In the interest of stabilizing Egypt further, Horemheb ensured that he was succeeded by a well-regarded military man who had an accomplished adult son and a young grandson.

Horemheb's successor, Paramessu—already an old man at the time of his crowning—assumed the throne name of Ramesses I. His son, Seti I, succeeded him several years later and, with the kingship passing once more from father to son, established the 19th Dynasty (*c.* 1293–1185 BCE) of the New Kingdom. It is Seti I's Temple at Abydos that displays evidence of the powerful potential for renewal in the restoration of Ma'at and her fellow deities throughout the land and in the hearts of its people.

Return to Ma'at: Personal Piety and the Natural Order

Studying the ethics of the ancient Egyptians means examining

Maat in the context of the Egyptian experience with

"knowledge/wisdom" and with the Egyptian's sense of the divine,

his piety. (Lichtheim, *Maat in Autobiographies* 7)

---

[52] Tutankhamun is the king whose tomb was discovered nearly intact in 1922 by Howard Carter. The worldwide tour of his treasure in the 1970s broke records for attendance, attesting to the unabated interest inspired by ancient Egypt.

In her book *Maat in Egyptian Autobiographies and Related Studies* Miriam Lichtheim examines the "triangle [of] ethics-wisdom-piety" and the evolution of personal piety described in ancient Egyptian literature. Lichtheim illuminates Ma'at's role in shaping a code of right action, offering a detailed textual study focused on autobiographical inscriptions that extend back as early as late 5th Dynasty (Old Kingdom, *c.* 2686–2160 BCE), in which "the Egyptians declare and define their doing and thinking of Maat" (7).

With the founding of the 19th Dynasty, the movement toward an ever-greater sense of personal piety—within the guidelines of ancient Egyptian tradition—took hold in the minds and lives of the majority of the population. More than ever, "doing Ma'at" included doing what was just and right through a sense of devotion and joy. The goal was to create a way of living that was imbued with a religious attitude, a deep piety—a way of being that invited the interest of and interactions with the deities.

One way personal piety manifested over the evolution of Egypt's historical period was the tending of one's relationship with a specific deity, or deities, that held personal meaning. As described in chapter 4, throughout previous generations the culture saw increasingly widespread access to the religious insights necessary to transform oneself in keeping with the teachings of one goddess in particular: Ma'at. This is evidenced in the New Kingdom, with personal piety becoming standard regardless of social status. Ma'at's teachings were not specifically directed toward any one deity or theological system. Instead her precepts were guidelines for the development of consciousness that included a devotional stance in general and encompassed the ancestral realm.

The evidence of piety can be seen, as well as read, in the images selected to be inscribed and painted in the tombs and temples—an often-overlooked source of cultural record on ritual practices and beliefs. The ancient Egyptian culture certainly ranks as one of the foremost producers of a plentiful and explicit record of such depictions. Taking the time to decipher and interpret the symbolic language coded into various gestures and other specific details can be rewarding, adding layers of insights beyond those gleaned from the literature and historical inscriptions.

Though approximately half of a century had passed since the end of Akhenaten's rule, the work of reestablishing Egypt's stability and balance was still under way. Seti I waged successful military campaigns against Egypt's enemies, the Hittites, and continued Horemheb's program of rebuilding Egypt's cults and temples. Seti's rule was guided by a return to the ancient rituals and relationships with the gods and goddesses, and with Ma'at in particular. Moreover, the 19th Dynasty, also referred to as the Ramesside period, is noted for a level of personal piety in the culture as a whole that had not been realized before this time (Roberts, *My Heart My Mother* 48; Hornung, *Conceptions of God* 196). This implies a recognition by Seti I and his son, Ramesses II, that Egypt's stability and prosperity was founded on each person's commitment to doing Ma'at and saying Ma'at.

Seti I's commitment to re-initiating Ma'at's order, harmony, justice, and truth is reflected in one translation of his choice of throne name: Men-Maat-Re, or "Established is the Justice of Re." Other translations are possible, however. For example, *Men* can also be interpreted as "eternal" or "fixed"—a reference to *djet* time, which is associated with the concept of "stability, of remaining, lasting, being permanent; its sign is that of the earth, its symbols are stone and mummy" (Assmann, *Mind of Egypt* 18). *Djet* is "a sacred dimension of everness" and that which has "ripened to its final form" (18).

The *Ma'at* in Seti I's throne name is normally translated as "Justice." Given that Seti I's reign reflects a wider commitment to Ma'at's purview, however, it's important to avoid limiting the suggested meaning of her name to one specific aspect. The *Men-maat-re* hieroglyph within its cartouche shows a seated Ma'at holding an *ankh*, which suggests the wider application of her purview. Ma'at is also associated with *djet*. Her order is the perfection of First Occasion, the lasting permanence of the ripened forms and patterns of the cosmos. And of course, *Re* aligns Seti I with the solar god, who is the divine king in all his fullness and movement through the complete cycle of renewal.

The art and architecture of the Temple at Abydos reveals that Seti I ascended to the throne of Egypt with the heartfelt mandate to recreate what had been thrown into chaos. Interestingly, his given name, Seti, means "the man of Seth." As explored in chapter 4, Seth is the god often associated with *isfet*, "wrongdoing," "chaos," "upheaval"—the opposite of Ma'at. But as with all archetypal energies, Seth expresses both aspects of this spectrum. Once his will is aligned with Ma'at, he is an indispensable force of strength and vigilance.

The temple's images reveal that Seti I was committed to reestablishing Ma'at, and to fostering his relationship with Amun-Re and all the gods, through acts of devotion and offerings of gratitude in celebrations, rituals, and processions that (as described in chapter 4) create an exchange of energy between the human, divine, and ancestral realms. It was necessary to attract the divine and feed them, sustain them, particularly after the circulation of energy had been damaged by Akhenaten's imposition of his personal beliefs.

One responsibility of the ascending king, as dictated by tradition, was to expand on his predecessors' works. Seti I followed the guidelines to a tee, for he engaged in military expansion, securing Egypt's interests, reinstating the cults and ancient traditions, repairing temples and monuments, and building his own temples and tomb. Rebuilding the eternal residences of the gods and goddesses and the Blessed Dead was a tangible response to the threat from Akhenaten's ideas and actions, and Seti I left no room for ambiguity, constructing them with permanence in mind.

Sacred Patterns and Archetypes in Stone

Early in the Dynastic Period, the Egyptians became masters of working with stone, with the great stone pyramids, temples, and tombs surviving as testimony. While homes, administrative buildings, and even palaces were made of sunbaked adobe bricks, an impermanent material, their temples ("Houses of Life") and tombs ("Houses of Eternity") were fashioned of cut stone or excavated into the mountainsides.

A stone structure is an "eternalized form of reality"; it is made to last (Assmann, *Mind of Egypt* 56). Construction of temples and tombs as permanent homes was a sacred offering suitable for *neters* and ancestors alike. The temple or *Per-ankh* ("House of Life") in particular was the home for the gods in the phenomenal world (Wilkinson, *Complete Gods* 42). The hieroglyphic symbols and images inscribed on the walls and ceilings were also sacred—a record of the eternal relationship with the divine. The energy contained within the images and spaces was activated and kept alive through the performative power of daily rituals that fed this connection between the human, divine, and ancestral realms. It was the primary responsibility of the king to ensure the precise observation of the ritual regulations so the connections between the realms would remain unbroken

(Assmann, *Mind of Egypt* 72). Any break in this reciprocal movement of energy was devastating to both the inner and outer dimensions of life, resulting in a one-sidedness that threatened to stall cultural expression in the same way it would stall the Solar Barque in its circulation between the Day World and the Night World.

Temples were the focal point of the daily performance and maintenance of rituals and festivals intended to enable participation in the maintenance of the cosmos and in perpetuating renewal. Their design was based upon established sacred patterns and was a physical representation of the "cosmography," the divine patterns made visible (Assmann, *Mind of Egypt* 65). The temple functioned as a model of the cosmos, a place where the physical and supernatural worlds interfaced. It was "the center of the cultural endeavor to preserve and ensure the ongoing progress of cosmic, political, and social life" (73).

The temple complex housed the shrines, altars, and activated images of the deities and ancestors, and provided a place for the devotional acts that maintained the reciprocal relationships. Each city or town had a temple or ritual space— ranging from simple in design to elaborate, from small to monumental—and these served as a focal point for the population. Their imposing edifices dotted the land along the entire length of the Great River. Though the general public did not enter the shrine areas, the presence of the temple served as a core from which emanated the ongoing energies of the sacred practices within. Weekly processions and frequent festivals brought the sacred barques that embodied the deities out among the people.

The architectural features of the temple complexes reflected archetypal patterns, with the most elementary symbolism the horizon or "seam between this world and the next, peopled by gods and the deceased" (Hornung, *Idea Into Image* 115–16). The east–west axis orientation represented the sun's daily path and was perpendicular to the south–north direction of the Nile's flow (rather than to magnetic north). A mud-brick wall surrounded the temple precinct, symbolic of the edge of Nun's waters—positioning the temple as the primordial mound, and echoing the lifting up of Nut to create the pocket for creation to emerge. The encircling wall can also be thought of as the *ouroboros* protecting Re in the Solar Barque on its nightly journey.

Gestures are hieroglyphic symbols, too, and the images inscribed and painted on the walls of the temples give specific information and act as a cultural record of ancient Egypt's rituals and practices. Wilkinson describes the coded gestures and positions of the figures as "simply hieroglyphs made large," complementing the hieroglyphic symbols' depiction of what is being offered (*Complete Gods* 90). In other words, a temple image must be considered and interpreted as a whole—with text alongside image, including groupings, gestures, eye contact, and direction of gaze.

Comparative studies aid us in this task of interpretation. Scientific methodologies may provide us with factual information, but reading the symbolism also requires responding to the hunch, the resonance, and the intuitive insight that are part of a creative response, an interaction with the images that may render multiple viewpoints. The result is a holoscopic combination of elements; it is more akin to a creative process than to a linear progression.

The Temple of Seti I at Abydos

One of the ways Seti I overcame the destruction initiated by Akhenaten was to construct temples throughout Egypt. Seti's Temple at Abydos is, by all accounts, "one of the most impressive religious structures in Egypt" (Wilkinson, *Complete Temples* 146). On the southwest side of the complex and just off of the 2nd Hypostyle Hall, a long hall contains the famous "Abydos King List"—a timeline of cartouches for many of the dynasties, stretching from Menes, the presumed founder of a united Egypt (*c.* 3100 BCE), to Seti I (*c.* 1291–1279 BCE). The interior walls throughout are divided into upper and lower registers, with scenes in all, including on the pillars. Exquisite raised bas-relief carvings indicate offerings made to—and received by—the many gods and goddesses. Seti I's devotion is easily discerned through his depiction in each scene. He is shown either making offerings on behalf of himself and all his subjects or receiving blessings from the deities.

As the king, Seti I was the divinized link between the *neters*, the ancestral realm of the kings, and the human realm. Throughout the temple he is envisaged as a vigorous king at the height of his strength and beauty. Depictions of him as a youth and as a divine child being attended to by a mother goddess—Isis, Hathor, Mut—emphasize that his divinity was preordained. He is shown as a beloved child of the goddesses who are the sacred womb, breast, lap, and nurse for the king as a child (see fig. 30).

The king does not become fully divinized until he has ascended to the throne and been accepted by the Two Ladies, Nekhbet and Wadjet, who embody the Red and the White crowns of Egypt. The images covering the walls portray

Seti I as the divinized king wearing the *uraeus* that symbolizes the Two Ladies as well as the Daughters of Re. He is an aspect of both Re and Osiris, for he is the king who will die one day and become Osiris, passing the throne to his son.

The cult center of Abydos (Abtu, in ancient Egyptian) was the main seat of worship of Osiris, Lord of the Underworld, from the beginning of the Dynastic Period onward. Menes and other 1st Dynasty kings have their tombs or cenotaphs[53] in the desert further west, in a remote spot "close to a great gap in the mountain peak" (Roberts, *My Heart My Mother* 48). Here the tomb of King Djer "was venerated as the sacred tomb of Osiris" (48).

Abydos had long been the site of an annual pilgrimage and elaborate festival that celebrated the mysteries of Osiris, including the lamentations of Isis and Nephthys—a ritual reenactment of the gathering and rejoining of Osiris's dismembered parts (described in chapter 5). Mock battles took place between the followers of Horus contending with Seth and his companions. The mysteries of rebirth and renewal were played out. Osiris, Isis, and their posthumously conceived son, Horus, formed the dynamic trinity that received the most popular devotion in ancient Egypt (West 381). Their mythologem shaped kingship and determined the succession necessary to create a dynasty—grandfather to father and father to son—Shu to Geb, Geb to Osiris, Osiris to Horus.

The largest temple in Abydos is the temple complex of Seti I, which "the writers of antiquity called the Memnonium" (Verner 363). The complex includes a mortuary temple primarily built by Seti I but finished after his death by Ramesses II. It is called "The House of Millions of Years of Menmaatre Rejoicing in the Heart of Abydos" (363).

---

[53] A symbolic tomb.

The Osireion—the symbolic tomb of Osiris—is west of the temple, built on the same axis. Gigantic storerooms were included within the walled complex on its south side. Seti I "endowed the temple with revenues from the gold mines in present-day Wadi Abadi" (364) to ensure its continuation.

When the Temple of Seti I (fig. 41) is viewed as a floor plan (see fig. 42), the many layers of symbolism and sacred geometry underlying the temple's design become apparent. The entrance through the first pylon into the outer courtyard is on the east side of the complex. Moving from the entrance in the east toward the west, each section is raised in height, suggesting the primordial mound that rose from the waters of the nun. Shrines to the gods and goddess are housed in individual chapels on the west end and are accessed through two columned halls known as "hypostyle" halls, from an ancient Greek word meaning "under columns," which simply means that columns support a roof. The huge columns and stone slabs of the roof create a dim interior meant to symbolize the primordial papyrus swamp where all life began. The columns are styled as massive individual papyrus stalks recreating this environment. Within this primordial stone forest, a person feels tiny in relationship to the closely spaced rows of columns in the semi-dark. It is a womb of creation.

The temple's inner halls and chapels were not open to the general population, as these areas were sacred, the home of the deities who resided there. Priests and priestesses attended to the private rituals within the temple, while others led the publicly performed ceremonies during the great festivals and celebrations—a restriction intended to preserve the holiness of the inner sanctum as well as to protect those who had not been ritually prepared for the potent energies of the deities that are activated through ritual.

Figure 41. Temple of Seti I at Abydos. The view is from the south end of the hall, looking toward the north wall (Calverley and Broome, "Plate 4"). Credit: Courtesy of the Oriental Institute of the University of Chicago. Reprinted with permission by copyright holder.

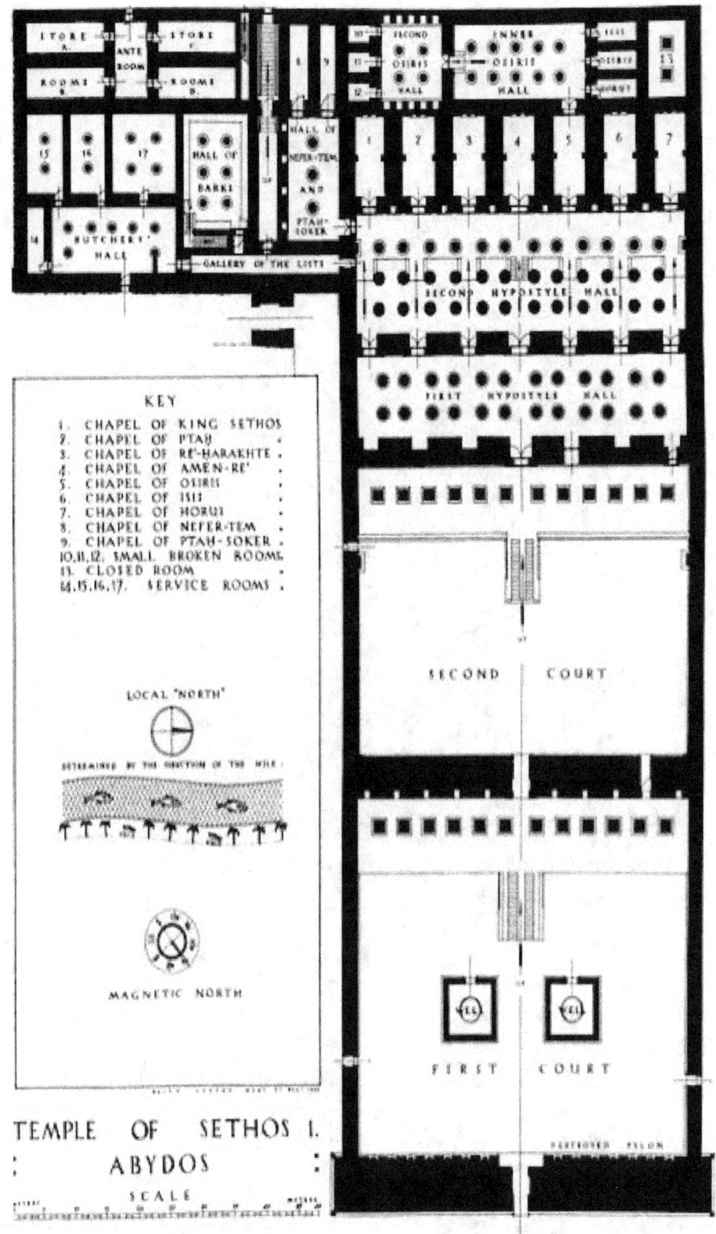

Figure 42. Diagram of the layout of the Temple of Seti I at Abydos (Calverley and Broome, "Plate 2"). Credit: Courtesy of the Oriental Institute of the University of Chicago. Reprinted with permission by copyright holder.

The Temple of Seti I at Abydos houses seven main chapels that honor the deities

critical to the state-observed religion of the New Kingdom, including the king (Roberts,

My Heart My Mother 50). Amun-Re's chapel (position #4 in fig. 42) holds the central

position, with chapels to its north dedicated to Osiris (#5), Isis (#6), and Horus (#7), and

to the south, Re-Harakhte (#3), Ptah (#2), and Seti I (#1). An inner sanctum accessed

through an opening at the back of the primary Osiris chapel, houses three more chapels

dedicated to Isis, Osiris, and Horus, as well as a columned hall with ten pillars that

connects to a smaller, four-pillared chamber. The Hall of Barques, the Hall of Nefertem

and Ptah-Sokar, and the chapels of Nefertem (#8) and Ptah-Sokar (#9) are also located at

the west end of the temple.

Although it is not indicated in fig. 42, and is inaccessible from the temple itself,

the Osireion is located directly behind the temple's west end, as mentioned earlier.

Exploring the Osireion's unique design and symbolism is beyond the scope of this study,

but its proximity is significant because it underscores Seti I's intention for the complex as

a whole: namely, reviving the worship of the deities who had been excluded and

disregarded during Akhenaton's reign—in particular Osiris, Ptah, and Amon (all chthonic

deities) and Isis and the many goddesses who are essential to the function of both cosmos

and state, aiding and protecting the gods. All were seen as "in residence" in this temple.

Earlier chapters of this study detail the history and cultural significance of the

ancient Egyptian *Amduat*. During his reign Akhenaten had rejected this essential

mythologem, which seriously threatened the stability of the culture. The nightly journey

made by the solar god and his companions was pivotal to the renewal and regeneration of

all life. It imparted the much-needed flexibility and dialectic, the connection with between conscious and unconscious, life and death, light and dark. The longstanding

practices, observations, cults, and festivals surrounding this journey bestowed the

renewal that kept this culture alive. Symbols of this journey that are featured in the

images on the north wall of the temple are amplified below.

The North Wall: A Story in Symbols

The north wall of the 2nd Hypostyle Hall is located in an area Amice Calverley

and Myrtle Broome refer to, in their four-volume collection, *The Temple of King Sethos I

at Abydos*, as the Alley of Horus (fig. 43). As one enters the 2nd Hypostyle Hall from the

east, this processional way is on the far right-hand side. Its north wall features the images

investigated below. The reliefs located in the upper registers are badly damaged in

several places, and some are unreadable. This study focuses on the reliefs featuring Ma'at

that are in the lower registers on the north wall adjacent to the entrance to the Chapel of

Horus—#7 and #10 on the floorplan below.

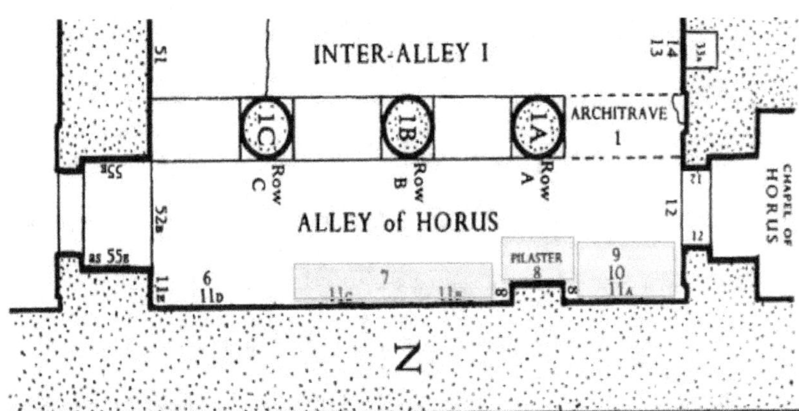

*Figure 43. Detail from the plan of the 2nd Hypostyle Hall, and the alleys leading to the
seven chapels*. This diagram features the north wall and the placement of the images (:
#7, #8, and #10) that are the focus of this chapter (Calverley and Broome, vi). Credit:
Courtesy of the Oriental Institute of the University of Chicago. Reprinted with
permission by copyright holder.

In addition, this study addresses the pilaster[54] (#8 in the diagram above) in between the two images showing the king with Ma'at—a beautiful bas-relief image of the *djed* pillar,[55] revealing symbolism related to Osiris and his central image (fig. 48). A border running along the base of the walls displays a repeating image of the fertility god Hapy (#11 a-e), kneeling and presenting various offerings. Each aspect of Hapy is wearing a headdress composed of the hieroglyphic symbols for the different nomes that make up the regions of Upper Egypt (twenty-two nomes) and Lower Egypt (twenty nomes).[56]

The images are hieroglyphic "texts" in their own right and should be considered in relationship to one another. In addition, the scenes relate to the nearest chapel, comprising what can be considered a meta-narrative. Since the north wall is perpendicular to the Chapel of Horus, the images tell a story about the living king, Seti I (as Horus) and his relationship to Osiris, both the dead king (his father) and the god— whom Seti I himself will one day become. For this temple is also the basis for Seti I's funerary cult; it was intended as a place of ongoing worship after his death.

Powerful positioning.

This study focuses on the two reliefs that feature Ma'at. Relief #7 is in the middle of the north wall, as shown on the floorplan above. The entire scene is shown below (fig. 44), with Osiris enthroned inside a large shrine and accompanied by five goddesses. The scene also includes two groupings on either side of the shrine containing the god Osiris

---

[54] A pilaster is a rectangular pillar that comes out from the wall.

[55] The *djed* pillar is the hieroglyphic symbol meaning "stability," and is an alternative image of Osiris. Raising the pillar is a ritual act that emphasizes his stabilizing effects.

[56] The border images are not shown here but can be accessed online thanks to the generosity of the Oriental Institute of the University of Chicago, which is striving to make scholarly works available digitally.

Figure 44. The central reliefs on the north wall of the 2nd Hypostyle Hall. Position #7 on the floor plan in fig. 43 (Calverley and Broome, "Plate 7"). Credit: Courtesy of the Oriental Institute of the University of Chicago. Reprinted with permission by copyright holder.

and the five goddesses, Nepthys, Imentet, Isis, Ma'at, and Renpet. The images in the upper register are badly damaged but appear to repeat some of the same or similar elements.

Details of this scene provide a closer look (figs. 45–47). As depicted in fig. 45, the three goddesses standing behind Osiris are, from right to left, Isis, Imentet, and Nephthys. Standing in front of Osiris and facing him are Ma'at and Renpet. Each deity is identifiable by her headdress and the hieroglyphs in front of her. These inscriptions offer additional insight into the context of this scene and are deciphered below.

Figure 45. The shrine's interior. Detail of fig. 44. From left to right: Nephthys, Imentet, Isis, Osiris, Ma'at, and Renpet. The shrine's roof is made of seventy rearing cobras. The five goddesses are wearing close-fitting sheaths of linen, carved in great detail to resemble wings wrapping the body (Isis and Ma'at), a net of beads (Nephthys), or sheer linen (Imentet and Renpet).

The scene continues beyond the shrine enclosure, as shown in fig. 46. On the left-hand side of the illustration, an Ennead is depicted, indicated by three rows of three mummiform deities each (3 x 3 formula), all wearing curved beards and facing into the shrine. In fig. 47, on the right-hand side of the relief, Seti I is standing outside (but facing) the shrine containing Osiris and the five goddesses. Between the shrine and Seti I

Figure 46. The Ennead behind Nephthys, Imentet, Isis and Osiris. Detail of fig. 44.

Figure 47. Ma'at, Renpet, and Seti I. Detail of fig. 44.

are seven vertical rows of hieroglyphic symbols and two altar tables with offerings (fig.

47). In his left hand, Seti is holding a smoking incense arm, and his right hand is raised in

the gesture that indicates he is speaking or chanting. His body is leaning forward,

indicating his deference. The hieroglyphic inscriptions give the fourteen names or

epithets of Osiris. Because hieroglyphic symbols are living entities, they should be

considered as yet another divine presence amplifying the scene and not merely as words

written as a caption. The scene in the upper register appears to repeat the offering to the

god and goddesses as well as the rows of hieroglyphs.

Fig. 48 shows the next scene that follows as one moves west toward the Chapel of

Horus. It is on the pilaster, #8 on the floorplan—an image of the *djed* pillar, with the king

wearing the Red Crown doubled at the bottom of the *djed*, supporting or stabilizing the

pillar. The same image is repeated directly across the hall, on the south wall's pilaster.

The *djed* is also known as the backbone of Osiris, and its hieroglyphic meaning is

"stability."

Moving further west, the last relief on the north wall in the lower register (#10)

features the Presentation of Ma'at ritual. It is situated just before the Chapel of Horus.

This depiction of the Presentation of Ma'at is explored in depth in chapter 4 (fig. 34). To

recap briefly: Osiris is enthroned inside his shrine, and his throne rests upon the plinth,

Ma'at's primordial symbol. Isis and Horus stand behind him. Isis has her right arm

protectively around Osiris and is raising her left hand in a gesture of greeting. She is

wearing the horned crown of Hathor and the vulture headdress of Mut. Horus is wearing

the Double Crown of a united Upper and Lower Egypt, and is holding a *was* scepter in

his left hand and an *ankh* in his right. Outside the shrine, Seti I is bowing and extending

Figure 48. Djed *pillar from the pilaster.* (Position #8 on the floor plan in fig. 43.) The pilaster is located between the reliefs shown in fig. 44 and fig. 34 (Calverley and Broome, "Plate 4"). Credit: Courtesy of the Oriental Institute of the University of Chicago. Reprinted with permission by copyright holder.

his right arm with the seated figure of Ma'at holding her *ankh* cupped in his hand. His left arm is raised in the gesture of praise. A lotus is in full bloom on the altar table in front of him, symbolizing renewal and resurrection.

The upper register above relief #10 is not shown in this study. It comprises the king kneeling in front of an enthroned Horus, who is wearing the Double Crown and the tail of the bull, indicating Horus is the ruler and bears the title "the Bull of his Mother," an ancient epithet harkening back to predynastic times. Horus is offering Seti the insignias of kingship.

Isis is also enthroned, seated behind Horus. The goddess Hathor is standing behind Seti I, holding a scepter made up of the symbols for "millions of years"—the *shen* ring, a frog, and a notched palm stem. Both thrones have the *sema* symbol in the inner rectangle and are resting on the plinth, which is filled with alternating *ankhs* and *was* scepters, twenty-four of each. Isis holds an *ankh* in her right hand and has raised her left hand in the gesture of praise. The easternmost scenes on the north wall are also not illustrated in this study. They depict Seti I before Osiris, Horus, and Isis, making offerings and being well received.

Read as a whole, these images illustrate the daily ritual actions that the king, and his appointed representatives, undertook to uphold Ma'at. The king is committed to and in alignment with Ma'at's order. As expounded in this study, this enables the energy contained in all the offerings to circulate between the human, ancestral, and divine realms. The daily ritual enacting the Presentation of Ma'at also validates the king's right to rule. The energies inherent in the food, drink, and other gifts placed on the altar are what nourish the gods—Ma'at again. The images and actual objects are akin to vessels that carry the numinous energies of life. These energies are the source of the constant regeneration that has the capacity to reanimate all the body's, and the soul's, functions after death.

Osiris's symbols amplified.

In addition to the illustration above, the recent images shown below (figs. 49–51) offer greater detail of the scene shown in fig. 44. This enables a more detailed look and conveys a sense of the living presence rendered by the exquisite artistry of these bas-reliefs. In the first image (fig. 49), Osiris's distinctive attributes are clear: the curved beard that denotes a god; the *nemes* headcloth; and the *afet* crown, which is composed of the *hedjet* (the White Crown of Upper Egypt) with two curled ostrich plumes (one on either side) and a solar disc.

In addition to being the hieroglyphic phonogram for Shu and the ideogram for Ma'at (see chapter 3), the ostrich feather is symbolic of Osiris's cult. The feather is an apt way to describe and visualize what is otherwise invisible: its movement reveals the breath of the gods. The ancient Egyptians loved to use language in a poetic fashion, stretching its capacity to spark the imagination and connect multiple metaphors, generating a big-picture image of the concepts they were exploring.

In fig. 49 the fire-spitting solar Eye goddess, *iret* or *Wadjet*, is rearing on the brow of Osiris. As explored in chapter 3 she is related to fiery protection and rulership and is one manifestation of the Daughter of Re, and therefore is related to Ma'at. Her presence emphasizes the Two Ladies (introduced in chapter 3) that represent the unity of Upper and Lower Egypt. The ram's horns, spiraling out from either side of Osiris's crown, refer to the god Amun, whose name means "the Hidden," and to Khnum, who is

Figure 49. Osiris and the four goddesses, from left to right: Imentet, Isis, Ma'at, and Renpet. Photo credit: Richard Mortel, from the flickr photo album: "Temple of Seti I at Abydos." Photographed on 14 January 2016. Original photo has been cropped and the contrast and color altered to enhance details. Creative Commons, some rights reserved. Web. 9 March 2018.

also a ram-headed creator god who forms (with the assistance of Neith) the body and its double, the *ka*, on his potter's wheel. Amun is one aspect of the solar god and also a chthonic symbol of the Great *Ba*-soul, which separates from the body upon death. The *ba* is that aspect of the eternal soul that maintains the ability to move about freely, in any form it chooses, once the deceased has successfully passed the Weighing of the Heart ordeal in the Hall of Double Ma'at.

Osiris's right hand holds the *heka* staff—a long shepherd's crook—indicating that he is "great of magic." In his left hand are the short crook and flail of kingship. His two fists come together at the solar plexus, the heart region of his body—a gesture that focuses the viewer's attention on the heart as the source of his kingly power and strength. This focus echoes both Seti I's name—Man of Seth, Beloved of Ptah—and the importance of the heart as the seat of the highest form of intelligence and the center of all acts of creation. It also relates Osiris to Ptah, the cosmogonic god who creates with his heart and tongue. Ptah is one of the seven deities who have a chapel in this temple; in fact, Ptah has two chapels (see fig. 42). Osiris is seated on a throne that rests on a plinth; both are potent hieroglyphic symbols naming the goddesses Isis and Ma'at, respectively.

Isis presenting Osiris to Ma'at, Renpet, and Seti I.

Feminine deities are often depicted standing behind the king or god. Though this can be interpreted as indicating they are of lesser rank, that is not necessarily the case. Instead these goddesses can be viewed as offering a protective, stabilizing presence; their hands are often raised in praise and embracing various parts of the individual before them. Thus it appears they are lending their energies to the god, the king, or the deceased person rather than assuming a subservient position.

The main emotional engagement in these images above is conveyed by the intense eye contact between the deities. This is an example of what Alison Roberts names the solar gaze (introduced in chapter 3 of this study), an "instrument of divine energy and power that is projected into the world" (*Hathor Rising* 9). The solar gaze directs the viewer's attention from one group of deities to the other and back again.

In addition to the intense gaze, Isis is standing directly behind Osiris and her arms are making the common gesture of presentation or offering (fig. 50). It appears, from Isis's gesture and eye contact, that she is offering Osiris to the goddesses who are standing in front of them: Ma'at and Renpet. Isis is wearing a combination headdress—her hieroglyphic symbol of the throne and vulture headdress.

The vulture headdress is related to the goddess Mut, whose name means "mother" and who also embodies Daughter of Re attributes, and suggests the shared iconography with the rearing cobra that often symbolizes the Two Ladies. During the Middle Kingdom and the New Kingdom, Mut's role evolved to include her roles as chief consort of Amun-Re and mother of Khonsu, their divine son and a moon deity, at Thebes (Pinch, *Handbook* 168–69). Many of the goddesses illustrated in the reliefs in the Temple of Seti I at Abydos are wearing the vulture headdress in addition to their own hieroglyphic symbols and headdresses.

Figure 50. Imentet, Isis, and Osiris. Detail from fig. 48. Photo credit: Richard Mortel, from the flickr photo album: "Temple of Seti I at Abydos." Photographed on 14 January 2016. Original photo has been cropped and the contrast and color altered to enhance details. Creative Commons, some rights reserved. Web. 9 March 2018.

Imentet and Nephthys.

Behind Isis, standing with their arms by their sides and looking straight ahead, are the goddesses Imentet, the Mistress of the Beautiful West, and Nephthys (figs. 45 and 46). Nephthys is the sister of Isis and Osiris, and Mistress of the Sacred Enclosure, as well as the Night Barque. Imentet is wearing the traditional headdress of the goddess of the west, comprising the primordial mound with a falcon perched on it. Allen identifies her headdress as sign R13, the ideogram for "west" (*Middle Egyptian* 493). In this instance the falcon is also wearing the Double Crown of a united Egypt, thus pointing toward the kingship role of the deceased—or to Osiris as Lord of the Underworld.

Naydler points out, in his book *Temple of the Cosmos,* that *amentet* (his preferred spelling) is one of three names used to identify the underworld (215). Wilkinson identifies Imentet as the "personification of the necropolis" that is usually located on the western side of the Nile Valley (*Complete Gods and Goddesses* 145). She is often depicted welcoming the newly deceased and offering them water, akin to Isis (145) or to Hathor and Nut in their Tree of Life manifestation.

Nephthys's headdress is also her hieroglyphic symbol. *Nephthys* is a Greek word; her Egyptian name is a title that can be translated as "the mistress at the head" (Gover).[57] Her hieroglyphic symbol is a combination of sign V30, a basket (*nbt*), and sign O6, the symbol for an enclosure (*ḥwt*); both are from Gardiner's Sign List (Allen 489). A literal translation for her name might be "Mistress [or Lady] of the Sacred Enclosure." Both of these titles suggest much more than the common portrait provided in most books on Egyptian mythology, where her name is translated as "Mistress of the House" and she is

---

[57] The archaeologist Andrea Gover translated the hieroglyphic inscriptions in this scene and submitted her findings in a private communication.

identified as a sort of housekeeper, nursemaid of Horus, illegitimate lover of Osiris, and spouse of her murderous brother Seth. These characterizations of Nephthys were probably first introduced by the ancient Greeks as attempts to create narratives from the oral traditions and sacred texts of the Egyptians.

In contrast, the literature and images of the ancient Egyptians emphasize the crucial roles Nephthys played in the recovery, lamenting, and resurrecting of Osiris; her aspect as the Night Barque, which is the sacred vessel that protects Re and his companions and battles Apophis with fiery breath; and her role as the mirror opposite of Isis, in their dual capacity channeling the flow of energy back and forth and raising into consciousness content from the hidden or unconscious realms. This aligns much more closely with the interpretation of her name as either "the mistress at the head"—a reference to the head of Osiris's corpse—or "Mistress of the Sacred Enclosure," where enclosure is understood to mean the holy of the holies, the innermost shrine-room in the temple or the burial crypt in the tomb. Like Seshet, another goddess with whom she is often equated, Nephthys is named as "First in the House of Life"; as discussed earlier, "House of Life" means "temple." This epithet names them both as serving a crucial role in the temple where the three realms connect—and in its libraries that are the repositories of the wisdom of the ages.

The combination of these three goddesses expands the normal dyad of Isis and Nephthys into a triad. The dyad represents the duality that "pervades Egyptian culture and is at the heart of the Egyptian concept of the universe itself" (Wilkinson, *Complete Gods* 74); the triad is also a familiar grouping, suggesting a family unit or plurality, as in the formula of *3 x 3* that embodies the sacred knowledge inherent in the Ennead. In this case the relationship seems to point toward the unity of cyclic renewal that these particular goddesses embody. The three goddesses are also related to Osiris, as the fourth member, calling to mind the symbolism of four—in particular the creation of the material world, the four cardinal points, the four quarters of heaven and earth, and stability in general (as discussed in chapter 5). The number four also symbolizes totality—as in the totality of the cyclic renewal that includes both the Day World and the Night World in its circuit. All this, it would seem, is what Isis offers to Ma'at, Renpet, and Seti I, who is in the act of calling forth the fourteen names of Osiris.

Figure 51. The goddesses Ma'at and Renpet. A close-up of two of the goddesses in the middle scene on the north wall of the 2nd Hypostyle Hall in the Temple of Seti I, Abydos. Photo credit: kairoinfo4u, from the flickr photo album: "Abydos." Photographed on 24 February 2009. Creative Commons, some rights reserved. Web. 9 March 2018.

Ma'at and Renpet.

Standing in front of and facing Osiris are two beautiful goddesses (fig. 51). The one directly in front of Osiris is Ma'at, with her distinctive headdress, the curled ostrich feather of truth. Her gaze is direct, eye to eye, and her expression is calm, focused, and intense. Her back is straight, and her arms are down at her sides. Her posture and Renpet's suggest they are receiving the offering that Isis's gesture indicates.

Ma'at is the personification of the cosmic pattern, the embodiment of *djet*, or fixed time, perfect ripeness. This is the aspect of time that recreates First Time every day—for it isn't a one-off event that happened in the far distant past. Osiris, Re, and Ma'at are the archetypal forces that engage in a "continuous process of creation and regeneration (*creation continua*), all in the service of the *one* who is called, in the Amduat, the Great *Ba*-soul" (Schweizer 41). Osiris, Isis, Nephthys, Thoth, and all the companions who make the journey with Re, play a part in the regeneration, "the rebirth and renewal of life in the depths of the netherworld" (42). This is the goal of the nightly/daily journey, and each image must be read with this goal kept firmly in mind.

Behind Ma'at in the image above is a goddess who is visually her double but for her garment and headdress. She is wearing the notched palm rib, which denotes the word for "year." This time-based symbol creates an energetic symmetry when paired with the goddess behind Isis, who is also a representation of another form of time—*nehen*, eternal renewal. As introduced in chapter 2, both forms of time are referred to as "eternal," but *djet* is eternal in that it is "fixed and unchanging"; it "remains, endures, and continues" (Schweizer 42).

Fixed is a word that can lead to confusion, because in contemporary language that which is *fixed* is static or "set in stone." This is antithetical to ancient Egyptian theology, which is based on *constantly becoming. Djet* time is related more to the idea of ripeness and to the alchemical term *fixation*. As Lyndy Abraham explains in *A Dictionary of Alchemical Imagery*, fixation is "the converting of spirit into body so that it can endure the fire and not fly away" (78). It reflects the process of coagulation and is one half of the primary transformative process in alchemy—the iteration of dissolving and coagulating the *prima materia* that eventually leads to the creation of the gold, the Philosopher's Stone, known as *solve et coagula* (78). This is an ongoing process of transformation, of continuous becoming, that relies on concentrated focus and the circulation of psychic and physical energies.

This is the very heart of this image, which illustrates that the Osiris mysteries combine the two halves of time, *djet* and *nehen*—Yesterday and Tomorrow, Osiris and Re, or Aker the double lion—to promote the renewal and therefore the flourishing of both the individual and the culture. The one-sidedness of Akhenaten's view of the cosmos created a rupture when he eliminated the gods Amun (the embodiment of the Great *Ba-soul*) and Osiris (the murdered and dismembered god whose re-membering leads to regeneration and renewal) and the goddesses (the necessary vessels that provide protection, attention, and creative energy to empower the unification necessary to create eternally renewing life) from his vision of the divine.

The dismemberment of Osiris, or the nightly death of the solar god, hints at "the dissolution of the old conscious attitude," and "in the midst of the decomposition and dissolution" emerges the little understood ordering principle of the collective unconscious, which Schweizer refers to as the "waterhole" of the sixth hour. Schweizer uses the Twelfth Gate image from *The Book of Gates* to illustrate this insight (fig. 40). At its bedrock, it is the understanding that regeneration begins in the darkest hour.

Nehen has the quality of cyclic renewal; it is "the everlasting and continuous transformation at work in the cosmos, the ongoing process of death and revival in nature" (Schweizer 176). Thus the positioning in fig. 45 seems to suggest that the Ennead, Nephthys, Imentet, Isis, and Osiris (on the left-hand side of the image) are related to the cyclic renewal inherent in the natural order of creation—the rising and falling of all life. They represent life flowing into life, which is Osiris's gift.

On the right-hand side are the two goddesses, Ma'at and Renpet; Seti I; and the holy hieroglyphic inscriptions that give the fourteen names of Osiris, which form a substantial body of text and embody his archetypal energies. The visual cues indicate that Ma'at, Renpet, and Seti are receiving Isis's gesture of offering—the offering of Osiris.

What does this mean? As articulated in chapter 5 (in the Afterlife section), Osiris is the movement toward the renewal of life, while Re is the movement toward death: "Two gods personify the cycle of life and death: Re, who with his living manifestation moves towards death, and Osiris, the dead god, who represents the process of rebirth" (Piankoff vii). This is an alteration in the way most people in our time think about the relationship of life to death and death to life. Here it seems that Osiris holds the primary point in the flow and is present on both sides of the scene, as a deity and as manifested in Seti I's recitation of Osiris's fourteen names.

The hieroglyphic symbol of the palm stem is used in words that originate in the Old Kingdom, such as *renpet*, for "year,"[58] and *ter*, for "time" or "season" (Wilkinson, *Reading Egyptian Art* 119). This symbol also signifies kingship, strengthening the identification of Seti I with Osiris in this temple where the annual rituals of Osiris's mysteries are celebrated.

Translation of the hieroglyphic inscriptions.[59]

Beginning with Osiris and reading toward the left, the hieroglyphic inscriptions read: "Words spoken by Osiris, resident in the House of Life of Men-maat-re. | Words spoken that may give you (Seti I) all health. | Words spoken that may give this each and every happiness [joy]. | Words spoken that may give you eternally all of this food [the offerings]."

Osiris states, "with words spoken," that he is in residence in Seti I's temple, using Seti I's throne name, Menmaatre. The repeated phrase *words spoken* is closely related to the understanding that hieroglyphs are "the writing of the gods"—and a reminder that the literal translation of the Egyptian word for hieroglyphs, *mdw-ntr*, is (according to Gover) "the words of the gods." This implies that reading, speaking, or chanting the symbols is the act of conjuring the archetypal energies inherent in the symbols, the gods' words— that is, the performative power of the ritual relies on this fact.

The hieroglyphic symbols above Isis are: "Words spoken by Isis, giving you life and power." Her gesture of presentation underscores her words. Isis has her left arm just under Osiris's right arm, while her right arm is raised. This is the symbol for presenting,

---

[58] Sign M4 in Gardiner's Sign List of hieroglyphic symbols.
[59] The following translations are provided by Andrea Gover in a private communication.

or making an offering. The "you" is likely the same one as Osiris named—those in front of her, to which she is directing her solar gaze: Ma'at, Renpet, and Seti I.

Imentet is the next goddess, and her hieroglyphic inscription reads: "Words spoken by Imentet. | Words spoken that may protect with all of the protection every day." Nephthys' inscription reads: "Words spoken by Nephthys, resident in the House of Life of Men-maat-re. | Words spoken that may give to you all health. | Words spoken that may give to you all life and all power."

Back at the center, a line of text between Osiris and Ma'at is oriented in the same direction as Ma'at and Renpet's hieroglyphic inscriptions. The caption for the scene reads: "Divine ones of the priesthood of Nekhen with the goddesses of time." Nekhen is the sacred city in Upper Egypt that is often represented by the jackal-headed companions of Re. The nine deities who compose the Ennead on the far left side of the image are probably the "divine ones of the priesthood of Nekhen." And of course, "goddesses of time" refers to the five goddesses who represent both *nehen* and *djet* time—the two poles of the image that pass the flow of reciprocal energy back and forth.

The hieroglyphic inscriptions in front of Ma'at read: "Ma'at, Daughter of Re, Mistress of the Sky, giving all life, stability, and power." These epithets accentuate Ma'at's cosmic dimensions and her relationship to royalty as well as her fellow deities. To Seti I, too, she bequeaths life, stability, and power.

The inscriptions in front of Renpet are: "Words spoken by Renpet, Mistress of Eternity. | Your daughter Renpet and Men-maat-re are joined for million and millions forever, forever." As if to emphasize the idea of the "joining" of Renpet and Seti, her notched palm stem headdress actually embraces the cartouche of Seti's throne name,

Meenmaatre, with a tender, intimate movement suggesting the vow of an eternal sacred marriage, forever, forever.

It seems that the presentation of Osiris, like the Presentation of Ma'at, bestows generous gifts: eternal life, health, power, stability, protection, and joy, and a share in all offerings to sustain Seti I in eternity, forever, forever. With his incense and offerings, his commitment to upholding Ma'at's ordering, harmonizing, balancing, Seti I activates the many attributes of Osiris as he chants aloud the names to celebrate this bounty of mutual love and respect, carved into stone and lasting forever, forever, millions and millions of years. This scene is an actualization of the "umbilical point through which the energies of eternity break into time" (Campbell 41).

Additional symbols: throne, *sema*, and plinth.

The shape of the throne (fig. 52) is similar to the hieroglyphic symbol in Nephthys's name—*hwt*,[60] for "sacred enclosure," which comprises a large upright rectangle with a smaller square in the lower corner. Gardiner describes this glyph as the "plan of a rectangular enclosure" and the ideogram for "temple, tomb, enclosure." ("Gardiner's Sign List"). In other words, the symbolism behind the throne's physical form is an enclosed sacred precinct, a temenos, with its holy-of-holies shrine room. Temple and tomb architecture locates that which is most precious and sacred in the holy of holies, the inner sanctum—the shrine that contains the sacred Solar Barque protecting the image of the god or goddess within. In this image, the smaller square—the holy of holies—contains *sema,* the hieroglyphic symbol meaning "union" or "unity."

---

[60] Sign O6 in Gardiner's Sign List.

Figure 52. Close-up of the throne of Osiris and the plinth. Detail from fig. 48. The image features both the *sema* symbol and the plinth filled with the *nebet*, *ankh*, and *was* symbols. Photo credit: kairoinfo4u, from the flickr photo album: "Abydos." Photographed on 24 February 2009. Creative Commons, some rights reserved. Web. 9 March 2018.

Sema, one of the keystone symbols of ancient Egypt, is the embodiment of Ma'at's natural order and cosmic patterns (see the introduction to this term in chapter 3). It is an image of the all-important uniting of Upper and Lower Egypt, both a historical fact and an ever-present reality that must be the focus and prime responsibility of the king (who sits on the throne, the lap of the Great Mother, Isis) and his administrators. This same throne design is found in early examples such as the throne of King Khefren from the 4th Dynasty. It is also the symbol of uniting all opposites—inner and outer, above and below, conscious and unconscious—and of filling and balancing the holy of the holies, the heart center with the rebirthing energies of love that feed the flourishing of life.

Figure 53. Sema—*the "unity" symbol on Osiris's throne.* Photo credit: Richard Mortel, from the flickr photo album: "Temple of Seti I at Abydos." Photographed on 14 January 2016. Original photo has been cropped. Creative Commons, some rights reserved. Web. 9 March 2018.

The plinth (fig. 54) is probably the oldest hieroglyphic symbol for Ma'at. Symbolic of the earth and the foundation of Egypt, it bestows stability to those who sit on the throne. Ma'at's plinth represents a firm foundation, supporting the throne of the king—the base on which Egyptian society was built (Pinch, *Egyptian Mythology* 159). The plinth is also believed to symbolize the primordial mound that rose with First Time.

Figure 54. Close-up of the plinth. Detail from fig. 48. Image features the plinth filled with the *nebet*, *ankh*, and *was* symbols. Photo credit: kairoinfo4u, from the flickr photo album: "Abydos." Photographed on 24 February 2009. Creative Commons, some rights reserved. Web. 9 March 2018.

Osiris's feet are firmly placed upon the foundational plinth—grounded in Ma'at—and he is seated on the lap of the divine Mother, emblematic of his sister and wife-partner Isis. The heart's wisdom and cosmic order are fully embodied. Here the plinth is filled with fifteen baskets (with *nb* or *nbt*[61] as the hieroglyphic symbol), each displaying an *ankh* and two *was* scepters facing it on either side. The *was* scepters are doubled, emphasizing "dominion" and "divine power." With the plinth indicating foundation, the primordial mound, and straightness as opposed to crookedness; the *nb* basket meaning "all" and/or "lord" (or *nbt*, "lady"); the *ankh* as the breath of life; and the *was* scepters denoting divine power and dominion—together the plinth's symbols can be read as a declaration of authority and perhaps an epithet: *The Divine Power of the Lord of Life Is Founded Upon the Cosmic Order of Ma'at, originating from the Lap of the Great Mother, the Source of Life.*

A Story of Renewal

Uniting the individual symbolic elements of the images in the Temple at Abydos and our historical insights into the reign of Seti I tells a story that highlights the restoration of ancient Egyptian traditions during Seti I's reign. It might be told something like this:

> *Osiris sits on the sacred lap of Isis, the divine throne. She offers Osiris to double Ma'at—Ma'at and Renpet—representing the eternal perfection of time and its annual renewal, and to Seti I, Menmaatre, the Horus-king who will become Osiris. Ma'at and Renpet, combined with Osiris, Isis, Imentet, and Nephthys, establish the "breathing hole" where the energies of eternity break*

---

[61] The "t" ending is added to indicate the feminine form.

into time. Outside of the shrine, Seti I offers incense and the blooming lotus—purification and eternal renewal. Seti I is Menmaatre, joining with Renpet, the perfection of the eternal cycles, for millions and millions, forever, forever.

Offerings are gifted to Seti I by each of the deities and witnessed by the Ennead, which represents all the many deities, confirming and nourishing Seti I with the breath of life, providing him with the food and drink so his eternal life flourishes. Double dominion and divine power are granted to him, now and for all eternity. His focus is clear, his heart is true, his devotion recognized. He sees Ma'at, does Ma'at, upholds Ma'at—for Ma'at is great. She is the Mistress of the Sky, the Daughter of Re. She is the seed and the fulfillment of the king's duty. In his responsibility as the living Horus king, he embodies his duties and serves the divine to uphold and rebalance the sacred order that is Ma'at.

As the deceased king, Seti-Meenmaatre will become one with Renpet, becoming Re-Osiris—majestic, the eternal light, and illumination of renewal. His heart's knowing, his intuition, and his wisdom are in alignment with Ma'at's natural order. His feet are firmly planted on the foundation of Ma'at's eternal cosmic pattern, harmonizing and balancing all life. He dedicates his work to unifying Upper and Lower Egypt, as it was in the First Time, is now, and ever shall be.

This reverie calls to mind an ancient hymn of praise to Re, introduced in chapter 4 ("O Re, Lord of Ma'at!"), for here in Seti I's Temple at Abydos, Osiris is in his full expression as the Lord of Life forever united with Re, the Lord of Light. At this temple the mysteries of renewal and transformation and how humans participate in the regeneration of the gods are celebrated in their fullest expression each year. May the pilgrimage, processions, rituals, feasting, and days of celebrating these mysteries never end. Here, Re and Osiris are joined forever in the renewal of all life.

Chapter Summary

After a brief but devastating break from tradition, the first rulers of the 19th Dynasty strove to recapture and reconstruct the temples and cults of their forefathers, and to restore stability and balance to ancient Egypt. The king Seti I came to the throne guided by a return to the old ways, including the renewal of order through relationships and rituals founded on Ma'at's principals of harmony, justice, and truth. He oversaw the rebuilding of destroyed temples up and down the Nile so they would once again mirror the cosmic order and thus the gods themselves.

Comparative studies are basically an art form, however much they are based on factual information. By interacting with the images and symbols, we open up to a creative process in figuring out how the details go together. This process is as important to the arts and humanities as laying the foundation of knowledge is to the sciences—a movement toward a new way of combining the elements to determine new meaning. This is the approach taken here to glean new understanding from the images at Abydos.

Seti I established a Temple at Abydos to honor Osiris in his full expression as the Lord of Life, joined by the gods and goddesses that Akhenaten had attempted to expunge.

With this temple of offerings, Seti I—in his capacity as representative of humankind—ensured that Ma'at was honored properly and that the mysteries of the divine realm and the cyclic processes of life and death were celebrated. Facing disruption and disharmony—a disconnect between the above and the below—he restored the principles of order and balance.

In the mysteries of renewal recorded in the *Books of What's in the Underworld*, Seth and Isis work in partnership from the bow of the Night Barque during the seventh hour of the night, when the threat of standstill is the greatest. Alert and engaged, together they protect Re and his companions from Apophis—and thus overcome the primal urge toward lethargy and unconsciousness, and instead promote regeneration and renewal. The divine, human, and ancestral realms participate in and benefit from the ongoing, repetitive, performative actions required to ensure this renewal and avert the diminishment and devastation of life—the opposite of Ma'at's cosmic order and creative potential.

Seti I demonstrates what is possible when one has undertaken the difficult psychological work of harmonizing the opposites within. His birth name, Seti, translates as "Man of Seth," to which he added Merenptah, "Beloved of Ptah," indicating that he is devoted to Ptah, the creator god of Memphis who brings forth creation with his heart and tongue. Seti I's throne name identifies him as Menmaatre—he is devoted to Ma'at and a model for channeling Seth's instinctual energies into creative, life-supporting endeavors. His inherent leadership skills go toward the purpose of creating, rather than causing chaos and harm to fulfill self-serving appetites and greed. In other words, his Sethian powers uphold Ma'at, serve Re-Osiris, and perpetuate the conditions necessary for life to flourish in all three realms. He is able to bring his creative energies into alignment with his desire to be of service to the ancestors, to the gods and goddesses, and to Egypt herself.

Chapter 7. Navigating Transformation: The *Hymn to Ma'at*

Ma-a-t means course of life, the order of indestructible life,

resurrection and return in the world of nature and of man. Her

natural component reveals itself in the regular course of things.

The eternal life of the sun god is the order of Ma-a-t. But her

activity was mostly perceived in the life of the earth, which

underneath all changes is eternal. (Kristensen 59)

What is needed by a culture struggling to endure through hardships that seem

implacable? Ma'at, as indestructible life, would naturally be a source of comfort and a

reminder that conflicts are opportunities to seek balance. She is the reminder of what is

truly important: harmonizing the world's opposites in order to promote the circulation of

energy required to maintain life. Polarization and standstill are abhorrent and only serve

to birth further loss and destruction. Faith in the indestructibility of life—in Ma'at—

would certainly provide a touchstone for these ancient people.

Hymn of Heart, Hope, and Harmony

When the Persians conquered Egypt late in its history—during the 27th Dynasty

(*c.* 521–486 BCE), in the Late Period—a work now known as the *Hymn to Ma'at* was

composed and inscribed on the wall of the Temple of Amun at el-Hibis to commemorate

the crowning of a foreign ruler.[62] Clearly this defeat would have been humiliating for the

ancient Egyptians. Yet in this difficult historical moment, this hymn gave voice to their

profound hope that the new Persian king, Darius I, would embrace Ma'at.

---

[62] The Temple of Amun at el-Hibis was rebuilt by the incoming Persian ruler, Darius I (*c.* 550–486 BCE). Evidence indicates an older temple was on this site that dated to the New Kingdom.

Figure 55. Relief depicting Ma'at. In the collection of the Museo Archeologico Nazionale, Firenze, Italia. New Kingdom. Photo credit: Laurie Larsen. Used with permission of copyright holder.

The hymn makes clear an important distinction: the ancient Egyptians recognized the heart, not the head or brain, as the seat of intelligence. Several Egyptian deities are identified as creator gods who use both heart and tongue to bring forth all creation, signifying the alignment of the heart with the power of the spoken word. In fact many ancient cultures believed the heart to be both the source of emotions and the center of divine intellect, or intuition. As revealed in chapter 3, the heart was the only organ left in the body during mummification, and a carved scarab amulet was placed over it to ensure its safety. Later, the Greeks named this center of intelligence *nous* and claimed it is "independent of body and thus immune from destruction" (Uždavinys, *Philosophy as a Rite* 312). The Greek philosopher Plato "distinguished *nous* from *dianoia*—discursive reason," which is what contemporary culture considers "intellect," knowledge, and "intelligence" (312). To the ancients, including Plato, discursive reasoning was a lower form of intelligence than direct apprehension, or *nous*.

The hymn also illustrates that Ma'at represents the pragmatic recognition of the ebb and flow of life, and that it is vital to master putting oneself into harmony and balance with the eternal forces of transformation. Ma'at's wisdom helped Egyptians become proficient in this endeavor.

Speaking Creation with the Lords of Ma'at

There are at least six main cosmologies[63] in ancient Egyptian mythology. Although they share common elements, each variant has its own organization around a particular creator god. In the first two lines of the hymn, Ma'at is identified with four of the six known cosmologies, and the first stanza alone delineates Ma'at's relationship to three of the creator gods: Re, Ptah, and Thoth.

Praise to you, Ma'at, daughter of Rē, consort of god, who Ptah

loves | The one who adorns the breast of Thoth, who fashioned her

---

[63] The study of the other cosmologies has been taken up by scholars of Egyptian religion and culture. See Alison Roberts, Jeremy Naydler, R. T. Rundle Clark, Geraldine Pinch, whose books are listed in the Works Cited section.

own nature, foremost of the Souls of Heliopolis; | Who pacified the

two falcon gods through her good will, | filled the Per-wer shrine

with life and dominion. (Foster 122)

Initially, Ma'at is named "daughter of Rē," the solar god whom Ma'at

accompanies both day and night on his essential journey, either guiding his Solar Barque

or standing behind him protectively. Throughout the history of Egypt, Re is the kingly

archetypal principle who embodies, among other things, the solar consciousness that

submits to the daily cycle of life, death, and rebirth. One of the most important functions

Re fulfills is uniting with Osiris in the sixth hour, midway through his underworld

journey. Through this mysterious union both Re and Osiris are regenerated and, in turn,

both the Night World and the Day World are renewed as well. The solar god is never

alone—day or night—as the success of his journey relies on his companions' diligent

attention and protection. They too are renewed in this effort when the Solar Barque

emerges reborn, resurrected from the Netherworld.

Ma'at is also named as "consort of god, who Ptah loves." Ptah, whose attestation

from the 1st Dynasty onward indicates an origin in prehistoric periods (Wilkinson,

Complete Gods 123), is the artisan creator god of the Memphite cosmology. He functions

as a divine masculine figure who creates with his "heart and tongue," bringing all

creation into being with the spoken word that originates in his conscious, awakened heart.

Ptah is commonly known as a "Lord of Ma'at."

Figure 56. Lord of Ma'at. Bust of high-ranking official. Late Period, 26th Dynasty (664–525 BCE). The detail on the right shows a close-up of Ma'at, both wearing and holding her feather of truth—double Ma'at. This artwork is in the Museo Egizio, Torino, Italia (C. 3075). Photography: Nicola Dell'Aquila, courtesy of the Museo Egizio, Torino, Italia. Copyright 2015. Copyright holder: Museo Egizio. Reprinted with permission granted by copyright holder.

The next line identifies Ma'at as the "one who adorns the breast of Thoth." Thoth (or Djehuty) was also a Lord of Ma'at, as well as a moon god (a role that probably dates back to a time before the ascendency of the solar aspects in Egyptian spiritual beliefs). He is the creator in the Hermopolitan cosmology, named so for his cult center at Hermopolis. He is also named as a high priest of Ma'at—one of the impartial judges who were commonly referred to as Lords of Ma'at (fig. 56). These priests wore a chain of gold with a golden Ma'at figure to symbolize that they kept Ma'at foremost in their heart, their awakened consciousness. In other words, Ma'at is the source of the "heart's wisdom" for each priest of Ma'at. Her emblem "adorns" each priest's breast (and thus Thoth's) and identifies him as a just and fair judge. As the "tongue of the gods," the high priest Thoth is the vizier to Re, noted for his eloquent and thoughtful speech on behalf of the *neters*. He is referenced as the consort of Ma'at, and Budge even saw Ma'at as the feminine half of Thoth, so closely related are their functions.

After enumerating Ma'at's intimate relationship with the three creator gods, the hymn declares that Ma'at is "foremost of the Souls of Heliopolis" and that she "fashioned her own nature"—a potent line that suggests she is a self-creator or co-creator. Deepening into the exploration of this idea, we can connect Ma'at's "nature" as the cosmic pattern of Order, where she is the form and personification of Order—and she is named as the daughter of Atum, or "Order," in the *Coffin Texts,* Spell 330. This sacred text (discussed in chapter 4) relates the Heliopolitan creation myth.

Ma'at's role in creation is substantiated by the fact that Ma'at's order is related to *djet* time, the eternal, unchanging, perfection of creation in that First Occasion. This is further underscored by the line of the hymn that names her as "foremost of the Souls of Heliopolis." It references Ma'at's place in the Heliopolitan cosmology and her relationship to Atum—yet another creator deity.

Over time Re became the name most often employed when identifying the solar or sun god. As is true of many of Egypt's deities, Re has multiple aspects. At dawn he might be thought of as Khepri the scarab beetle—or of Nefertem, the divine child who is born when the first lotus emerges from the primal waters of Nun and blossoms with the first light. In the evening as the sun sets, he is known as Atum, the old man walking with a cane. In the underworld journey to renewal, he may become Amun, the ram-headed god whose name means "hidden."

Schweizer states that together Re and Ma'at "created the world in the infinitely remote past, or what Egyptians called the First Occasion" (37). Re and Ma'at's relationship calls to mind other mythologies that might have been influenced by this example. For instance, in Jewish mysticism and Hermeticism,[64] the Feminine—Shekhinah and Sophia, respectively—was identified as a joyous daughter for whom creation was play (to the delight of her father, the creator god). Ma'at, too, shared this distinction, as Hornung points out: "Not only did she descend to earth at the time of creation, she is also the favorite child of the creator, and she remains near him and continually entertains him" (*Idea Into Image* 134).

Transforming Chaos into Order and Unity

As delineated throughout this study, Ma'at is not only order but also the embodiment of a number of other primary characteristics—natural laws, justice, straightness, harmony, balance. In total, Ma'at's individual aspects add up to her role of transforming chaos, the undifferentiated inertia and blackness of the Nun, into harmonious, interconnected systems of creation. Ma'at is equated with the net as symbolic of the cosmos, where the interstices between the interconnecting cords of time

---

[64] It is well attested that early Greek, Hebrew, and Christian forebears lived in Egypt, at least for a time, and studied with the Egyptian priests and sages, therefore influencing the evolution of Greek philosophy and monotheistic religions. See Robert Strassler, editor, *The Landmark Herodotus: The Histories*; Karl Luckert, *Egyptian Light and Hebrew Fire: Theological and Philosophical Roots of Christendom in Evolutionary Perspective*; Garth Fowden, *The Egyptian Hermes: A Historical Approach to the Late Pagan Mind*; Jeremy Naydler, *The Future of the Ancient World: Essays on the History of Consciousness*.

and space are the "breathing hole"—where the renewing wind of eternity enters the stream of time and space (Schweizer 178–81).

As the organizing principle of the Egyptian culture, Ma'at's natural order can be either adhered to or disrupted by the actions of the people—in all their thoughts, words, and deeds, their saying and doing. As this study has established, Ma'at was the underlying pattern of the social structure, and long before the inscription of the *Hymn to Ma'at* it was assumed that the well-educated individual would do his or her part in propagating and perpetuating Ma'at's natural order and cosmic laws. The Egyptians' pragmatic thoughts on these matters were shaped by their astute observations of what did and did not promote social cohesion and the flourishing of life. Their spiritual feelings, reflected in their cosmologies, rituals, and practices, joined with their pragmatism to create codes of behavior that functioned to sustain and renew social interactions.

Herein is the unity outlined in the myth *The Contendings of Horus and Seth* (explored at length in chapter 4), referenced in the line that identifies Ma'at as she "who pacified the two falcon gods through her good will." The "two falcon gods" refers to Horus and Seth, and this description names the time when their battles over who would inherit the throne of the murdered Osiris threatened to destroy creation. The solution to their disagreement provides an example of *sema* (unity) and Ma'at's laws in action. *Sema* is upheld through good will and a commitment to Ma'at's ethical balance and harmony, rather than just through strength of arms.

Being a skilled strategist and a powerful warrior was definitely expected and praised in the king and his army. Yet Ma'at's laws, both cosmogonic and natural, are upheld because they promote the flourishing of life, not because one king has more might and a better army than the other—at least when addressing the balance of power within Egypt. Her laws are based on what works to perpetuate life's flourishing, which means all life (at least all Egyptian life) is in harmonious balance.

Sema is the image of unity that amply illustrates this. It is not a one-sided solution or a win-lose situation. It involves uniting in the common interest of the whole, and its achievement bestows the breath of life; it makes life possible. As *sema* illustrates with the image of a double Hapy (the god of inundation and the fecundity it brings), unity of opposites restores and renews.

As discussed in chapter 4, several genres of ancient Egyptian literature developed to express and give explicit details of this ideal of *sema* and other principles of Ma'at. During the second half of the New Kingdom (*c.* 1550–1069 BCE, including the reign of Seti I, explored in chapter 6), it was generally recognized that both the intellectual and the emotional energies of each person who hoped for eternal life must be focused on upholding *sema* with their thought, words, and deeds. The literature made clear the ethical expectations for attaining a favorable judgment during the Weighing of the Heart in the afterlife. Both the enjoyment of life and the hard work and psychological effort of aligning oneself with Ma'at and her natural order were critical in order for *sema* to flourish. This was the unity of heart and mind, inner and outer, above and below, and it required the daily practice of reciprocity with the divine and ancestral realm. It also included spending time reflecting on and preparing for your death—creating the life that would ensure a favorable outcome when one's heart was weighed against Ma'at or her feather.

Another image that illustrates Ma'at's cosmic order is Aker, the double lion who guards the two gates of the horizon, who "watches over renewal and the mystery of regeneration" (Schweizer 111). As guardian of the east and the west, the double lion demonstrates the necessity for the harmonious blending of life and death, of sunrise and sunset. Aker speaks to both sides of any pair and to the circulation of life force, of energy, that guarantees this continuity. Ma'at resides in the midpoint of that lemniscate of flowing energy. She is the right proportion, the right measure; her balance is reflected in the image of her scales that weigh the heart in the Hall of Double Ma'at.

Harmonizing with Ma'at's order and balance is also served in the acknowledgment that momentous transformation takes place in the darkest hour. The greatest danger in the transformation process comes as the newly emerging renewal begins to ascend, to be embraced by the dawn's light. It is then that the giant serpent of the depths, Apophis—who would unmake all consciousness and creation, and keep the solar god and his many companions in the black and inert waters of the Nun—rises up and must be attended to. It is at this moment that one's companions in the barque, one's resources and consciousness, must be most alert.

The hymn goes on to claim Ma'at is the one "who filled the Per-wer shrine with life and dominion." Ma'at's "dominion" extends from Upper Egypt in the south (where Luxor and the Valley of the Kings are located) to Lower Egypt in the north, where Heliopolis and Memphis are located. The "Per-wer [Great House] shrine" belongs to the tutelary Nekhbet, the vulture goddess, one of the Two Ladies who are the premier symbol for the unification of Upper and Lower Egypt (fig. 57). Wadjet, the cobra goddess of Lower Egypt—whose shrine is called Per-nu or Perneser (*pr nsr*), or "House of Flame"—

is the other. As described in chapter 3, they too symbolize *sema*: the personification of the two crowns of Egypt, both Red and White—Ma'at's ordering, balancing, and harmonizing through the highest authority and consciousness of the crown chakra. The symbol of their unity is central to the ancient Egyptian cosmogonic structure that permeates all life.

Figure 57. Relief of the "Two Ladies" on a pillar in the courtyard of the Temple of Kom Ombo. The tutelary goddesses of Upper and Lower Egypt are standing back-to-back on their *nebet* baskets. On the left is *Wadjet*, wearing the Red Crown. She is the cobra goddess who embodies Lower Egypt. On the right is *Nekhbet*, the vulture goddess who embodies Upper Egypt. Both have their wings embracing a *khu* fan and a *shen* symbol, meaning "infinity." Photo credit: Olaf Tausch. Photographed on 11 March 2011. Creative Commons, some rights reserved. Web. 29 March 2018.

Nourishing and Guiding Humanity

It was believed that the king's relationship to Ma'at greatly influenced his ability to mediate and maintained the necessary reciprocal relationships with the gods and goddesses, as discussed in chapter 4. This is how the social structures and the natural order were upheld, and this was the king's number one responsibility. The hymn continues with a reference to the Presentation of Ma'at ritual with the statement about "daily offerings for those who are on duty":

> Skilled one who brought forth the gods from herself | and brought
>
> low the heads of the enemies; | Who herself provides for the House
>
> of the All-Lord, | brings daily offerings for those who are on duty. |
>
> Magnificent her throne before the judges—and she consumes the
>
> enemies of Atum. (Foster 122–23)

This stanza juxtaposes Ma'at as the "skilled" one—provider, nourisher, creatrix bringing forth "gods from herself"—with the word-image of her as the warrioress bringing "low the heads of the enemies." Those falcon-headed Neolithic goddesses with their arms raised and ample bodies tall and strong are calling to imagination, acknowledged as the source of life, the provider.

The majesty of Ma'at is clear in the last line of the stanza, where once again juxtaposition is used to weave the both/and image of her "[m]agnificent . . . throne" indicating justice and her vengeful hunger as she "consumes the enemies of Atum." "[T]hose who are on duty" are the faithful companions who are necessary to the successful execution of state and religious duties. The Lords of Ma'at, the priests and priestesses—indeed, all who contribute, who take their duty seriously and attend to seeing Ma'at's justice, order, harmony, and balance upheld—will be nourished by her beneficence.

The next stanza makes this clear:

> She is just, and there is no injustice in the Son of Rē, who lives
>
> forever. | She comingling with Thoth—his body is filled, through
>
> her, with mankind | which he offers to Amen-Rê, Ptah, and Amun
>
> of Hibis. | And the Great Ennead is powerful | in the House of the
>
> Prince in Heliopolis. (Foster 122–23)

What does this enigmatic statement mean? The first line gives a hint, as it points to Ma'at's justice. It equates the justice of the Persian king Darius ("the Son of Rē") with her own justice, reassuring the people of Egypt that he will uphold Ma'at's just nature, recognizing it (despite his foreignness) as the sacred duty of the Egyptian king.

Thoth is identified as the consort of Ma'at, who fills his body "with mankind." In other words, Thoth, the awakened heart and silver tongue of all the gods—and himself a creator—is the vessel for humanity, which he brings forth to three gods: Amen-Re, Ptah, and Amun of Hibis. Most likely these represent a trinity important to this specific sacred site.

Thoth (as we learned earlier in this chapter) is the impartial judge, the Lord of Ma'at, who is beyond all greed and self-interest. His capacity in this regard is as a model of excellence that exists to inspire and guide the humans in the implementation of Ma'at's precepts. As the vizier he is the gold standard, and in him humanity is meant to find its own path to excellence. Therefore, Ma'at herself—at one ("comingling") with Thoth—has filled his body with the doing and saying that humans can call upon in fulfilling their responsibilities to the divine and ancestral realms. This is what ensures the human realm will flourish. Anything less will reap discord and the negative consequences of violating Ma'at's precepts.

> Rise splendidly, O Rê, | how beautiful you are because of Ma'at! |
>
> As Ma'at shines splendid from the heart of Rê, | so are you
>
> splendid, O King, Son of Rê, who lives forever; | You too are
>
> beautiful because of Ma'at | see her who comes to the Son of Rê,
>
> who lives forever! (Foster 122–23)

Beauty, beauty, beauty—to make the heart sing, to awaken the joy and love of life, to experience the desire to promote what is good! Here, the "Son of Rê" (Darius, the king) carries on his shoulders a dual weight. To be the embodiment of Ma'at's beauty requires that he set aside self-interest so he can shine forth Ma'at, from the very "heart of Re." Ma'at is a resident in Re's heart center; he is awakened and enlivened by her presence there. In turn, Re too resides in Ma'at's heart center, shining forth in splendor.

A Plea to Ma'at

> O Ma'at, build your throne in the head, in the mouth, | of the King,
>
> Son of Rê, who lives forever! | May you make heaven and earth
>
> rejoice in Rê his father | from whom I, the King, have come forth.
>
> May you rise splendid from him on this beautiful day | in this your
>
> divine Name of Khayt—She who appears in beauty | And may
>
> your beautiful face give peace | to this good god, lord of the Two
>
> Lands, Darius, | Son of the Sun and living forever. (Foster 122–23)

In the closing verse of the *Hymn to Ma'at*, she is addressed directly as her subjects implore her to intervene for them with the foreign king (Foster 123). They ask Ma'at to influence ("build your throne") all his saying and doing ("in the head, in the mouth | of the King"). This line could also be read as follows: "O Ma'at, build your throne in the heart and on the tongue of Darius." The people are pleading with Ma'at to help the king align himself with her patterns and natural order.

In the next line Darius becomes the speaker, indicating his relationship to Re, his kingly father ("from whom I, the King, have come forth"), and thus (following through the familial lines) Ma'at, his sister by implication. Darius confirms Ma'at's authority, asking her to use her influence to "make heaven and earth rejoice."

The fourth line gives Ma'at a new sobriquet, a "divine Name"—Khayt—and calls forth the rising sun "on this beautiful day" along with the renewal and triumph that hour of the day intimates. But instead of the renewed and youthful Re-Harakhty, Nefertem, or Khepri being named as this dawning orb, it is Ma'at who is rising splendidly—Ma'at "who appears in beauty."

Figure 58. On a lintel in the descending passage into the Tomb of Nefertari. Photo credit: kairoinfo4u, from the flickr album "Tomb of Nefertari." Photographed on 19 March 2017. Original photo has been cropped. Creative Commons, some rights reserved. Web. 9 March 2018.

An important hymn to the rising sun also comes from the Temple of Amun at el-Hibis as well as from papyri of the 21st and 22nd dynasties. It has a similar structure and uses a similar name to identify Re as the rising sun. Assmann states that this earlier hymn offers an example of both a "liturgical text" and "a ritual style"—a reminder that it was chanted aloud in a temple space where the voices and accompanying instruments would add depth and power to the words being intoned (*Solar* 15).

In the earlier solar hymn, "Maat has appeared on your forehead"—undoubtedly as the *uraeus*. Remember, she is the most powerful one, so named by Atum in the Nun as creation was under way. In this solar hymn, Re is summoned by a name that recalls the *Hymn to Ma'at* title "Khaty"—in the line "Rise, Re | Shine as Akhty | Dark one with radiant face" (Assmann, *Egyptian Solar Religion* 15). In this verse, Re is the embodiment of Amun-Re Harakhty; Amun the ram-headed god of Thebes, who is best known as the Hidden One, is combined here with Re-Harakhty, the ancient solar falcon, Bull of His Mother.

These fluid combinations of widely varying aspects and deities, as well as the vast span of time they embrace (thousands of years), are a further testament to the ancient Egyptian holoscopic perspective. Tracing the lines, attempting to identify all the intersections and relationships, illustrates how the nimble, collective imagination of these people could wind together threads of numerous metaphorical trails to weave bright images speaking in poetic innuendos. Underneath it all resonates the oneness of the divine; the kaleidoscopic pieces are the jeweled radiance that celebrates a mystery so grand, it can only be pointed to and drawn with beauty, elegant words, and awe.

While the *Hymn to Ma'at* commends Ma'at to Darius and acknowledges many times over that he is now the legitimate king, the "Son of Re," it also proclaims that Ma'at is a powerful force to be reconciled with. The speaker addresses Ma'at directly, asking her to intervene and to influence this foreign conqueror with her wisdom. The hymn ends with their heartfelt desire: "may your beautiful face give peace" (Foster 122–23). This hymn of praise outlines how the ancient Egyptians experienced Ma'at. It reveals her relationships to the other gods and to the king, as well as the fervent hopes of the people. Its verses poignantly show that even at this late stage in their history—with just several centuries remaining until the Roman conquest—the Egyptians viewed Ma'at as the keystone of their civilization and as essential to the continued existence of their culture with its shared beliefs and values.

Chapter Summary

Darius I repaired the Temple of Amun at el-Hibis during his reign. Is it possible that he oversaw the inscription of the *Hymn to Ma'at*? Was he proclaiming his acknowledgment of Ma'at and assuring those who would read the inscription that he adhered to Ma'at and all she embodied?

As articulated throughout this study, the deities are one; their unique qualities come forth as differentiations that enable humans to know them and build relationship with them. The ancient Egyptians have left us mountains of evidence of their mastery in building their relationships with the divine—praise, joy, beauty, and an awakened heart are necessary for this journey, which then informs all our saying and doing. There is a map of consciousness available in their treasure trove of art and literature.

This hymn makes clear that Ma'at moves to dissolve the obstructions, rather than destroy or enforce a single-sided solution that brooks no cooperation. Her way is the middle way, the pragmatic recognition that life naturally ebbs and flows; mastering the actions of putting oneself into harmony and balance with those ebbs and flows is essential. Ma'at and her wise precepts help us become proficient in this.

The image below (fig. 59) combines hieroglyphic symbols to create Ma'at's scale, and reference her balancing and harmonizing. The base and central pillar are comprised of the *shen* as "infinity"; the *was* scepters as "power"; Khepri, symbolizing "eternally becoming"; and the Two Ladies as the rearing cobras encircling the solar disc say "unity." The beam is a combination of the *ankhs* as "life" and the *was* scepters as "power," supporting the *heb-sed,* or "jubilee pavilion," symbol. These form the pans of the scale, which appear to contain a stepped pyramid representing the primordial mound on the left and a temple or shrine on the right. All together the symbols create a core metaphor of Ma'at's truth as harmonized and balanced justice, eternally renewing all life. As a text this image can be read as follows: *The power of life is eternally renewing, harmonizing and balancing; this circulation of cosmic energy births regeneration.*

This *Hymn to Ma'at* is a beautiful example of the ancient Egyptians' multiple cosmologies and reveals the fluid interweaving of their multiple perspectives, their

Figure 59. Detail of the Full Moon scene in the Astronomical Ceiling in Hathor's Temple at Dendera (fig. 10). Photo credit: kairinfo4u, from the flickr photo album: "Dendera Temple." Photographed on 14 January 2016. Original photo has been cropped. Creative Commons, some rights reserved. Web. 9 March 2018.

holoscopic viewpoint. Each deity adds depth and breadth to the articulation of the sacred and its influences on the human realm. The hymn offers a rich framework elaborating Ma'at's multifaceted influence as the goddess who unites, harmonizes, and balances the sacred order. She is the coherent pattern that organizes all life. The *Hymn to Ma'at* recognizes her as a divine Feminine co-creator, an active participant in the manifestation of the world, and a dynamic cosmological pattern that orders and harmonizes all life.

This hymn speaks volumes to the ancient participatory way of knowing inherent in these sacred verses. It awakens a knowing, a remembering, in the heart. To celebrate daily and sing the praises of that which is held most dear—truth, justice, harmony, balance, joy, beauty—awakens that knowing, activates it, and brings it into being.

This knowing heart slumbers restlessly until the human realm reaches across the chasm created by our own profane way of knowing. Our way of knowing and being, our doing and our saying, has desacralized nature . . . has stripped the gods and goddesses of their gleaming robes . . . has laid bare and raw the earth herself. When awoken, this divine presence responds—immediately. The ancient Egyptians wrote of this knowing in stone so it would be eternal, a gift for all humanity.

Assmann's scholarship makes available the beauty extracted from two hymns that are bookends to the journey at the horizon, sunset and sunrise:

Sunset

Hail to you, master of endless repetition

Atum great one of endless duration

You have come in peace

You have reached land and joined the arms of Manu

Your Majesty has received venerableness

Moored at your place of yesterday

The arms of your mother protect you

Sunrise

Hail to you, who rises in the Primeval Waters

Who illuminates the Two Lands after his going forth

The assembled Ennead praise you

The Two Ladies . . . nurture you

Beautiful youth of love,

At whose rising people live

At whose sight the Ennead rejoices

(*Egyptian Solar Religion* 14)

Chapter 8. Conclusion: Finding Renewal in Ma'at

Man's task [is] to become conscious of the contents that press

upward from the unconscious. Neither should he persist in his

unconsciousness, nor remain identical with the unconscious

elements in his being, thus evading his destiny, which is to create

more and more consciousness. (Jung, *Memories, Dreams,*

Reflections 326)

The ancient Egyptians deeply questioned their part in maintaining the natural

balance and order of things, and sought ways they could promote the success and unity of

their culture. The structures and conventions of this culture changed over time even as

these people preserved traditions and beliefs that enhanced their quest—a process that is

recorded in their literature and images. Above all, it was thought that harmony and

unity—achieved through the rightness of one's actions, words, and thoughts—must

promote the flourishing and renewal of life. This hard-won wisdom of Ma'at is available

to our modern society, if we drop the thought habit of cultural superiority and the

evolutionary notion of steady progress that has characterized Western thought since the

so-called Age of Reason began.

Contemporary Western cultures have become entrenched in collective and

individual ego consciousness that places one's ego at the core of the great matrix of life,

constantly referring to one's own needs and wants and holding these as its central

concern and preoccupation. This anthropocentricism has resulted in a fragmented style of

thinking that calls to mind the image of shattered glass. It seems to be a primary source of

our collective sense of alienation and loneliness that so many poets, artists, philosophers, and psychologists have articulated in the past several hundred years. Only by rediscovering our capacity for resilience and renewal can we awaken the ancient wisdom in the modern heart and psyche and bring forth individual fulfillment and a flourishing culture.

Overview: Principal Themes

The concept of renewal is perhaps the greatest gift that the venerable ancient Egyptian culture can engender in each of us today; it is a reality that we have lost the power to imagine, and yet rediscovering its importance is critical for our own renewal—both individual and collective.

The ancient Egyptians lived within an interwoven cosmos and were part of its whole cloth, and this is evident in both their artwork and their literature. The unity engendered by their holoscopic perspective is also reflected in their language and the way they related to the mysteries of the natural world, to life and death, to the divine and the ancestral realms. Life depended on Ma'at. The gods depended on Ma'at. Access to eternal afterlife depended on Ma'at, too, and therefore the ancestors depended on Ma'at. Doing Ma'at was not a onetime thing, something to do now and then cross off the list forever; on the contrary, achieving balance in Ma'at required continual effort in this world and the next, for "[t]he same *maat* that guarantees success and continuance in life is also the standard of the Judgment of the Dead and leads to immortality" (Assmann, *Death and Salvation* 413).

Times of major social or political upheaval, such as the New Kingdom period of destruction and renewal—the long process of restoration and rebuilding following the chaos of Akhenaten's rule—offer a clear illustration of how resilience allows people to create and build rather than destroy and dismantle. The pragmatic recognition of the natural ebb and flow of life sustained and instructed these ancient people for thousands of years, through difficulty and destruction, through humiliation and obstruction, helping them discover the middle path of peace and renewal. These are things we should keep clearly in mind in our own times.

The rediscovery of ancient Egyptian culture has spawned an evolution in consciousness ever since Napoleon's scientific teams began publishing their discoveries at the end of the eighteenth century. Still today, there is much to learn from the ancient Egyptians, who clearly took great care to record their discoveries and preserve them for future generations. Our relationship with these ancient ancestors can be based in reciprocity: we offer our devotion to understanding their culture from their own perspective, and they are immortalized through being honored and remembered as they strove so hard to be. This two-way flow between our consciousness and the collective unconscious where their wisdom remains has the potential to open pathways to new insights and a much-needed transformation of consciousness.

Combined with the profound spiritual feelings reflected in their rituals and cosmologies, the pragmatism of the ancient Egyptians created an ethical viewpoint that evolved over the course of their long history and reached further into the social fabric, until people at all levels of society recognized their responsibility and capacity for contributing to the perpetuation of Ma'at.

New Insights and Understanding

As far as we can discern, the sole purpose of human existence is to kindle a light in the darkness of mere being. It may even be assumed that just as the unconscious affects us, so the increase in

our consciousness affects the unconscious. (Jung, *Memories,*

Dreams, Reflections 326)

The ancient Egyptians learned to leverage a resilient cultural model that endured all the challenges both nature and humanity could throw at them. Their discoveries are pertinent today as they help us develop a crucial understanding: when the rituals that promote and ensure a healthy society are no longer vibrant and alive . . . when our myths lose their elasticity and meaning . . . when our inherent desire for harmony, balance, and order ossifies into rigid laws, intolerance, and inflexibility . . . then eros can irrupt as the fierce, creative feminine principle, and in each of us her aspect might very well become a scorching solar Eye or raging lioness. Then we become hell-bent, stuck in a cycle of disintegrating logos, wanton destruction, greedy consumption, and self-serving isolation. Until we choose the soothing moisture of unity and cohesion—until Ma'at renews us, purifies us—life will languish, and the earth and all her creatures will suffer.

The value of an ethical model in shaping a culture cannot be underestimated. The ancient Egyptians used their ethical standards as a method to govern actions and interactions and as a model of excellence. What is destructive to social order and the overall flourishing of life was seen as needing to be tempered and put into right proportion, harmonized, and balanced.

In ancient Egypt the duties of the king were well defined, and people were aware of whether or not the king was fulfilling his role, because his success was reflected in the quality of life for all. The king was held responsible for the annual inundation, for drought, for famine, war, and pestilence . . . so the king and his administrators planned for the future and took these things into account. Perhaps they followed Ma'at's counsel to prepare for the worst and enjoy the present.

The Contendings of Horus and Seth is a crucial mythologem that transmitted the value of unity and harmonizing the conflictual elements in ancient Egypt. The lessons in this story in particular could be applied as a way to observe and then remedy the breakdown in our twenty-first-century sociopolitical systems—the polarization that has caused such ineffectiveness in resolving conflicts or in promoting the flourishing of life.

Following Ma'at's ethical model and reinforcing her principles in one's daily life was the foremost way an ancient Egyptian individual could ensure he or she would enjoy eternal life—in the sense of living meaningfully and thus becoming worthy of being remembered well. Ma'at's mysteries challenge us to be conscious of how our interactions influence and aid life, or impede and distort the natural flow of energy, of libido. It is the duty of each human being to maintain and preserve Ma'at's balance. By articulating the practices that embody Ma'at, we can develop rituals and traditions that enhance and increase Ma'at—a missing and much-needed energy pattern in our contemporary world.

In his book *Re-Visioning Psychology*, the archetypal psychologist James Hillman asks us to consider how images are related to health and psychological well-being. Hillman names one of the four cornerstones of his re-envisioned psychology as "personifying," which he describes as "the spontaneous experiencing, envisioning and speaking of the configurations of existence as psychic presences" (12). Personifying is an act, an experience, an ensouling—it brings soul and heart into consciousness, into images that are warm-blooded and alive. Personifying "also offers another avenue of loving, imagining things in a personal form so that we can find access to them with our hearts"

(12). Hillman makes the case that through psychological faith in psychic reality, we develop the sense of having and being a transcendent soul:

> Psychological faith begins in the love of *images*, and it flows mainly through the shapes of persons in reveries, fantasies, reflections, and imaginations. Their increasing vivification gives one an increasing conviction of having, and then of being, an interior reality of deep significance transcending one's personal life. (*Re-Visioning Psychology* 50)

Our faith bestows a sense of meaning. Our sense of having an eternal soul comes from our capacity to imagine. This fact cannot be overemphasized.

Yet in today's society our inherent imaginal capabilities are often dismissed as superfluous. Think of the spontaneous stream of mental images produced by an individual day and night, waking and sleeping. We call these images "dreams," "daydreams," "memories," "fantasies," or "insights," and think of them as random, meaningless, or unfathomable. Yet these images are a critical, natural function of the psyche, and this is its metaphorical communication style—the very foundation of all our experiences, because "consciousness depends on these images" (23).

We often repress and exclude these images from our consciousness, judging them, perhaps embarrassed by their content or even unaware of their presence at all—with unhealthy consequences. For when a metaphorical image is not embraced and consciously explored, it "returns in concrete form" (46). This can result in illness and psychological pathologies that have become concretized in the body and soul. A failure of imagination results in meaninglessness and a barren one-sidedness that is rigid and demonic in its need for primacy. Contemporary culture seems to be in the grips of this fearful coldness, this emptiness.

We have turned away from personifying, labeling it pathological, and turned instead to personalizing and literalizing our psychic metaphors. As a result we have shrunk the "soul into the narrow confines of the human skin" (Hillman, *Re-Visioning Psychology* 48) and inflated the ego to monomaniacal, overbearing, titanic proportions. Yet symptoms, psychopathologies, depression, and the sense of emptiness remind us that we are not this one-sided "me," that there is a whole host or world of beings, of autonomous complexes living alongside and underneath the ego consciousness, which often spring to life unbidden.

A lack of emotional connection to instinctual knowing—and the inability to see how our actions impact the quality of life for all—is a symptom of the fissure in our soul. Recognition of the consequences is a call to action. How can we be complacent, content to hand these pressing, multipronged issues on to our beloved children and their children? It is past the time to begin differentiating the pernicious roots feeding the multitude of crises in our world. Together we must take action to stem the rising destruction, no matter how modest our individual contributions. *The movement of renewal we so urgently need must be imagined and held in our hearts before it will become a reality.*

Searching the cultural signs and observing historical evidence reveals the forces aligning, birthing a transformation of consciousness that is reflected in our cultural expressions as both challenges and breakthroughs. As our ancestors since time immemorial have known, any difficult and dangerous passage is best begun by gathering the healing stories and images arising from our creative source, the wellspring of consciousness, the soul. The psyche's native language is imaginal, and it communicates from its multiple levels of knowing with images, metaphors, dreams, somatic insights, and synchronicities. Nature, too, offers up a whole host of communiqués—that is, if we are paying attention.

We are not in this dilemma alone, nor is this impasse unique to current conditions (although it can certainly feel that way). If we awaken to our inner knowing that flows beneath the surface of the everyday solar "I," or ego consciousness, and if we share the essence of what arises from the pulsing current, we might find a community of beings to partner with—even if their existence dates back to the very beginning of our recorded histories. We can discover with one another and truly listen as others share their own impressions from this wellspring.

As Ma'at and her people have shown us, within the relational union between complementary opposites lies the potential for awakening wisdom that brings forth both a flourishing individual life and dynamic transformative traditions. The dual movement between *human* and *divine* reestablishes the multiple perspectives of the psyche and rebuilds what is critical for transformation and renewal to occur. Within the multiplicity of the psyche's many perspectives is the awakened heart, which directs our doing and saying—and has done so for thousands of years of humanity.

Expanding on the Thesis and Research Questions

1. What unifying elements give the ancient Egyptian civilization its vibrant, creative resilience and its capacity for renewal?

2. How do the ancient Egyptians depict their experience of the archetypal energies of Ma'at and the renewal that she represents?

3. What do the myths, rituals, and prescriptions surrounding Ma'at reveal about the participatory way of knowing and the power of renewal derived from seeking harmony with Ma'at?

Studying the cultural works of the ancient Egyptians reveals examples of the human psyche honoring the relational unity among complementary opposites. It is likely that the participatory way of knowing was a main source of their resiliency and flexibility. Furthermore, their insistent resilience propagated rituals of renewal that fostered their connection to their awakened heart, even in trying times. Exploring their culture-wide devotion to fostering reciprocal relationships with the divine provokes comparison with the profane and materialistic style of consciousness prevalent in our contemporary cultures.

Ma'at's prominence in Egyptian history reveals the collective psyche's inherent capacity for renewal and resilience. In their own era, the images, literature, and other cultural works devoted to Ma'at enabled human consciousness to transcend opposites and achieve harmony, unity, and peace with the laws of nature. These works permit an awakening in the human heart to the mysteries at the foundation of the cultures of yesterday—and also those of today. We modern humans are every bit as capable of this awakening to renewal and harmony. What remains to be seen is whether we can translate the guidance of the ancient Egyptians and their ongoing relationship with Ma'at into our struggling society.

Future Lines of Inquiry

The passionate longing of the human heart has always been to press beyond the boundaries of the known, to break through the limitations of our understanding, to extend the horizon of our awareness. This is perhaps our most fundamental and essential freedom. (Baring 536)

This study imagines the ancient Egyptian capacity for resilience as a model of excellence. Key components of this civilization's success are anchored in their deeply held spiritual beliefs that fostered an evolution in consciousness. A flexible holoscopic perspective, self-reflection, and mindfulness—in combination with the daily acknowledgement of the reciprocal relationships between the human, ancestral, and divine realms—are proven techniques that cultivate the capacity to extend the horizons of awareness and enliven participatory practices that perpetuate life.

Life Flowing into Life

Joseph Campbell and David Kudler (in *Myths of Light*) tell us, "The portal to transcendence [is the realization that] life feeds on life. This is the absolute affirmation of the world as it is" (23). And if we take that principle and extend it, expand it, give it chthonic roots that sink into the deep, dark soil, this holds true for the transformation of energy and the patterns it weaves through our attention and reciprocity. Fig. 60 depicts an image of this, Thoth-Djehuty is offering the *Wedjat*-eye to Khepri, the becoming one. Khepri holds the encircled star, which is the symbol for the Amduat, the Underworld. Beneath Khepri is the solar disc emitting its rays of light below. Above each baboon is the *shen* symbol of infinity and protection—forever, forever. This is the core of Ma'at's mysteries and the focus of this study. Energy transforms from physical into spiritual and back again, over and over. This the very heart of the ancient alchemical maxim: *As above, so below.*

Figure 60. Double Djehuty offering double Wedjat *to Khepri.* Limestone relief from the Late Period, 30.9 x 39.3 x 6 cm. Credit: Purchase, Fletcher Fund and The Guide Foundation Inc. Gift, 1966. Accession #66.99.73. Metropolitan Museum of Art, New York. Public domain. Web. 19 March 2018.

The Great Goddesses of the ancient world, a few of which have migrated into the current era—such as Shakti, Kali, Isis, Wisdom/Sophia, Shekhinah, and the Great Mother as the Christian Madonna—hold this transcendent knowledge, for they are envisioned as the portal of birth, life, death, and rebirth; the continuous womb-to-tomb-to-womb journey is their domain. Like a powerful underground river their presence continues to surface in myriad ways, as the springs and pools of living waters that nourish the heart and give hope and courage to demoralized and oppressed people. The overpowering reality of this is palpable when one enters the side chapel of a great European cathedral and senses the living presence of the Madonna, a heartbroken mother herself, comforting the praying women whose lives are full of hardship and loss.

Ma'at and the other goddesses of the ancient Egyptian pantheon are the embodiment of this active energy of the cosmos and were revered in their own culture for millennia, representing life, death, rebirth, and protection. Their energy wove in and out like the infinity symbol, like the threads on the loom, merging to create cloth. They beckon now, reminding us of various aspects to the archetypal patterns, and of the tension—and the dynamism—between the complementary pairs of opposites.

The One and the Many—there is no difference. We are the embodied expressions of the individual characteristics reflected in the numerous deities acknowledged in ancient traditions. Once we recognize this, it is not a sense of duty, or the threat of going to hell, or the judgment of sinfulness that stirs us and moves us. Rather it is the burning desire—the choice. We must ask ourselves to choose: "Which aspects of the One do I embody? Which ones do I want to model for my children?"

Upholding Ma'at in Our Sethian Times

The political and social breakdown presented in chapters 6 and 7 is, of course, not restricted to ancient Egypt. We can recognize this same dynamic—the struggle to shape collective identity or maintain cultural continuity—in our own times as well. We live in a dangerous age, surrounded by volatility, upheaval, and distress. Many are suffering a sharp decline in well-being and security. The very few are accumulating vast fortunes, with little to no concern for the long-term effects of their practices and ideologies. The fierce individualism of contemporary Western culture presents a stark contrast to the concept of renewal rooted in the cooperative actions of the ancient Egyptian community.

The deterioration of a living relationship with the divine means the majority no longer see the interrelationship between individual integrity and a flourishing society. The breakdowns in society and the upheavals in the biosphere—namely, the crisis of a rapidly changing climate—are seen as unrelated to the rampant corruption and political stalemate that have been amplifying for decades. As Hornung points out, we are living "in an age that has focused attention on fragmentation while continuing to cling to a history of absolutes"—yet "the idea that there is no single answer, that everything is flow and every answer provisional, is worth investigating" (*Idea Into Image* 13–14).

Moreover, it seems that culturally we have lost the moral compass fostered by that living relationship with the divine. Thus the majority also fail to see the connection between individual integrity and the flourishing of *life itself*. Instead integrity is viewed as a matter of personal choice—and has even become a "quaint" idea, an unnecessary luxury if one wants to be successful and "get ahead" in life.

America is in the throes of a great unraveling, with the destruction of numerous environmental protections, societal support systems, and political upheaval, all of which reflect a diminishment of guiding ethical values. Collectively, it seems, we have turned a blind eye to the very obvious decline of conditions in both the United States and the world. What possible reason could there be for portions of our population to vote so obviously against their own best interests? Why should the degradation of the earth continue to be bankrolled by consuming resources and developing destructive practices in the name of endless, exponential growth? Why do we measure our financial health merely by the growth of our economy, a model that fails to consider the cost (financial and otherwise) of the environment's depletion and destruction, of the poisoning of water, air, and soil? The damage to irreplaceable habitats is only the beginning of the spiraling consequences. It might be possible to reverse the trajectory—but only if the will of enough people were ignited toward that end.

This division is a time of potential societal collapse and disorder—a Sethian time, a precarious time. Equally, this division creates a powerful opportunity by demanding transformation of the collective consciousness and providing opportunities for the individual to manifest the needed change at the many levels of our existence.

We are being urgently challenged, both individually and collectively, to recognize the interrelationship between our actions and their consequences as *reciprocal opposites*, not as rivals that cancel out one another. Self-reflexivity and social-emotional intelligence have long been recognized as abilities that can be taught and learned, dating back to an ancient participatory way of knowing. Mindfulness practices are shown to stimulate intrinsic values such as empathy and compassion—hallmarks of a healthy, resilient person and culture. *Yet today our capacities to discern, distinguish, and deploy self-reflexivity, social-emotional intelligence, and empathy seem to be at an all-time low.*

During the 1980s and 1990s the *LA Weekly* published articles by the journalist Michael Ventura, calling attention to a pervasive lack of discernment in the public as a whole, which he named *societal dysfunctions*. His January 12, 1990, article declares:

> Your health cannot be disengaged from the society's and the
>
> society's health cannot be disengaged from the planet's. And until
>
> we accept these facts—nobody can say truly that they are healthy. .
>
> . . To be physically astute and psychologically tended, yet morally
>
> insulated and conceptually blind—is to be crazy, not healthy. (111)

One of the most poignant examples of this societal dysfunction is the failure to take appropriate action to address human-caused climate change. Unsustainable increases in the concentration of atmospheric carbon dioxide are a direct result of human actions. Evidence has mounted to the level of scientific fact, whether or not we chose to acknowledge it.[65]

In our denial and inaction we are jeopardizing our children's and grandchildren's future as well as that of the countless species that inhabit this world with us. The current situation separates us from previous climate events because it is of our own making. What other species fouls its own nest repeatedly and expects life to flourish or its offspring to survive? These are the actions of an ill animal, disconnected from its instinctual self and floundering in an out-of-balance society. A much-needed course correction is long overdue, and the question remains: Do we have the psychological tools and emotional intelligence to find our way forward?

Aligning the Soul with Nature

If Ma'at embodies the mysteries of the awakened heart that are fundamental to the needs of human culture, then psychologically we modern humans have this capability of awakening in common with the ancient Egyptians, hidden though it may be beneath the millennia and the many layers of our own worldview.

---

[65] In 2017, thirteen federal agencies of the US government concluded that evidence for a changing climate can be observed in our atmosphere as well as in our oceans (Friedman). In 2007 the fourth assessment of the United Nations Intergovernmental Panel on Climate Change (IPCC) reported that the warming of the climate system is unequivocal and that "most of the observed increase in global average temperatures since the mid–twentieth century is very likely due to the observed increase in anthropogenic [i.e., caused by humans] greenhouse gas concentrations" (IPCC).

The *Hymn to the Rising Sun* gives an example of how living enveloped in the arms of nature, within its cycles and rhythms, shaped the consciousness and reality of the ancient people of Egypt:

> Hail to you! | Re in your rising, concealed as Amun in your going to rest, | You shine down from your mother's back, appearing gloriously as King of the Ennead. | Nut gives greeting at your appearance; the arms of Ma'at protect you night and day. | . . . | The hearts of the gods delight to see you in the Day Barque, and you shall have a following breeze; | the Night Barque has destroyed him who attacked it. | You traverse your two heavens triumphantly, with the Nine Great Gods accompanying you; | Your mother, Nut, embraces you, and all is flourishing wherever you have been. | . . . | Let me worship you, with your beauty in my heart, and may your Power grow fruitful in my breast.[66] (Foster 41–42)

As aspects of the solar god, Re (the rising sun) and Amun (the setting sun) bookend the day/night journey. Re is associated with the king, the ruler of the land, who is either Horus (the living king) or the deceased king and related therefore to Atum-Re or Amun-Re. The "concealed" Amun makes the night passage into the underworld, seeking union with Osiris, the god of renewal and rebirth. Both halves of the journey embody the order of Ma'at, and she stabilizes and nourishes their functions.

---

[66] From the tomb of Kheruef, inscribed at the end of the 18th Dynasty. He was the chief steward to the Queen Tiye, the Great Royal Wife of Amenhotep III, New Kingdom.

The Feminine is present as the archetypal Great Mother—both Nut (the goddess of the sky) and Ma'at, the sun's protector "night and day." She is the Night Barque and the Day Barque, the vessel that transports the king, his companions, and the many gods and goddesses. In this hymn, the Night Barque's protective guardianship destroys the enemy who attempts to attack the sun god. The hymn ends with a celebration of life ("all is flourishing")—in both heavens, upper and lower, day and night. The high steward Kheruef longs to fill his heart with the beauty of this harmonious vision and to foster Re's power, encouraging its fruitfulness—its ability to multiple forever, to renew—for such is the power of the heart.

As we reach the close of this study, it seems clear that our collective Solar Barque—the one in which our nation travels—is caught in the coils of Apophis. The companions have failed in their appointed tasks, turning a blind eye to the truth and order of Ma'at. They have been seduced by greed, and the solar god's renewal is aborted. Collectively we have fallen asleep, as in the fairy tale about Sleeping Beauty, when the entire castle lies under a spell, in the pall of a deathlike, hundred years' sleep, encircled by a deadly, impenetrable hedge of thorns.

All those very aspects of psyche that the Egyptians were most vigilant about, knowing from experience the utter destruction that awaited all who succumbed to their pull—laziness, lethargy, denial, unconsciousness, crookedness, profanity, greed, avarice—are absolutely rampant in our country right now, cultivating instability. Amid the hot-bellied appetites that consume beyond all measure . . . the out-of-balance greed . . . the forgotten rituals for propitiating the divine forces . . . the neglected daily offerings that might otherwise nurture the reciprocal relationship between the realms . . . our only recourse is to wake up and remember our appointed tasks as companions in the barque. It is time to come to attention, shed the complacency of Apophis's pull, and begin the individual and collective tasks necessary to overcome these destructive habits of mind and the corrupt and dissolute pathways they unfold.

This observation can be applied to today's "debate" about climate change in light of the numerous physical consequences and economic costs of rising temperatures and seas—and the lack of leadership and vision to address this long-standing crisis. It seems self-evident that life is not flourishing in our modern world, on many levels. Evasion of, unreasonable compromise on, and simple failure to address the issues invites societal upheaval and breakdown of infrastructure that will take years to rebuild.

The UN Secretary-General's Special Representative for Disaster Risk Reduction, Robert Glasser, names it "a failure to understand" how our actions, and inaction, are intensifying the crisis. Yet more critical than a failure to understand, it is a culture-wide failure of imagination and empathy that keeps us locked into our own tiny concerns and blocks the compassion necessary to promote a flourishing of life for the well-being of the whole.

> We must realize that these disaster events are not natural
>
> phenomena but are a result of a built environment which is not fit
>
> for [its] purpose and a failure to understand how we are
>
> intensifying the cocktail of disaster risk by not adequately
>
> addressing poverty, land use, building codes, environmental
>
> degradation, population growth in exposed, vulnerable settings

and, most fundamentally, greenhouse gas emissions. (United

Nations Office for Disaster Risk Reduction)

Adopting a Ma'atian perspective could awaken a much-needed course correction,

through the reevaluation of business-as-usual practices and the identification of those that

result in harm, depletion, and impairment. Ma'at's standpoint places the goal on the

actions that result in the flourishing of all life, in both the short and the long term.

Actively developing our relationship with Ma'at and her principles could

replenish the well of the living imagination, the source of the living waters we so urgently

need right now. Ma'at's healing wisdom can renew our fractured relationship with the

natural order and right proportions that are a joy to uphold. Her wings fan insights that

create pathways into this source of life, so we can participate in the renewal so

desperately called for on earth.

> Whenever cultural development threatens to stagnate, there is need
>
> of a reorientation rooted in the past in order to create the future.
>
> New life emerges from what was once alive and is now decayed.
>
> This is a law of nature valid for the inorganic world and no less for
>
> the world of the spirit. (Schweizer 127)

The ancient Egyptians have gifted us with their literature, artifacts, and images

galore, and these symbolic, pragmatic, and aesthetic works speak to us—if we know the

language of the psyche and how to read its imaginal messages. Their texts—both image

and word—stir our imaginations, awaken our knowing, excite and fascinate us. But they

also disturb and perturb us, and this healthy sign should not be ignored. These jarring

sensations are letting us know that we are awakening from a long sleep, and that we are being met from other levels of being, through our conscious and unconscious psyche, which is personal, collective, and transpersonal.

Across more than three thousand years of their civilization, the Egyptians (like many other peoples) wove their very essence, their etheric souls into the web of light and energy that surrounds our beautiful blue planet. They are the intangible molecules of our pure atmosphere. As their own cultures began the long slide into oblivion, they might have intuited that one day people would come to their lands, discover their treasure troves, decipher their wisdom teachings. They might have sensed that these curious people would be driven by a looming cultural crisis similar to those they had learned to weather. They may have assumed that these future ones loved the natural world as they did, with its diversity and amazing life forms, but had lost the ability to protect and sustain all life. They would have known from their own experiences that we future generations would need their discoveries to help us endure and overcome the darkness and chaos, to heal and renew the earth and all life.

The ancient Egyptians tantalize us with the remnants of their culture. Their images and literature have captured our attention for many centuries, though their unfamiliar ways and customs make us uncomfortable at times and might incite our judgments. These treasures call to the deep layers of psyche, awakening this knowing: that the heart belongs to our Mother—the Mother Earth—and that she will testify on our behalf if we uphold her prime directive: *Keep Ma'at in your heart. Do and say Ma'at, and take joy in being alive.*

These actions—the saying and the doing of Ma'at from a sense of joy—make life flourish. But if we deny or defile Ma'at's cosmic laws, we are unworthy of her greatest gift: life everlasting, right here on our home planet and reflected in the starry skies that taught us long ago how to live in harmony and balance. *The movement of renewal we so urgently need must be imagined and held in our hearts before it will become a reality—and each of us is capable of that!*